Arthur

Plays: T

The American Clock, The
Two-Way

In *The American Clock* (1980), Miller c
society during the Great Depression and harks back to those q
and values which helped America to survive. It is also a warning from Miller to his fellow Americans: 'There's never been a country that hasn't had a clock running on it,' says one of his characters, 'so I keep asking myself – how long?' 'Freewheeling, humorous, melancholy and full of unsentimental sympathy for the men and women, brave and bigoted, garrulous and grasping, who went under or survived . . . spellbinding.' *Sunday Times*

Set in an Eastern European capital, in a room which is probably bugged, *The Archbishop's Ceiling* was written in 1977, in the aftermath of Watergate, and is a powerful elegy for the fate of the individual in an age when power is the sole remaining ideology of both East and West. It deals with the question of how 'real' human behaviour can be under the ubiquitous threat of surveillance, where everyone is turned into performers. 'A complex, gritty, intellectually teasing play.' *Guardian*

Two-Way Mirror (1982) consists of two short plays: *Elegy for a Lady* and *Some Kind of Love Story*. In the first play, an aging, married businessman comes into a classy boutique searching for a present for a dying lover who has cut off all contact with him. It has been described by the author as 'a play of shadows under the tree of death'. *Some Kind of Love Story* is a deeply ironic thriller in which an innocent man has been jailed for murder and the police and the judiciary appear to have played an active role in this miscarriage of justice.

Arthur Miller was born in New York City in 1915. After graduating from the University of Michigan, he began work with the Federal Theatre Project. His first Broadway hit was *All My Sons*, closely followed by *Death of a Salesman*, *The Crucible* and *A View from the Bridge*. His other writing include *Focus*, a novel; *The Misfits*, first published as a short story, then as a screenplay and as a novel; *In Russia*, *In the Country*, *Chinese Encounters* (all in collaboration with his wife, photographer Inge Morath) and '*Salesman*' *in Beijing*, non-fiction; and his autobiography, *Timebends*, published in 1987. Among his other plays are: *The Ride Down Mount Morgan*, *The Last Yankee*, *Broken Glass*, *Mr Peters' Connections*, *Resurrection Blues* and *Finishing the Picture*. His novella, *Plain Girl*, was published in 1995 and his second collection of short stories, *Presence*, in 2007. He died in February 2005 aged eighty-nine.

by the same author

plays
After the Fall
All My Sons
The American Clock
The Archbishop's Ceiling
Broken Glass
The Creation of the World and Other Business
The Crucible
Danger: Memory!
Death of a Salesman
An Enemy of the People (*adapted from Ibsen*)
Finishing the Picture
The Golden Years
Incident at Vichy
The Last Yankee
The Man Who Had All the Luck
A Memory of Two Mondays
Mr Peters' Connections
The Price
Resurrection Blues
The Ride Down Mount Morgan
Two-Way Mirror
Up From Paradise (*musical*)
A View from the Bridge

screenplays
The Crucible
Everybody Wins
The Misfits
Playing for Time

fiction
Focus
I Don't Need You Any More
Jane's Blanket (*for children*)
Plain Girl
Presence: Stories

non-fiction
The Crucible in History and Other Essays
Echoes Down the Corridor: Collected Essays 1944–2000
On Politics and the Art of Acting
Salesman in Beijing
Situation Normal
The Theatre Essays of Arthur Miller

with Inge Morath
Chinese Encounters
In Russia
In the Country

autobiography
Timebends

ARTHUR MILLER

PLAYS: THREE

The American Clock
The Archbishop's Ceiling
Two-Way Mirror

Introduction by Arthur Miller

Methuen Drama

METHUEN DRAMA WORLD CLASSICS

1 3 5 7 9 10 8 6 4 2

This edition first published in Great Britain in 1990
by Methuen Drama

Reissued with a new cover design 1994, 2000, 2009

Methuen Drama
A & C Black Publishers Ltd
36 Soho Square
London W1D 3QY

www.methuendrama.com

The American Clock first published in Great Britain 1982 by Methuen London Ltd

The Archbishop's Ceiling first published 1984 by Methuen London Ltd

Two-Way Mirror first published 1984 by Methuen London Ltd
Revised and reprinted in 1989

A CIP catalogue record for this book
is available from the British Library

ISBN 978 1 408 11132 1

Contents

Arthur Miller

Chronology of professionally produced plays

	First US production	First UK production
The Man Who Had All the Luck	23.1.44	28.4.60
All My Sons	29.1.47	11.5.48
Death of a Salesman	10.2.49	28.7.49
An Enemy of the People (adapted from Ibsen)	28.12.50	
The Crucible	22.1.53	9.11.54
A Memory of Two Mondays	29.9.55	29.9.58
A View from the Bridge		
(one-act version)	29.9.55	
(two-act version)	28.1.65	11.10.56
After the Fall	23.1.64	31.10.67
Incident at Vichy	3.12.64	10.1.66
The Price	7.2.68	4.3.69
The Creation of the World and Other Business	30.11.72	17.8.74
Up from Paradise (musical)	23.4.74	
The Archbishop's Ceiling	30.4.77	1.4.85
The American Clock	24.5.80	18.4.83
Two-Way Mirror	26.10.82	1.89
Playing for Time (adapted from his screenplay)	22.9.85	10.11.05
Danger: Memory!	8.2.87	6.4.88
The Golden Years	(world première)	6.11.87
The Ride Down Mount Morgan	17.7.97	11.10.91
The Last Yankee	5.1.91	21.1.93
Broken Glass	9.3.94	4.8.94
Mr Peters' Connections	17.5.98	20.7.00
Resurrection Blues	3.8.02	14.2.06
Finishing the Picture	21.9.04	

Introduction

Obviously there are two distinct kinds of theatre in our time, the Majority one and the Other. The Majority includes the musicals, light comedies, melodramas of reassurance and farces – anything that takes peoples' minds off their troubles.[1] The Other, in contrast, is devoted to generating anxiety rather than reassurance, or escape through hermetically circular ironies. Other comedy tends toward snarling parody of love or any similar implication of pure human intentions, and has far more prestige in academic circles. Other theatre is most eager to become part of the future, the Majority is perfectly content with immediate acceptance at the highest possible ticket prices. Few seriously discuss the Majority theatre, the Other gets written about in articles and books and its authors are treated as seers and philosophers. The Majority theatre has only practitioners, no seers. In fact, the Majority theatre practitioner who visibly aspires to become a seer is quickly thrown out of both camps and ends in poverty unless he has saved money in his pre-seer period.

How to tell a Majority work from the Other kind is often a tricky problem. A show is Majority when it runs a long time, although some can close in a week or less (in New York). However, the Other kind may also run a long time but almost always in small theatres. One can only theorize that their audiences must abhor large crowds while Majority people like it best when surrounded by thousands in big halls or stadiums. Television they find most enjoyable of all probably because they know they are watching along with millions of others, a fact which in itself is likely to raise suspicions of fraudulence in the Other audience.

There are differences as well in the receptivity of both audiences. The Majority expects to be reached by a play, and to be able to

[1] Of course, Shakespeare, the most-produced playwright of all time, is an anomaly. The majority, by all laws inherent in such matters, should be too dull to enjoy him but they persist in thinking he is a popular writer.

understand what is taking place more or less when it is happening. The Other audience seems to prefer not to understand what is going on, at least not too precisely, probably in order to exercize their own imaginations, much as they have to in real life where most things people do are unanticipated, if not incomprehensible. It follows that the Other audience, disregarding its antipathy for naturalism, harbours an unacknowledged taste for it while the Majority audience prefers a theatre based on the archaically formalized relationship to real life behaviour.[2] (One need only stand listening to snatches of conversation on a subway platform to realize the passengers are unknowingly performing what amounts to a real-life Other play.)

In general, life is a mystery to the Other no less than to the Majority theatre, the difference being that the latter claims to have cleared it up in two hours. The very idea of clearing anything up is anathema to the Other theatre; indeed, if in the course of time and repeated productions an Other play seems to have become clarified to the point of easy comprehensibility, it is gradually absorbed into the Majority repertoire and its author correspondingly becomes richer and richer until, slowly but surely, he is despised.[3]

Many ordinary people – people who never stop to analyze anything, are apt to wonder what the point is of having the Other theatre when it is attended by so ludicrously few poeple, and when even those who do show up cannot often agree on what it was they saw. But these people overlook a fundamental point about Other art – that its object is to analyze *them*, the Majority, in particular their middle-class stupidities, Puritanical or materialistic illusions about money, sex and war, and general bourgeois dimness. So naturally the Majority is unlikely to catch on that it is, for example, a Rhinoceros, or that despite appearances of immense activity it is really standing around awaiting the non-arrival of the Lord, or that its idealistic patriotism is simply a clever means of enriching the ruling class through warfare. Those are some of the basic proposals of Other theatre, and should one ask why, if Other theatre is truly attempting to heal the Majority with its wisdom it does not search

[2] Namely, actors pretending to really feel emotions rather than mocking them – or pretending to mock them.

[3] Again, Shakespeare only serves to confuse analysis. The ambiguousness of his meanings is only that for scholars, the Majority audience remaining content to imagine they understand precisely what he is driving at.

out some way, difficult though this might be, to make itself Majority-comprehensible, one is likely to run into a philosophical conundrum; for if the Majority were ever convinced that it is a dangerous conformist Rhinoceros, or that all its wordly strivings, fanatical shopping, money-lust, automobile-fixations etc., are futile attempts to escape the true and pointless conditions of existence, then – converted to the truth of these radical propositions – the Majority would cease to exist as such and would turn into the Other. In which case, one might ask, would the old Other separate itself from this new Other, detesting it as a *nouveau* or *faux* Other, while turning its back on the original Other theatre as outmoded and passé, or historically exhausted, declaring that they, the original Others, are *not* Rhinoceroses and are *not* waiting around for a god who never shows up, thereby moving over inadvertently into former Majority positions? In other words, does the fundamental question finally come down to whether it is preferable to sit in a small theatre with few people or a large theatre with many?

The issue is complicated in addition by whether the definition of Other theatre is or is not linked with immediate comprehensibility. There is – or was – no more Majority text than the Holy Bible whose stories have been drummed into immense mobs of people for close to two millenia. Indeed, whole wars have been launched against people who refused to accept it as God's truth, wars that mobilized hundreds of thousands of passionate Bible readers – or hearers – since most have been illiterate. Yet there is probably no book in whose narratives so much remains inexplicable. Why did Cain have to kill Abel? There is no straightforward explanation, it just happens. Where did Noah learn to build a veritable *Queen Mary*, especially having lived on a desert, no less? And if Adam and Eve were the first and only humans, with what people was Cain sent to live in exile in the land East of Eden so that they could curse him? Where did they come from? This is Other literature if there ever was any; indeed, the entire creation of the world takes less linear space than a cooking recipe, surely an example of Other condensation and elypsis. Yet most Other audiences are sure to consider it fit only for the Majority mentality and its lusting after clear and simple situations.

The possibility of some gross error would seem to open before us, a confusion of matter with manner, of the merely customary with the decrepit. In New York – to step aside from theatre for illustration – a new architectural style has set Greek pediments and columns on top of fifty-storey buildings in revolt, we are told, against the boring Bauhaus form-follows-function shibboleth. Instead, we are apparently to have form-tops-function since the working interiors of these immense buildings devoted to money-making and therefore impervious to useless add-ons, remain exactly the same as all other skyscraper designs of the past. One has to wonder whether the problem is not so much architecture as simple boredom. Since in other periods a large new building was a rare event, and in pre-industrial times one that took years and even generations to complete, perhaps we are so accustomed to immense new structures suddenly springing up that the sight of them is unlikely to inspire the effort to look up from the street, and so the architect's job, especially the Other architect, is to entertain and draw attention to his performance as much as to make something intrinsically unified and beautiful. In short, art now is an assault on the boredom of excess and the unnecessary with which life overflows, at least for the favoured, in this, one of the longest periods of peace between the great-powers in all history.

Perhaps something similar is at work in theatre where boredom, of course, has always been the cardinal sin. In Majority theatre an event once strove above all for credibility, and to this end was carefully prepared for in advance, impressing the audience with the wonderful, or menacing, inviolability of cause-and-effect. In Other theatre, in contrast, nothing is as valued as the unanticipated, the event which, if at all possible, violates every imaginable system of logic to the point of total arbitrariness. It is striking how this mode of perception more and more reflects like qualities that now glare forth from life. For example, the Soviet system, thought to be set in concrete, breaks up without foreign intervention, causing the implosion of vast edifices of Western armed war preparation without a shot being fired. The whole anti-Communist soufflé has simply slid down to the bottom of the pot just like the pro-Communist one. The Other style reflects the elevation to his country's Presidency of a playwright – of all things – who a few short months earlier had been jailed for his views. Other theatre, the theatre of the unanticipated, would seem to have its roots in the common, blatant world after all, would seem – ironically enough – not to have been as pure a flight of imaginative liberation as it would like to have seemed, but one quite as influenced, if not determined by social and political circumstances as the Majority theatre, with its boring enslavement to the logic of psychological-social-political realities. Other theatre is hitched to a different cart, but it is hitched.

What does it all come to? The same old thing, of course – those radiating images, compact imitations of people that inflame the imagination with intimations of completeness; images of the self-defrauded Lear and Oedepus, of the abandoned Estragon, of fatuous Tartuffe, the infinite Alice, pining Bovary; God-hungry Ahab – the qualities of earthly existence, each bearing its self-contained interior system of logical inevitability. In such super-informing images the Majority and the Other merge, fall apart, in fact, into a mutuality of understanding that transcends the size of their theatres, the hipness of their audiences, or the modes they use to get themselves created – in short, despite everything. In the end, the long run, the informing human image – by whatever means it is brought to life – is. The rest is gossip.

Arthur Miller 1990

THE AMERICAN CLOCK

To Inge and Rebecca

NOTE ON PRODUCTION

The American Clock was first produced at the Harold Clurman Theatre, in New York City, and opened at the Spoleto Festival's Dockside Theatre in Charleston, South Carolina, on May 24, 1980, directed by Dan Sullivan.

It opened at the Biltmore Theatre in New York on November 20, 1980, under the direction of Vivian Matalon. The scenery was designed by Karl Eigsti; the lighting was by Neil Peter Jampolis; and the costumes were by Robert Wojewodski. The cast, in order of appearance, was as follows:

LEE BAUM	William Atherton
MOE BAUM	John Randolph
CLARENCE, WAITER, ISAAC, JEROME, PIANO MOVER	Donny Burks
ROSE BAUM	Joan Copeland
FRANK, LIVERMORE, MAN IN WELFARE OFFICE, STANISLAUS	Ralph Drischell
GRANDPA, KAPUSH	Salem Ludwig
FANNY MARGOLIES, MYRNA	Francine Beers
CLAYTON, SIDNEY MARGOLIES, RALPH	Robert Harper
DURANT, SHERIFF, PIANO MOVER, TOLAND	Alan North
TONY, TAYLOR, DUGAN	Edward Seamon
WAITER, BICYCLE THIEF, RUDY, PIANO MOVER, RYAN	Bill Smitrovich
JOE, BUSH	David Chandler
DORIS, ISABEL, GRACE	Marilyn Caskey
IRENE	Rosanna Carter
JEANETTE RAMSEY, EDIE, LUCILLE, ATTENDANT	Susan Sharkey

CHARACTERS

ARTHUR ROBERTSON
CLARENCE, *a shoeshine man*
LEE BAUM
MOE BAUM, *Lee's father*
ROSE BAUM, *Lee's mother*
FRANK, *the Baum's chauffeur*
FANNY MARGOLIES, *Rose's sister*
GRANDPA, *Rose's father*
DR ROSMAN
WILLIAM DURANT, JESSE LIVERMORE, ARTHUR CLAYTON — *financiers*
TONY, *a speakeasy owner*
WAITER
DIANA MORGAN
HENRY TAYLOR, *a farmer*
MRS TAYLOR, *his wife*
HARRIET, *their daughter*
CHARLEY
JUDGE BRADLEY
BREWSTER
FRANK HOWARD, *auctioneer*
SIDNEY MARGOLIES, *Fanny's son*
DORIS GROSS, *the landlady's daughter*
JOEY, *a boyhood friend*
RALPH, RUDY — *students*
ISABEL, *a prostitute*
RYAN, *supervisor of a federal relief office*
MATTHEW R. BUSH, GRACE, KAPUSH, DUGAN, IRENE, TOLAND, LUCY — *people at the relief office*
EDIE, *a comic strip writer*
LUCILLE, *Rose's niece*
STANISLAUS, *a seaman*

ISAAC, *a lunch-counter proprietor*
SHERIFF
FARMERS
DEPUTIES
PIANO MOVERS

This version of *The American Clock* was used as the basis of the Birmingham Repertory Theatre's production in 1983.

Act One

The set is a flexible area for actors. The few pieces of furniture required should be openly carried on by the actors. An impression of a surrounding vastness should be given, as though the whole country were really the setting, even as the intimacy of certain scenes is provided for. The background can be sky, clouds, space itself, or an impression of the United States' geography.

Light rises on LEE BAUM *who enters and faces the audience. In his fifties, greying hair, wears tweed jacket and has a vaguely preppy look, a journalist.*

LEE. There have been only two American disasters that were truly national. Not the first or second World Wars, Vietnam or even the Revolution. Only the Civil War and the Great Depression touched nearly everyone wherever they lived and whatever their social class. (*Slight pause.*) Personally, I believe that deep down we are still afraid that suddenly, without warning, it may all fall apart again. And that this fear, in ways we are rarely conscious of, still underlies every . . . (ARTHUR ROBERTSON *has entered. In his seventies, a corporate leader. In blue blazer, white turtle neck, white shoes, carrying a cane. Tends to grin ironically.*)

ROBERTSON. Sorry, but I don't think that kind of collapse is really possible again. And I don't mean only the stock market. I mean the emotional collapse. By the year 1929 you had a general belief that every

American was inevitably going to get richer every year. People are a lot more sophisticated now, they expect ups and downs, they are much more sceptical . . .

LEE. Is it scepticism or a deep fear that the whole thing can suddenly cave in and that nothing is really under control?

ROBERTSON. Well whatever it is you can always get out of the way if you use your head. I made more money in the Depression than I ever had before. And I think it's interesting why I wasn't destroyed by the Crash. In 1927 – the height of the boom – I read that the Wright Aeronautical Company was building the plane that would take Lindbergh across the Atlantic. I bought Wright stock, and in one morning it went up sixty-seven points. That was the day I ceased to believe in the permanency of the boom. Only an illusion can multiply itself sixty-seven times in three hours, and I began to remove myself from the market. In two years, it was lying all over the floor. (ROSE BAUM *appears, softly playing the piano, a romantic light on her.*)

LEE (*the sight of her moves him*). But there were people who could not pull out because they believed. And with all their hearts. For them the clock would never strike midnight, the dance and the music could never stop . . .

ROBERTSON (*recalling, mournfully*). Oh, I know, yes – the Believers. (CLARENCE, *a black shoeshine man enters, sets his box down. As* ROBERTSON *approaches him,* LEE *moves in another direction towards* ROSE.) How you making out, Clarence? (*Puts his shoe up on the box and slipping off his grey wig, tosses it offstage – he is in his forties.*)

ROSE (*to* LEE). Sing, Darling!

Tossing his greying wig offstage, and with a boyish air

... LEE *sings first line of 'For I'm just a vagabond lover ...' Blackout on* ROSE *and* LEE.

CLARENCE (*taking bill from his pocket*). Mr Robertson, I like to lay another ten dollars on that General Electric. You do that for me? (*Hands bill to* ROBERTSON.)

ROBERTSON. How much stock you own now, Clarence?

CLARENCE. Well, that ten ought to buy me a thousand dollars' worth, so altogether I guess I got me about hundred thousand dollars in stock.

ROBERTSON. And how much cash you got home?

CLARENCE. Oh, I guess about forty, forty-five dollars.

ROBERTSON (*slight pause*). All right, Clarence, let me tell you something. But I want you to promise me not to repeat it to anyone.

CLARENCE. I never repeat a tip you give me, Mr Robertson.

ROBERTSON. This isn't quite a tip, this is what you might call an un-tip. Take all your stock, and sell it.

CLARENCE. Sell! Why just this morning in the paper Mr Andrew Mellon say the market's got to keep goin' up. *Got* to!

ROBERTSON. I have great respect for Andrew Mellon, Clarence, but he's up to his eyebrows in this game – he's got to say that. You sell, Clarence, believe me.

CLARENCE (*drawing himself up*). I never like to criticise a customer, Mr Robertson, but I don't think a man in your position ought to be carryin' on that kind of talk! Now you take this ten, sir, put it on General Electric for Clarence.

ROBERTSON. I tell you something funny, Clarence.

CLARENCE. What's that, sir?

ROBERTSON. You sound like every banker in the United States.

CLARENCE. Well I should hope so!

ROBERTSON. Yeah, well . . . good-bye. (*He goes.* CLARENCE *takes his shoeshine box off. Light rises on* ROSE *at the piano, dressed for an evening out. She plays 'Vagabond Lover' softly. Two valises stand centre stage.*)

LEE (*glances at* ROSE *as he removes jacket and pulls ups his trousers to make knickers of them*). Lindbergh had flown the Atlantic because he believed; Babe Ruth kept smashing home runs because he believed; a tremendous broad-shouldered woman named Gertrude Ederle swam the English Channel and Charley Paddock, the World's Fastest Human, won a race against a racehorse – because he believed – and one afternoon my mother came home and she had bobbed her beautiful long hair in which I had always believed. (ROSE *sings the opening line of 'Vagabond Lover'.* LEE *tries to join in but his voice is quavering. She stops.*)

ROSE. What's the matter with you? (*He can only shake his head – 'nothing'.*) Oh, for God's sake! Nobody's going to bother with long hair anymore. All I was doing was winding it up and winding it down . . .

LEE. It's *okay*! I just didn't think it would ever . . . happen!

ROSE. But why can't there be something new!

LEE. But why didn't you *tell* me?

ROSE. Because you would do exactly what you're doing now! – Carrying on like I was some kind of I-don't-know-what! Now stop being an idiot and *sing*. (LEE *starts the song again. Spoken.*) You're not breathing, dear. (MOE *enters in tuxedo, carrying a phone.*)

MOE. Trafalgar five, seven-seven-one-one. (*He joins them in the song.* FRANK, *in chauffeur's uniform, enters, applauding.*)

ROSE. Rudy Vallee is turning green.

MOE (*in phone*). Herb? I'm just thinking maybe I ought

to pick up another five hundred shares of General Electric – good. (*Hangs up.*)

FRANK. Car's ready, Mr Baum.

ROSE (*to* FRANK). You'll drop us at the theatre and then take my father and sister to Brooklyn and come back for us after the show. And don't get lost please.

FRANK. No, I know Brooklyn. (*He goes off with the baggage.* FANNY *enters –* ROSE*'s sister, with four walking sticks and two hat boxes.*)

FANNY (*apprehensively*). Rose . . . listen . . . Papa really doesn't want to move. (*A slow turn with rising eyebrows from* MOE*;* ROSE *is likewise alarmed.*)

ROSE (*to Fanny*). Don't be silly, he's been here six months.

FANNY (*fearfully, voice lowered*). I'm telling you . . . he is not happy about it.

MOE (*resoundingly understating the irony*). He's not happy.

FANNY (*to* MOE). Well, you know how he loves space, and this apartment is so roomy.

MOE (*to* LEE). He bought himself a grave, you know, it's going to be in the cemetery on the aisle. So he'll have a little more room to move around . . .

ROSE. Oh, stop it.

MOE. . . . Get in and out quicker.

FANNY. Out of a grave?

ROSE. He's kidding you, for God's sake!

FANNY. Oh! (*To* ROSE.) I think he's afraid my house'll be too small; you know, with the girls and Sidney and us and the one bathroom. And what is he going to do with himself in Brooklyn? He never liked the country.

ROSE. Fanny, dear – make up your mind – he's going to love it with you.

MOE. Tell you, Fanny – maybe we should *all* move over

to your house and he could live here with eleven rooms for himself and we'll send the maid every day to do his laundry . . .

FANNY. He's brushing his hair, Rose, but I know he's not happy. I think what it is, he still misses Mama, you see.

MOE. Now *that's* serious – a man his age still misses his mother . . .

FANNY. No, *our* mother – *Mama.* (*To* ROSE, *almost laughing, pointing at* MOE.) He thought Papa misses his own mother!

ROSE. No he didn't, he's kidding you!

FANNY. Oh you . . .! (*She swipes at* MOE.)

ROSE (*walking her to the doorway*). Go, hurry him up. I don't want to miss the first scene of this show, it's supposed to be wonderful.

FANNY. See, what it is, something is always happening here, but in our house it's . . . very *quiet*, you know? . . .

MOE (*in phone*). . . . Trafalgar five, seven-seven-one-one.

FANNY. . . . I mean with the stock market and the business . . . Papa just loves all this! (GRANDPA *appears. Suit, cane, overcoat on arm. Very neat, proper – and very sorry for himself. Comes to a halt, already hurt.* FANNY, *deferentially.*) You ready, Papa?

MOE (*to* GRANDPA). See you again soon, Charley! (*On phone.*) Herb? . . . Maybe I ought to get rid of my Worthington Pump. Oh . . . thousand shares? And remind me to talk to you about gold will you? – Good.

FANNY (*with* ROSE, *getting* GRANDPA *into his coat*). Rose'll come every few days, Papa . . .

ROSE. Sunday we'll all come out and spend the day.

GRANDPA. Brooklyn is full of tomatoes.

FANNY. Not so much anymore, you'd be surprised.

They're starting to put up big apartment houses now; it's practically not the country anymore. (*Happy reassurance.*) On some streets there's hardly a tree! (*To* ROSE, *of her diamond bracelet.*) I'm looking at that bracelet! Is it new?

ROSE. For my birthday.

FANNY. It's gorgeous.

ROSE. He gave exactly the same one to his mother.

FANNY. She must be overjoyed.

ROSE (*with a cutting smile to* MOE). Why not?

GRANDPA (*a sudden despairing announcement*). Well? So I'm going! (*Shaking his head disapprovingly, as he starts off.*)

LEE. Bye-bye, Grandpa!

GRANDPA (*goes to* LEE, *offers his cheek, gets his kiss, then pinches* LEE*'s cheek*). You be a good boy. (*He strides past* ROSE, *huffily snatches his hat out of her hand, and goes out.*)

MOE. There goes the boarder. I lived to see it!

ROSE (*to* LEE). Want to come and ride with us?

LEE. I think I'll stay and work on my radio.

ROSE. Good, and go to bed early. I'll bring home all the music from the show and we'll sing it tomorrow. (*Kisses.*) Good night, darling. (*She has a fur stole over her arm and swings out.*)

MOE (*to* LEE). Whyn't you get a haircut?

LEE. I did, but it grew back, I think.

MOE (*realising* LEE*'s size*). Should you talk to your mother about college or something?

LEE. Oh no, not for a couple of years.

MOE. Oh. Okay, good. (*He laughs and goes out, perfectly at one with the world.* ROBERTSON *appears and walks over to an armless couch and lies down.* DR ROSMAN *appears and sits in a chair behind* ROBERTSON*'s head.*)

ROBERTSON. Where'd I leave off yesterday?

DR ROSMAN. Your mother had scalded the cat. (*Pause.*)

ROBERTSON. There's something else, Doctor. I feel a conflict about saying it . . .

DR ROSMAN. That's what we're here for.

ROBERTSON. I don't mean in the usual sense. It has to do with money.

DR ROSMAN. Yes?

ROBERTSON. Your money.

DR ROSMAN (*turns down to him alarmed*). What about it?

ROBERTSON (*hesitates*). I think you ought to get out of the market.

DR ROSMAN. Out of the market!

ROBERTSON. Sell everything.

DR ROSMAN (*pauses. Raises his head to think, speaks carefully*). Could you talk about the basis for this idea? When was the first time you had this thought?

ROBERTSON. About four months ago. Around the middle of May.

DR ROSMAN. Can you recall what suggested it?

ROBERTSON. One of my companies manufactures kitchen utensils.

DR ROSMAN. The one in Indiana.

ROBERTSON. Yes. In the middle of May all our orders stopped coming.

DR ROSMAN. Completely?

ROBERTSON. Dead stop. It's now the end of August and they haven't resumed.

DR ROSMAN. How is that possible? The stock keeps going up.

ROBERTSON. Thirty points in less than two months; this is what I've been trying to tell you for a long time now, Doctor – the market represents nothing but a state of mind. (*Sitting up.*) On the other hand, I must face the possibility that this is merely my personal fantasy . . .

DR ROSMAN. Yes, you've always had a fear of approaching disaster.

ROBERTSON. But I've had meetings at the Morgan Bank all week and it's the same in almost every industry – the warehouses are overflowing, we can't move the goods, that's an objective fact.

DR ROSMAN. Have you told your thoughts to your colleagues?

ROBERTSON. They won't listen. Maybe they can't afford to – we've been tossing the whole country on to a crap table in a game where nobody is ever supposed to lose . . .! I sold off a lot two years ago but when the market opens tomorrow I'm cashing in the rest. I feel guilty for it, but I can't see any other way.

DR ROSMAN. Why does selling make you feel guilty?

ROBERTSON. Dumping twelve million dollars in securities could start a slide. It could wipe out thousands of widows and old people . . . I've even played with the idea of making a public announcement.

DR ROSMAN. But that could start a slide in itself, couldn't it?

ROBERTSON. But it would warn the little people.

DR ROSMAN (*with mounting anxiety*). But . . . you might end up responsible for a collapse.

ROBERTSON. But knowing what I know, and saying nothing, I'm responsible too, aren't I?

DR ROSMAN. Yes, but selling out quietly might not disturb the market quite so much. You *could* be wrong, too.

ROBERTSON. I suppose so. Yes . . . Maybe I'll just sell and shut up. You're right. I could be mistaken.

DR ROSMAN (*relieved*). You probably are. – But I think I'll sell out anyway.

ROBERTSON. Fine, Doctor. (*Stands.*) And one more thing. This is going to sound absolutely nuts, but ... when you get your cash, don't keep it. Buy gold.

DR ROSMAN. You can't be serious.

ROBERTSON. Gold bars, Doctor. The dollar may disappear with the rest of it. (*Extends his hand.*) Well, good luck.

DR ROSMAN. Your hand is shaking.

ROBERTSON. Why not? If they heard this there aren't two great bankers in the United States who wouldn't agree that Arthur A. Robertson had lost his mind. – Gold bars, Doctor ... and don't put them in the bank. In the basement. Take care now. (*He goes. Then* ROSMAN. *Light rises on Tony's Speakeasy. An offstage orchestra is playing the latest hit, waiters are setting the table where two stately men in evening clothes take chairs, drinking their brandy. Now* LEE *enters observing all this. – He once again is in his grey wig.*)

LEE. Ah yes, the Great Men. (ROBERTSON *enters. He too is grey now.*)

ROBERTSON (*chuckling*). Oh indeed – the legendary Jesse Livermore, the genius of corporate finance, William Durant ...

LEE. When I think of how we idolised these gurus who were nothing but pickpockets in a crowd of pilgrims ...

ROBERTSON. Yes, but they too believed.

LEE. Oh what did they believe!

ROBERTSON. Why, they believed in the most important thing of all – that nothing is real! That if it was Monday and you wanted it to be Friday, and enough people could be made to believe it *was* Friday – then by God it was Friday! In fact, had they really been cynical, they and the country would have been a lot better off!

LIVERMORE. Tony?

TONY (*entering*). Yes, Mr Livermore? Little more brandy, Mr Durant?

LIVERMORE. About Randolph Morgan. Could you actually see him falling?

TONY. Oh yeah. It was still that blue light, just before it gets dark? And I don't know why, something made me look up. And there's a man flyin' spread-eagle, falling through the air. He was right on top of me, like a giant! (*Looks down.*) And I look. I couldn't believe it. It's Randolph!

LIVERMORE. Poor, poor man.

DURANT. Damned fool.

LIVERMORE. I don't know – I think there is a certain gallantry . . . When you lose other people's money as well as your own, there could be no other way out.

DURANT. There's always a way out. The door.

LIVERMORE (*raising his glass*). To Randolph Morgan. (DURANT raises his glass.)

TONY. Amen here. And I want to say something here – everybody should get down on their knees and thank John D. Rockefeller.

LIVERMORE. Now you're talking.

TONY. Honest to God, Mr Livermore, didn't that shoot a thrill in you? I mean there's a *man* – to come out like that with the whole market falling to pieces and say, 'I and my sons are buying six million dollars in common stocks.' I mean that's a bullfighter.

LIVERMORE. He'll turn it all around, too.

TONY. Sure he'll turn it around, because the man's a capitalist, he knows how to put up a battle. You wait, tomorrow morning it'll all be shootin' up again like Roman candles! (*Enter waiter, who whispers in* TONY's *ear.*) Sure, sure, bring her in. (*Waiter hurries out.* TONY *turns to financiers.*) My God, it's Randolph's sister . . . she don't know yet. (*Enter* DIANA.) How do you do, Miss Morgan, come in, come in. Here, I got a nice table for you.

DIANA (*the bright Southern belle*). Thank you!

TONY. Can I bring you nice steak? Little drink?

DIANA. I believe I'll wait for Mr Robertson.

TONY. Sure. Make yourself at home.

DIANA. Are you the . . . *famous* Tony?

TONY. That's right, miss.

DIANA. I certainly am thrilled to meet you. I've read all about this marvellous place. (*Looking about avidly.*) Are all these people literary?

TONY. Well not all, Miss Morgan.

DIANA. But this is the speakeasy F. Scott Fitzgerald frequents, isn't it?

TONY. Oh yeah, but tonight is very quiet with the stock market and all, people stayin' home a lot the last couple days.

DIANA. Is that gentleman a writer?

TONY. No, miss, that's Jake the Barber, he's in the liquor business.

DIANA. And these? (*Points to* DURANT *and* LIVERMORE. DURANT, *having overheard, stands.*)

TONY. Mr Durant, Miss Morgan. Mr Livermore, Miss Morgan.

DIANA. Not *the* Jesse Livermore?

LIVERMORE. Afraid so, yes!

DIANA. Well I declare! – And sitting here just like two ordinary millionaires! This is certainly a banner evening for me! – I suppose you know Durham quite well.

LIVERMORE. Durham? I don't believe I've ever been there.

DIANA. But your big Philip Morris plant is there. – You do still own Philip Morris, don't you?

LIVERMORE. Oh yes, but to bet on a horse there's no need to ride him. I never mix in business, I am only interested in stocks.

DIANA. Well that's sort of miraculous, isn't it, to own a place like that and never've seen it! My brother's in brokerage – Randolph Morgan?

LIVERMORE. I dealt with Randolph when I bought the controlling shares of IBM. Fine fellow.

DIANA. But I don't understand why he'd be spending the night in his office. The market's closed at night, isn't it? (*Both men shift uneasily.*)

DURANT. Oh yes, but there's an avalanche of selling orders from all over the country, and they're working round the clock to tally them up. The truth is, there's not a price on anything at the moment. In fact, Mr Clayton over there at the end of the bar is waiting for the latest estimates.

DIANA. I'm sure something will be done, won't there? (*Laughs.*) They've cut off our telephone!

LIVERMORE. How's that?

DIANA. I don't actually know – it seems that Daddy's lived on loans the last few months and his credit stopped, I had no idea! (*Laughs.*) I feel like a figure in a dream. I sat down in the dining car, absolutely famished, and realised I had only forty cents! I am surviving on chocolate bars! (*Her charm barely hiding anxiety.*) Whatever has become of all the money?

LIVERMORE. You mustn't worry, Miss Morgan, there'll soon be plenty of money. Money is like a shy bird: the slightest rustle in the trees and it flies for cover. But money cannot bear solitude for long, it must come out and feed. And that is why we must all speak positively and show our confidence. With Rockefeller's announcement this morning the climb has probably begun already. (CLAYTON *appears in the dim periphery with phone to his ear.*)

DURANT. If I were you, Miss Morgan, I would prepare myself for the worst.

LIVERMORE. Now, Bill, there is no good in that kind of talk!

DURANT. It's far more dreamlike than you imagine, Miss Morgan. Here I am chatting away while that gentleman at the end of the bar, that gentleman who has just put down the telephone, is undoubtedly steeling himself to tell me that I have lost control of General Motors.

DIANA. What! (ARTHUR CLAYTON *has indeed put down the phone, straightened his waist-coat, and is now crossing to their table.*)

DURANT (*watching him approach*). If I were you, I'd muster all the strength I have, Miss Morgan. (CLAYTON *comes to a halt before* DURANT.) Yes, Clayton? (TONY *enters, sets a glass of wine before* DIANA.)

CLAYTON. If we could talk privately, sir ... (TONY *glances knowingly at* CLAYTON, *goes.*)

DURANT. Am I through?

CLAYTON. If you could borrow for two or three weeks –

DURANT. From whom?

CLAYTON. I don't know, sir.

DURANT (*stands*). Good night, Miss Morgan. (*She is looking up at him, astonished.*) How old are you?

DIANA. Nineteen.

DURANT. I hope you will look things in the face, young lady. Shun paper. Paper is the plague. Good luck to you. (*He turns to go.*)

LIVERMORE. We have to talk, Bill ...

DURANT. Nothing to say, Jesse. Go to bed, old boy, it's long past midnight. (*He goes.*)

LIVERMORE (*turns to* CLAYTON, *adopting a tone of casual challenge*). Clayton . . . what's Philip Morris going to open at, can they tell?

CLAYTON. Below twenty. No higher. If we can find buyers at all.

LIVERMORE (*his smile gone*). But Rockefeller, Rockefeller . . .

CLAYTON. It doesn't seem to have had any effect, sir. (LIVERMORE *stands. Pause.*) I should get back to the office, sir, if I may. (LIVERMORE *is silent.*) I'm very sorry, Mr Livermore. (CLAYTON *goes.* DIANA *sees the excruciating look coming on to* LIVERMORE'*s face, and half stands.*)

DIANA. Mr Livermore? . . . (ROBERTSON *enters, in his forties now.*)

ROBERTSON. Sorry I'm late, Diana – how was the trip? (*Her expression turns him to* LIVERMORE. *He goes to him.*) Bad, Jesse?

LIVERMORE. I am wiped out, Arthur.

ROBERTSON (*trying for lightness*). Come on now, Jesse, a man like you has always got ten million put away somewhere.

LIVERMORE. No – no. I always felt that if you couldn't have *real* money, might as well not have any. Is it true what I've heard, that you sold out in time?

ROBERTSON. Yes, Jesse. I told you I would.

LIVERMORE (*slight pause*). Arthur, can you lend me five thousand dollars?

ROBERTSON. Certainly. (*Sits, removes one shoe.*)

LIVERMORE. What the hell are you doing? (ROBERTSON *removes a layer of five-thousand-dollar bills from the shoe, hands* LIVERMORE *one as he stands.* LIVERMORE *stares down at* ROBERTSON*'s shoes.*) By God. Don't you believe in anything?

ROBERTSON. Not much.

LIVERMORE. Well, I suppose I understand that. (*Folds the bill.*) But I can't say that I admire it. (*Pockets the bill. Looks down again at* ROBERTSON*'s shoes and shakes his head.*) Well, I guess it's your country now. (*He turns like a blind man and goes out.*)

ROBERTSON. Five weeks ago, on his yacht in Oyster Bay, he told me he had four hundred and eighty million dollars in common stocks.

DIANA (*turning to him from staring after* LIVERMORE). Is Randolph ruined too?

ROBERTSON (*takes her hand*). Diana . . . Randolph is dead. (*Both hands fly to her cheeks.*) He . . . fell from his window. (*Diana stands, astonished, seeing. All fade, except* ROBERTSON, *in spotlight, who turns front to audience.*)

ROBERTSON. Not long after, Mr Livermore sat down to a good breakfast in the Sherry-Netherland Hotel, and calling for an envelope addressed it to Arthur Robertson, inserted a note for five thousand dollars, went into the washroom, and shot himself. (*Light on* LEE, *as he rides in on a bike.*) How did an event like that strike you, out there in Brooklyn? Did it disturb your faith in the system at all?

LEE. Oh no, at that stage I didn't know there was a system. I thought that if a man was – say, like my father – hard-working and making the right goods, he got to be well-off. That's all. Life was a question of individuals, I think.

ROSE (*calling from offstage*). Lee?

ROBERTSON. Interesting. (*He walks into darkness as* ROSE *appears.*)

ROSE (*a small paper bag in her hand*). I want you to do something – oh, what a beautiful bike!

LEE. It's a Columbia Racer! I just bought it from Georgie Rosen for twelve dollars.

ROSE. Where'd you get twelve dollars?

LEE. I emptied my savings account. But it's worth way more! . . .

ROSE. Well I should say! – Listen, darling, you know how to get to Third Avenue and Nineteenth Street, don't you?

LEE. Sure, in ten minutes.

ROSE (*lifts out a diamond bracelet from bag*). This is my diamond bracelet. (*Reaches into bag and brings out a card.*) And this is Mr Sanders' card and the address. He's expecting you; just give it to him and he'll give you a receipt.

LEE. Is he going to fix it?

ROSE. No, dear. It's a pawnshop. Go, I'll explain sometime.

LEE. Can't I have an idea? What's a pawnshop?

ROSE. Where you leave something temporarily and they lend you money on it, with interest. I'm going to leave it the rest of the month, till the market goes up again. I showed it to him on Friday and we're getting a nice loan on it.

LEE. But how do you get it back?

ROSE. You just pay back the loan plus interest. But things'll pick up in a month or two. Go on, darling, and be careful! I'm so glad you bought that bike . . . it's gorgeous!

LEE (*mounting his bike*). Does Papa know?

ROSE. Yes, dear. Papa knows . . . (*She starts out when* JOEY *hurries on.*)

JOEY. Oh, hya, Mrs Baum.

ROSE. Hello, Joey . . . did you get thin?

JOEY. Me? – (*Touches his stomach defensively.*) No, I'm okay. (*To* LEE *as well – as he takes an eight-by-ten photo out of envelope.*) See what I just got? (ROSE *and* LEE *look at the photo.*)

ROSE (*impressed*). Where did you get that!

LEE. How'd you get it autographed?

JOEY. I just wrote to the White House.

LEE (*running his finger over the signature*). Boy . . . look at that, huh? – 'Herbert Hoover'!

ROSE. What a human thing for him to do! – What did you write him?

JOEY. Just wished him success . . . you know, against the Depression.

ROSE (*wondrously*). Look at that! – You're going to end up a politician, Joey. (*Returns to studying the photo.*)

JOEY. I might, I like it a lot . . .

LEE. But what about dentistry?

JOEY. Well, either one.

ROSE. Get going, darling. (*She goes, already preoccupied with the real problem.* LEE *mounts his bike . . .*)

LEE. You want to shoot some baskets later?

JOEY. What about now?

LEE (*embarrassed*). No . . . I've got something to do for my mother. Meet you on the court in an hour . . . (*Starts off.*)

JOEY (*stops him*). Wait, I'll go with you, let me on! (*Starts to mount the crossbar.*)

LEE. I can't, Joey.

JOEY (*sensing some forbidden area, surprised*). Oh!

LEE. See you on the court. (LEE *rides off.* JOEY *examines the autograph and mouths silently . . . 'Herbert Hoover'. Shakes his head proudly and walks off.* FRANK *appears in chauffeur's cap and overcoat and in mime dusts off a large limousine with a cloth from his pocket, blowing on a spot here and there. Carries a folded laprobe under one arm.* MOE *enters, stylishly dressed in fur-collared overcoat.)*

FRANK. Morning, Mr Baum. Got the car nice and warmed up for you this morning, sir. And I had the laprobe dry cleaned.

MOE (*hands* FRANK *a bill*). What is that, Frank?

FRANK. Oh. Looks like the garage bill.

MOE. What's that about tyres on there?

FRANK. Oh yes, sir, this is the bill for the new tyres last week.

MOE. And what happened to those tyres we bought six weeks ago?

FRANK. Those weren't very good, sir, they wore out quick. And I want to be the first to admit that.

MOE. But twenty dollars apiece and they last six weeks?

FRANK. That's just what I'm telling you, sir – they were just no good. But these ones are going to be a whole lot better, though.

MOE. Tell you what, Frank . . .

FRANK. Yes, sir. – What I mean, I'm giving you my personal guarantee on this set, Mr Baum.

MOE. I never paid no attention to these things, but maybe you heard of the market crash? – The whole thing practically floated into the ocean, y'know.

FRANK. Oh yes, sir, I certainly heard about it.

MOE. I'm glad you heard about it because I heard a *lot* about it. In fact, what you cleared from selling my tyres over the last ten years –

FRANK. Oh no, sir! Mr Baum!

MOE. Frank, lookin' back over the last ten years, I never heard of that amount of tyres in my whole life, since I first come over from Europe a baby at the age of six.

That is a lot of tyres, Frank; so I tell ya what we're gonna do now, you're going to drive her over to the Pierce Arrow showroom and leave her there, and then come to my office and we'll settle up.

FRANK. But how are you going to get around!

MOE. I'm a happy man in a taxi, Frank.

FRANK. Well I'm sure going to be sorry to leave you people.

MOE. Everything comes to an end, Frank, it was great while it lasted. No hard feelings. (*Shakes* FRANK*'s hand.*) Bye-bye.

FRANK (*all his uniformed stature suddenly gone*). But what . . . what am I supposed to do now?

MOE. You got in-laws?

FRANK. . . . But I never got along with them.

MOE. You should've. (*Hurrying off, calling . . .*) Taxi! (FRANK, *cap in hand, starts to walk aimlessly;* ROBERTSON *now appears, again in his seventies, and stares into* FRANK*'s face as he walks past and goes.*)

ROBERTSON (*gravely*). They just walked away . . . to nothing; no unemployment insurance, no social security, just fresh air. About that time I made a deal with a Negro chap who worked in my building – every night around six he'd line up seventy-five people and I'd march them into the Mcfadden Penny Restaurant, so-called, where you could buy a fair meal for seven cents. There were seventy-five new ones every night. It began to look like Germany in 1922 . . . and I worried about the banks. There were times I walked around with as much as twenty-five, thirty thousand dollars in my shoes. (LEE *has entered, pushing an armchair loaded with a small table and phone which he sets up.*)

LEE. The population jumped on that block – married children coming back home to live, parents moving back with their children . . . babies were crying where there hadn't been a baby in twenty years . . .

ROBERTSON. There you go, you see? – it revived the family. Progress through catastrophe! (*He and* LEE *go off in opposite directions as* GRANDPA *enters, carrying four or five walking sticks. He comes to a point and lays them on the floor. He is also carrying two hatboxes by their strings; he puts them down and sits in the chair, looking peevish.* ROSE *enters, carrying an unfolded bedsheet, wearing a house-dress, energetically at work.*)

ROSE (*sees the walking sticks on the floor*). What are you doing?

GRANDPA (*a final verdict*). There's no room for these in my closet . . .

ROSE. For a few *canes*?

GRANDPA. And what about my hats? – You shouldn't have bought such a small house, Rose.

ROSE (*starts to leave*). I'll be right down. (*Of the canes.*) I'll put them in the front-hall closet.

GRANDPA. No, I don't want them where they fall down, people step on them. – And where will I put my hats?

ROSE (*trying not to explode*). Papa, what do you want from me? We are doing what we can do!

GRANDPA. One bedroom for so many people is not right – you had three bathrooms in the apartment and you used to look out the window, there was the whole New York. Here . . . listen to that street out there, it's a Brooklyn cemetery. And this barber is *very* bad – Look what he did to me. (*Shows her.*)

ROSE. Why? It's beautiful. (*Brushes hairs straight.*) It's just a little uneven . . .

GRANDPA (*pushing her hand away*). I don't understand, Rose – why does he declare bankruptcy if he's going to turn around and pay his debts?

ROSE. For his reputation.

GRANDPA. His reputation! He'll have the reputation of a fool! – The reason to go bankrupt is *not* to pay your debts!

ROSE (*uncertain herself*). He wanted to be honourable.

GRANDPA. But the whole beauty of it is you don't have to pay anybody. He should've asked me. When I went bankrupt I didn't pay *nobody*!

ROSE (*deciding*). I've got to tell you something, Papa . . .

GRANDPA. And you'll have to talk to Lee – he throws himself around in his bed all night, wakes me up ten times, and he leaves his socks on the floor . . . (*Raises a foot to make a step.*) . . . I have to step over them.

ROSE. I don't want Moe to get aggravated, Papa. (*He is reached, slightly glances at her*). He might try to start a new business, so he's nervous.

GRANDPA. What did I say?

ROSE. Nothing. (*He remorsefully helps her to fold up the sheet. She suddenly embraces him, then glances at the canes.*) Maybe I can find an umbrella stand someplace.

GRANDPA. I was reading about this Hitler . . .

ROSE. I was just thinking before, when Mama used to stand in front of the mirror, her face was so fine, she looked like a China doll.

GRANDPA. . . . He's chasing all the radicals out of Germany. He wouldn't be so bad if he wasn't against the Jews. He won't last six months . . . Reminded me years ago when I used to take Mama to Baden-Baden this time of year . . .

ROSE. How beautiful she was.

GRANDPA. . . . One time we were sitting on the train ready to leave for Berlin. And suddenly a man gallops up calling out my name. So I says, 'Yes, that's me!' And through the window he hands me my gold watch and chain – 'You left it in your room, mein Herr.' Such a thing could only happen in Germany. This Hitler is finished.

ROSE. Please . . . (*Of the canes.*) Put them back in your closet, heh? (*She starts to leave.*)

GRANDPA. All I said was if he's declaring bankruptcy, then he –

ROSE. I don't want him to get mad, Papa! (*She cuts her rebellion short and loads him with canes and his hatboxes.*)

GRANDPA (*mutters*). Man don't even know how to go bankrupt. (*He goes off.* LEE *appears on his bike – but dressed now for winter. He dismounts, parks the bike just as* ROSE *lies back in the chair.*)

LEE. Ma! Guess what!

ROSE. What?

LEE. Remember I emptied my bank account for the bike?

ROSE. So?

LEE. The bank has just been closed by the government! It's broke. There's a whole mob of people yelling where's their money! They've got cops and everything! There is no more money in the bank!

ROSE. You're a genius!

LEE. Imagine! – I could have lost my twelve dollars! – Wow!

ROSE. That's wonderful. (*She removes a pearl choker and sits staring at it in her hand.*)

LEE. Don't you love Brooklyn, Ma? We ought to plant some kind of fruit tree in the backyard. Imagine, go out and pick an apple or something? (*Now he sees the pearls. Moved.*) Oh, Ma, really?

ROSE. I hate to; it was Papa's wedding present.

LEE. But what about Papa's business! Can't he? . . .

ROSE. He put too much capital in the market, dear – it

made more there than in his business. So now . . . it's not there anymore. (*A thief swiftly appears, and rides the bike Off.*) But we'll be all right. Be careful. Go. You can have a jelly sandwich when you come back. (LEE *stuffs the pearls into his pants as he approaches where the bike was; looks in all directions, his bones chilling. He runs upstage and down, and to left and right and finally comes to a halt, breathless, stark horror on his face. As though sensing trouble,* ROSE *leaves her chair and walks over to him.*) Where's your bike? (*He can't speak.*) They stole your bike? (*He is immobile.*) May he choke on his next meal. (*She embraces him.*) Oh, my darling, my darling, what an awful thing. (*He sobs once, but holds it back. She holds him by the shoulders, facing him, and tries to smile.*) So now you're going to have to walk to the hockshop like everybody else. (*She makes him laugh.*) Come, have your jelly sandwich.

LEE. No, I'd like to see if I can trot there – it'd be good for my track. By the way, I'm almost decided to go to Cornell, I think. Cornell or Brown.

ROSE (*an empty, congratulatory, exclamation*). Oh! – Well, there's still months to decide. (*She puts a hand over her eyes in sorrow. She goes.* ROBERTSON *enters.* LEE *is staring front*).

LEE. I guess that's when I knew there was a system. (*The crowing of a cock. Light transforming to dawn.*)

ROBERTSON. Meaning what, exactly?

LEE. Things that had always seemed fixed and frozen forever were melting, slipping away. One man alone began to seem like a ridiculous idea. (*A swelling crowd of farmers emerges, dressed in mackinaws, pea jackets, big sweaters, checked caps, denim caps; blowing on hands, kicking boots together for warmth.* HENRY TAYLOR *is sitting on the ground to one side.*) What could be a more conservative image? – the Iowa farmer! Yet there they were, turning over milk trucks, dumping thousands of gallons across the highways!

ROBERTSON. That was to create scarcity and raise prices. A perfectly conservative thing to do.

LEE. Huh! – Why did it seem so revolutionary?

ROBERTSON. Oh! – That was that other little number they started to do. (*He moves aside to observe as* BREWSTER *steps forward.*)

BREWSTER (*calling front to the crowd*). Just sit tight, fellas, be startin' in a few minutes.

FARMER 1. Boy, this is one hell of an August. Looks like snow up there.

FARMER 2 (*laughs*). Even the weather ain't workin'. (*Low laughter in the crowd.*)

BREWSTER (*heading over to* HENRY TAYLOR). You be catchin' cold, sitting on the ground like that, won't you, Henry?

HENRY. Tired out. Never slept a wink all night. Not a wink. (MRS TAYLOR *appears in overcoat, carrying a big coffee pot, accompanied by* HARRIET, *the fifteen-year-old daughter, who has a coffee mug hanging from each of her fingers.*)

MRS TAYLOR. You'll have to share the cups, but it's something hot anyway.

BREWSTER. Oh, that smells good, lemme take that, Mrs Taylor. (*She gives the coffee pot to* BREWSTER *and comes over to* HENRY, *her husband.* HARRIET *hands out the cups.*)

MRS TAYLOR (*sotto voce, irritated and ashamed*). You can't be sitting on the ground like that, now come on! (*She starts him to his feet; he stands.*) It's a auction – anybody's got a right to come to a auction.

HENRY. There must be a thousand men along the road – they never told me they'd bring a thousand men!

MRS TAYLOR. Well, I suppose that's the way they do it.

HENRY. They got guns in those trucks!

MRS TAYLOR (*frightened herself*). Well it's too late to stop 'em now. So might as well go around and talk to people that come to help you.

CHARLEY (*Rushes on*). Brewster! Where's Brewster!

BREWSTER (*steps forward from the crowd*). What's up, Charley?

CHARLEY (*points Off*). Judge Bradley! He's gettin' out of the car with the auctioneer! (*Silence. All look to* BREWSTER.)

BREWSTER. Well ... I don't see what that changes. (*Turning to all.*) I guess we're gonna do what we come here to do. That right? (*The crowd quietly agrees – 'Right,' 'Stick to it, Larry,' 'No use quittin' now,' etc. Enter* JUDGE BRADLEY, *sixty, and* MR FRANK HOWARD, *the auctioneer. Silence spreads.*)

JUDGE BRADLEY. Good morning, gentlemen. (*Looks about. There is no reply.*) I want to say a few words to you before Mr Howard starts the auction. (*He walks up on to a raised platform.*) I have decided to come here personally this morning in order to emphasise the gravity of the situation that has developed in the state. We are on the verge of anarchy in Iowa, and that is not going to help anybody. Now you are all property owners, so you –

BREWSTER. Used to be, Judge, used to be!

JUDGE BRADLEY. Brewster, I will not waste words; there are forty armed deputies out there. (*Slight pause.*) I would like to make only one point clear – I have levied a deficiency judgment on this farm. Mr Taylor has failed to pay what he owes on his equipment, and some of his cattle. A contract is sacred. The National Bank has the right to collect on its loans. Now then, Mr

Howard will begin the auction. But he has discretionary power to decline any unreasonable bid. I ask you again, obey the law. Once law and order go down, no man is safe. Mr Howard?

MR HOWARD (*with a clipboard in hand, climbs on to the platform*). Well, now, let's see. We have here one John Deere tractor and combine, three years old, beautiful condition. (*Three bidders enter together – and the crowd turns to look hostilely at them as they come to a halt.*) I ask for bids on the tractor and com –

BREWSTER. Ten cents!

MR HOWARD. I have ten cents. (*His finger raised, he points from man to man in the crowd.*) I have ten cents, I have ten cents . . . (*He is pointing towards the bidders, but they are looking around at the crowd in fear.*)

JUDGE BRADLEY (*calls*). Get over here and protect these men! (CALDWELL, *wearing a deputy's star, and four other deputies enter and edge their way in around the three bidders. The deputies carry shotguns.*)

MR HOWARD. Do I hear five hundred dollars? Do I hear five –

BIDDER I. Five hundred! (*Disciplined and quick,* CHARLEY *rushes up – and the farmers grab the deputies and disarm them; a shotgun goes off harmlessly.* BREWSTER *is instantly on to the platform where he pins the* JUDGE'S *arms and another man lowers a noose around his neck.*)

JUDGE BRADLEY. Brewster – Great God, what are you doing!

BREWSTER (*calling out towards other deputies off.*) You come any closer and we're gonna string him up! You all get back on that road or we string up the Judge! So help me Christ he goes up if any one of you deputies interferes with this action! Now let me just clear up one thing for you, Judge Bradley . . .

HENRY. Let him go, Brewster – I don't care anymore, let them take it!

BREWSTER. Just sit tight, Henry, nobody's takin' anything. That is all over, Judge. Mr Howard, just to save time, why don't you take a bid on the whole place? Do that, please?

MR HOWARD (*turns to the crowd, his voice shaking*). I . . . I'll hear bids on . . . everything. Tractor and combine, pair of mules and wagon, twenty-six cows, eight heifers, assorted tools . . . and so forth. Do I hear . . .

BREWSTER. One dollar.

MR HOWARD (*rapidly*). I hear one dollar. One dollar, one dollar? . . . (*Looks about.*) Sold for one dollar.

BREWSTER (*handing him a dollar*). Now will you just sign that receipt please? (MR HOWARD *scribbles, hands him a receipt.* BREWSTER *leaps off platform, goes over to* HENRY TAYLOR, *and hands him the receipt.*) Henry? Whyn't you go along now and get to milkin'. Let's go, boys. (*He stands, with a wave, and the crowd quickly follows him out.* BRADLEY *removes the noose and comes down off the platform, goes over to* HENRY TAYLOR, *who is staring down at the receipt.*)

JUDGE BRADLEY. Henry Taylor? You are nothing but a thief! (TAYLOR *cringes under the accusation. The* JUDGE *points to the receipt.*) That is a crime against every law of God and man! And this isn't the end of it either! (*He turns and stalks out.*)

HARRIET. Should we milk 'em, Papa?

MRS TAYLOR. Of course we milk 'em – they're ours. (*But she needs* TAYLOR'*s compliance.*) Henry?

HENRY (*staring at the receipt*). It's like I stole my own place. (*Near tears, humiliated,* TAYLOR *moves into darkness with his wife. The farmers disperse.* MOE *enters.*)

MOE. When you say three hundred dollars tuition . . . Lee! (LEE *enters from opposite side of stage with college catalogues.*)

LEE. . . . That's for Columbia. Some of these others are cheaper.

MOE. But that's for the four years.

LEE. Well, no, that's one year.

MOE. Ah. (*He lies back in chair, closes eyes.* LEE *flips a page of a catalogue.*)

LEE. Minnesota here is a hundred and fifty, for instance. And Ohio State is about the same, I think. (*Turns to* MOE, *awaits reaction.*) Pa? (MOE *is asleep.* LEE *closes catalogue and looks front.*) He always got drowsy when the news got bad. (*Moves downstage.*) And the mystery of the marked house began. You'd see the stranger coming down the street – poor and ragged – and he'd go past house after house, but at our driveway he'd make a nice self-assured turn right up to the back porch and ask for something to eat. Why us? (TAYLOR *appears at one side of the stage. In mackinaw, farm shoes, peaked hunter's cap, a creased paper bag under his arm. Looking front he seems gaunt, out of his element; now he rings doorbell. Nothing happens. He then summons courage and rings again.* LEE *goes to door.*) Yes?

HENRY (*shyly – still an amateur at the routine*). Ah . . . sorry to be botherin' you on a Sunday and all. (ROSE *enters, wearing house-dress and apron, wiping hands on a towel.*)

ROSE. Who is that, dear? (*She comes to the door.*)

LEE. This is my mother.

HENRY. How de do, ma'am, my name is Taylor and I'm just passing by, wondering if you folks have any work around the place . . .

MOE (*springs up*). Hey! The bell rang! (*Sees the conclave.*) Oh . . .

ROSE (*ironically*). Another one looking for work!

HENRY. I could paint the place, or fix the roof, electrical, plumbing, masonry, gardening . . . I always had my own farm and we do all that, don't you know. I'd work cheap . . .

ROSE. Well we don't need any kind of . . .

MOE. Where you from?

HENRY. State of Iowa.

LEE (*– it's the moon*). *Iowa!*

HENRY. I wouldn't charge hardly any more than if I could have my meals, don't you know. 'Course you'd have to provide materials.

MOE (*he is beginning to locate* TAYLOR *in space*). Whereabouts in Iowa?

ROSE. My sister's husband comes from Cleveland.

MOE. No – no, Cleveland is nowhere near. (*To* HENRY.) Whereabouts?

HENRY. You know Styles?

MOE. I only know the stores in the big towns.

HENRY (*a grateful chuckle*). Well! I never expected to meet a . . . (*He gets suddenly dizzy and breaks off and reaches for some support.* LEE *holds his arm and he goes down like an elevator and sits there.*)

ROSE. What's the matter!

MOE. Mister?

LEE. I'll get water! (*He rushes out.*)

ROSE. Is it your heart?

HENRY. 'Scuse me . . . I'm awful sorry . . . (*He gets on hands and knees as* LEE *enters with glass of water and hands it to him. He drinks half of it, returns glass.*) Thank you, sonny.

ROSE (*asking* MOE'S *opinion-agreement – she indicates within*). He better sit down.

MOE. You want to sit down? (HENRY *looks at him help-*

lessly.) Come in, sit down. (LEE *and* MOE *help* HENRY *to a chair and he sits.*)

ROSE (*bends over to look into his face*). You got some kind of heart?

HENRY (*embarrassed, and afraid for himself now*). Would you be able to give me something to eat? (*The three stare at him; he looks up at their shocked astonishment and weeps.*)

ROSE. You're *hungry*?

HENRY. Yes, ma'am. (*She looks at* MOE *whether to believe this.*)

MOE (*urgently*). Better get him something.

ROSE (*hurrying out immediately*). Oh my God in heaven!

MOE (*with a suspicious, even accusatory edge*). What're you doing, just going around? . . .

HENRY. Well, no, I come East when I lost the farm . . . they was supposed to be hiring in New Jersey, pickers for the celery? But I only got two days . . . I been to the Salvation Army four, five times, but they only give me a bun and a cup of coffee yesterday . . .

LEE. You haven't eaten since yesterday?

HENRY. . . . Well, I generally don't need too much . . . (ROSE *enters with tray, bowl of soup, and bread.*)

ROSE. I was just making it so I didn't put in the potatoes yet . . .

HENRY. Oh, beets?

ROSE. That's what you call borscht.

HENRY (*obediently*). Yes, ma'am. (*He wastes no time, spoons it up. They all watch him, their first hungry man.*)

MOE (*sceptically*). How do you come to lose a farm?

HENRY. I suppose you read about the Farmers' Uprisin' in the state couple months ago?

LEE. I did.

MOE (*to* LEE). What uprising?

LEE. They nearly lynched a judge for auctioning off their farms. (*To* HENRY, *impressed.*) Were you in *that*?

HENRY. Well, it's all over now, but I don't believe they'll be auctioning any more farms for a while, though. Been just terrible out there.

ROSE (*shaking her head*). And I thought they were all Republicans in Iowa.

HENRY. Well, I guess they all are.

LEE. Is that what they mean by radical, though?

HENRY. Well . . . it's like they say – people in Iowa are practical. They'll even go radical if it seems like it's practical. But as soon as it stops being practical they stop being radical.

MOE. Well, you probably all learned your lesson now.

LEE. Why! – He was taking their homes away, that judge!

MOE. So you go in a court and lynch him?

LEE. But . . . but it's all *wrong*, Pa!

ROSE. Shh! – Don't argue . . .

LEE (*to her*). But *you* think it's wrong, don't you? – Suppose they came and threw us out of *this* house?

ROSE. I refuse to think about it. (*To* HENRY.) So where do you sleep?

MOE (*instantly*). Excuse me. We are not interested in where you sleep, Mister . . . What's your name?

HENRY. Taylor. I'd be satisfied with just my meals if I could live in the basement . . .

MOE (*to* HENRY, *but half-addressing* ROSE). There is no room for another human being in this house, y'understand? – including the basement. (*He takes out two or three bills.*)

HENRY. I wasn't asking for charity . . .

MOE. I'm going to loan you a dollar and I hope you're going to start a whole new life. Here . . . (*Hands* HENRY *the bill, escorting him to the door.*) And pay me back but don't rush. (*Holds out his hand.*) Glad to have met you, and good luck.

HENRY. Thanks for the soup, Mrs . . .

ROSE. Our name is Baum. You have children?

HENRY. One's fifteen, one's nine. (*He thoughtfully folds the dollar bill.* GRANDPA *enters eating a plum.*)

ROSE. Take care of yourself and write a letter to your wife.

HENRY. Yes, I will. (*To* MOE.) Good-bye, sir . . .

MOE (*grinning, tipping his finger at him*). Stay away from rope.

HENRY. Oh yeah, I will . . . (*He goes.*)

LEE (*goes out on the periphery and calls to him as he walks away*). Good-bye, Mr Taylor!

HENRY (*turns back, waves*). Bye, sonny! (*He leaves.* LEE *stares after him absorbing it.*)

GRANDPA. Who was that?

MOE. He's a farmer from Iowa. He tried to lynch a judge so she wanted him to live in the cellar.

GRANDPA. What is a farmer doing here?

ROSE. He went broke, he lost everything.

GRANDPA. Oh. Well, he should borrow.

MOE (*snaps his fingers – to* LEE). I'll run down the street and tell him! He got me hungry. (*To* ROSE.) I'm going down the corner and get a chocolate soda . . . What do you say, Lee?

LEE. I don't feel like it.

MOE. Don't be sad. Life is tough, what're you going to do? Sometimes it's not as tough as other times, that's all. But it's always tough. Come, have a soda.

LEE. Not now, Pa, thanks. (*He turns away.*)

MOE (*straightens, silently refusing blame*). Be back right away. (*He strolls away across the stage, softly, tonelessly whistling. He goes.* GRANDPA, *chewing, the plum pit in his hand, looks around for a place to put it.* ROSE *sees the inevitable and holds out her hand . . .)*

ROSE (*disgusted*). Oh, give it to me. (GRANDPA *drops it into her palm and she goes out with it and the soup plate.*)

LEE (*still trying to digest it*). That man was starving, Grandpa.

GRANDPA. No – no, he was hungry but not starving.

LEE. He was, he almost fainted.

GRANDPA. No, that's not starving. In Europe they starve, but here not. Anyway, couple weeks they're going to figure out what to do and you can forget the whole thing . . . God makes one person at a time, boy – worry about yourself. (ROBERTSON *enters.*)

ROBERTSON. How did you react to that advice?

LEE. It was ridiculous – how could you only think of yourself when fellows with advanced degrees were out on the block throwing footballs around all day! – Some-big was wrong! – How'd it seem up where you were?

ROBERTSON. Well of course the rich are always quicker to be radicalised. Too much at stake to wait around waiting for something to happen. So the American Banking Association promptly asked the new Administration to nationalise the banks.

LEE. What!!

ROBERTSON. It had all gone out of control – they knew that. Did you know it?

LEE. All I knew was . . . (*He picks up a catalogue, opens it idly.*) . . . it was a very strange July. I'd graduated high school but nobody was mentioning college anymore. It was like having to . . . invent your life. (ROSE *has entered, sits reading a book.* LEE *points to catalogue.*) In

Cornell there's no tuition fee at all if you enrol for the bacteriology degree.

ROSE. None *at all*?

LEE. It's what it says. Maybe they're short of bacteriologists.

ROSE. That would be wonderful! Would you like that?

LEE (*stares; sees himself as bacteriologist. Sighs*). I don't know. Bacteriology?

ROSE (*wrinkles her nose*). Must be awful. Is anything else free?

LEE. It's the only one I've seen. – Boy, I wish I'd gotten better marks. I don't know what I was doing in school.

ROSE. You were in love with a baseball bat.

LEE. . . . I might've gotten a scholarship or something.

ROSE. I had a scholarship. But Grandpa couldn't wait to marry me off. (*Shakes her head.*) Two days before graduation the girl who was supposed to recite 'The Ancient Mariner' got a quinsy sore throat, so I had two days to learn 'The Ancient Mariner'.

LEE (*shakes his head*). Wow.

ROSE. And I got up there . . . without a mistake. They were spellbound.

LEE. I could never memorise like that.

ROSE. You've got a cat's head. You're always surprised – every morning the world starts up for the first time.

LEE (*mournfully*). I know. (*Thumbing a catalogue.*) Syracuse has –

ROSE. I've got to finish this before tomorrow. I'm overdue fourteen cents on it.

LEE. What is it?

ROSE. *Coronet* by Manuel Komroff. It's about this royal crown that gets stolen and lost and found again and lost again for generations. It's supposed to be literature, but I don't know, it's very enjoyable. (*She goes back to her book.*)

LEE (*closes all the catalogues, looks at her*). Ma?

ROSE (*still reading*). Hm?

LEE (*gently breaking the ice*). I guess it's too late to apply for this year anyway. Don't you think so?

ROSE (*turns to him*). Well, I guess probably for this year. I imagine so, dear.

LEE. Okay, Ma.

ROSE. I feel so terrible – all those years we were throwing money around, and now when you need it –

LEE (*relieved, now that he knows*). That's okay. I think maybe I'll try looking for a job. But I'm not sure whether to look under 'Help Wanted, Male', or 'Boy Wanted'.

ROSE. Boy. (*Their gazes meet. She sees his apprehension.*) Don't be frightened, darling – you're going to be wonderful! (*She hides her feeling in the book. She goes as the light dims.*)

LEE. (*coming centre, facing front*). Like all the winds had stopped, gone dead. (*Light on* SIDNEY *picking out a tune on a piano.*) So anything that moved at all seemed hopeful. (FANNY, SIDNEY'*s mother, enters, stands watching him, arms akimbo.*) And nothing could move like my aunt, Two-Gun Fanny Margolies. (*He goes.*)

FANNY. Sidney? (SIDNEY *sings opening line of 'Brother Can You Spare a Dime'.* FANNY *interrupts.*) Sidney? (SIDNEY *sings second line of song, oblivious.*) Sidney? (*He hears now but sings on.*) I have to talk to you, Sidney. (*He plays soft chords – evasively.*) Stop that for a minute!

SIDNEY (*stops playing*). Ma, look . . . it's only July. If I was still in high school it would still be my summer vacation.

FANNY. And if I was the queen of Rumania I would have free rent. You graduated, Sidney, this is not summer vacation.

SIDNEY. Mama, it's useless to go to employment agencies – there's grown men there – engineers, college graduates. They're willing to take anything. If I could write one hit song like this, just one – we wouldn't have to worry again. Let me have July, just July; see if I can do it. Because that man was serious – he's a good friend of the waiter who works where Bing Crosby's manager eats. He could give him any song I write, and if Crosby just sang it one time . . .

FANNY. I want to talk to you about Doris.

SIDNEY. What Doris?

FANNY. Doris! Doris from downstairs. I've been talking to her mother. – She likes you, Sidney.

SIDNEY. Who?

FANNY. Her mother! Mrs Gross. She's crazy about you.

SIDNEY (*not comprehending*). Oh.

FANNY. She says all Doris does is talk about you.

SIDNEY (*worried*). What is she talking about me for?

FANNY. No, nice things. She likes you.

SIDNEY (*amused, laughs incredulously*). *Doris?* – She's thirteen.

FANNY. She'll be fourteen in December. Now listen to me.

SIDNEY. What, Ma?

FANNY. It's all up to you, Sidney, I want you to make up your own mind. But Papa's never going to get off his back again and after Theresa's wedding we can forget about *her* salary. Mrs Gross says – being she's a widow, y'know? And with her goitre and everything . . .

SIDNEY. What?

FANNY. If you like Doris – only if you like her – and you would agree to get married. – When she's eighteen, about, or seventeen, even – if you would agree to it now, we could have this apartment rent-free. Starting next month.

SIDNEY (*impressed, even astounded*). Forever?

FANNY. Of course. You would be the husband, it would be your house. You'd move downstairs, with that grand piano and the tile shower . . . I even think if you'd agree she'd throw in the three months' back rent that we owe. I wouldn't even be surprised you could take over the bakery.

SIDNEY. The bakery! For God's sake, Mama, I'm a composer!

FANNY. Now listen to me . . . (DORIS *enters, sits at a distance and plays cat's cradle with string.*)

SIDNEY. But how can I be a baker!

FANNY. Sidney, dear, did you ever once look at that girl?

SIDNEY. Why should I look at her!

FANNY (*taking his arm, and turning him towards* DORIS). Because she's a beauty. I wouldn't have mentioned it otherwise. Look. Look at that nose. Look at her hands. You see those beautiful little white hands? You don't find hands like that everywhere.

SIDNEY. But, Ma, listen – if you just leave me alone for July, and if I write one hit song . . . I know I can do it, Mama.

FANNY. Okay. Sidney, we're behind a hundred and eighty dollars. August first we're out on the street. So write a hit, dear. I only hope that four, five years from now you don't accidentally run into Doris Gross somewhere and fall in love with her – after we all died from exposure!

SIDNEY. But Ma, even if I agreed – supposing next year or the year after I meet some other girl and I really like *her* . . .

FANNY. All right, and supposing you marry *that* girl and a year after you meet another girl you like better –

what are you going to do, get married every year? . . . But I only wanted you to know the situation. I'll close the door, everything'll be quiet. Write a big hit, Sidney. (*She goes out. Alone, he avoids looking in* DORIS'*s direction, goes in conflict to the piano, and touches the keys without sitting down. A pause. He turns towards* DORIS. *Then walks across to her. She continues playing cat's cradle. Slowly, he sits on his heels.*)

SIDNEY. Gee . . . you're really terrific at that, Doris. (DORIS *rises to him; they look – for different reasons – rather desperately at one another. He starts to walk, she catches up, and he slips his hand around hers as they go. Light on* MOE *and* ROSE*; she is in a housecoat and slippers, he in a business suit and hat. He is just giving her a peck.*)

ROSE. Good-bye, darling; this is going to be a good day – I know it!

MOE (*not too much conviction*). I think you're right. G'bye. (*He walks. Gradually comes to a halt. Much uncertainty and tension as he glances back towards his house and then looks down to think.* LEE *enters and* ROSE *gives him a farewell kiss. He wears a mackinaw and has a lunch bag and a book under his arm.*)

ROSE (*indicating his lunch bag*). Don't squeeze it, I put in some cookies . . . And listen – it doesn't mean you can *never* go to college.

LEE. Oh, I don't mind, Ma. – Anyway, I like it around machines. I'm lucky I got the job!

ROSE. All the years we had so much and now when you need it –

LEE (*cutting her off*). See ya! (*He leaves her; she goes; he walks and is startled by* MOE *standing there.*) I thought you left a long time ago!

MOE. I'll walk you a way. (*Doesn't bother explaining, simply walks beside* LEE, *but at a much slower pace than*

LEE *had before.* LEE *feels his unusual tension but can only glance over at him with growing apprehension and puzzlement. Finally.*) . . . Good job?

LEE. It's okay. I couldn't believe they picked me!

MOE (*nods*). Good. (*They walk again in silence, weaving all over the stage, the tension growing as* LEE *keeps glancing at* MOE, *who continuously stares down and ahead as they proceed. Now at last* MOE *halts and takes a deep breath.*) How much money've you got, Lee?

LEE (*completely taken aback*). . . . Money have I got?

MOE (*indicating* LEE'*s pockets*). I mean right now.

LEE. Oh! Well about – (*He takes out change.*) – thirty-five cents. I'm okay.

MOE. . . . Could I have a quarter? – So I can get downtown.

LEE (*an instant; astonished; then*). Oh sure, Pa! (*He quickly searches in his pockets.*)

MOE. You got your lunch – I'll need a hot dog later. (LEE *hands him a quarter.*)

LEE. It's okay. I have a dollar in my drawer . . . Should I? . . . (*Starts to go back.*)

MOE. No, don't go back. (*Proceeds to walk again.*) Don't, ah . . . mention it, heh?

LEE. Oh no!

MOE (*who has come to a halt*). She worries.

LEE. I know. (*To the audience, as* MOE *goes.*) We got on the subway together and it was hard to look at one another. So we pretended that nothing had happened. But something had. – It was like I'd started to support my *father*! And why that should have made me feel so happy, I don't know, but it did! And to cheer him up I began to talk and before I knew it I was inventing a fantastic future! (*Laughs.*) I said I'd be going to college in no more than a year, at most, two; and that I'd straighten out my mind and become an A student; and then I'd not only get a job on a newspaper, but I'd have my own column, no less! – By the time we got to Forty-Second Street the Depression was practically over! (*Laughs. Music.*) And in a funny way, it *was* – (*Touches his breast.*) – in here . . . even though I knew we had a long bad time ahead of us. – And so, like most people, I waited with that crazy kind of expectation that comes when there is no hope, waited for the dream to come back from wherever it had gone to hide. (*He turns and walks, putting on his cap, and as he passes out of his light,* ROBERTSON *appears – once again an old grey-haired man with a serious grin.*)

ROBERTSON. By my twenty-fourth birthday I had a seven-figure income; I considered retiring at twenty-eight. I've been a little of everything – war correspondent, ad-man, engineer – we built a section of the Sixth Avenue subway, in fact. – I've worked in many countries, but I guess the most shocking thing I ever saw was from the window of my Riverside Drive apartment. It was like Calcutta, thousands of people living in cardboard boxes, tin shanties along the Hudson River right below the Drive – at night their campfires flickered right down the length of Manhattan Island, like an army encampment. Some nights I'd go down and walk among them; remarkable, the humour they still had, and of course people still blamed themselves rather than the government. But there's never been a society that hasn't had a clock running on it and you couldn't help wondering – how long? How long would they stand for this? There were nights you could almost hear it in the air . . . (*He clucks his tongue like a clock, glaring out, continuing until . . .*)

Curtain.

Act Two

ROSE *is discovered walking up and down in agitation near the piano. She halts, stares, speaks.*

ROSE. But this piano is not leaving this house. Jewellery, yes, but nobody hocks this dear, darling piano. (*Plays, sings opening line of 'I Can't Give You Anything but Love, Baby'.*) The crazy ideas people get. Mr Warsaw on our block, to make a little money he started a race-track in his kitchen, with cockroaches. Keeps them in matchboxes with their names written on – 'Alvin', 'Murray', 'Irving' . . . They bet nickels, dimes. (*Picks up sheet music.*) Oh, what a show, that 'Funny Face'. (*Sings opening lines of 'He Loves and She Loves'.*) The years go by you and don't get to see a show and Brooklyn drifts further and further into the Atlantic; Manhattan becomes a foreign country and a year can go by without ever going there. (*Sings more of 'He Loves and She Loves'.*) Wherever you look there's a contest; Kellogg's, Post Toasties win five thousand, win ten thousand. Maybe I ought to try but the winners are always in Indiana, somehow. I only pray to God our health holds up because one inlay and there go the new hinges for the refrigerator. Sing! (*She sings opening of 'Do-Do-Do What You Done-Done-Done Before'.*) I must go to the library – I must start taking out some good books again; I must stop getting so stupid. I don't see anything, I don't hear anything except money, money, money . . . (*Plays Schumann. Then stops in frus-*

tration and walks into darkness. LEE *emerges in the spotlight with three fellow students wearing graduation caps and gowns. He is in a sweater. They are a quartet, singing, 'Down by the Old Mill Stream'. He steps forward as the others hum their harmony.* ROBERTSON *emerges, observes.*)

LEE. The very best place to be was school. Two pairs of socks, a shirt, a good shirt, and a mackinaw; part-time job in the library maybe – you could live like a king and practically never see cash.

ROBERTSON. Could that be why it held together as well as it did? – People saw how little they really needed, and maybe that gave them a new happiness.

LEE. You could keep the razor blade sharp for six months by rubbing it around in a drinking glass – you got to know that razor blade.

ROBERTSON. And naturally there were some tremendous new opportunities – banks foreclosing on some first-class properties that you could pick up for a song.

LEE (*rejoins quartet to finish song*). Boy, I hope next year's batch of guys can sing. (*He hugs his old friend* JOEY.) Is it possible, Joe!

JOE. What?

LEE. You're a dentist! (ROBERTSON *goes, smiling.*)

RALPH (*extending his hand*). Well, it was nice knowing you, Lee.

LEE (*shaking hands*). You decide what to do?

RALPH. There's supposed to be a small aircraft plant still working in Louisville . . .

LEE. Too bad you picked propellers for a specialty.

RALPH. Oh, they'll make aeroplanes again; if there's ever a war, you'll see.

LEE. How could there be another war?

JOE. Long as there's capitalism, baby.

RALPH. There'll always be war, y'know, according to the Bible. But if not, I'll probably go into the ministry.

LEE. I never knew you were religious.

RALPH. I'm sort of religious. They pay pretty good, you know, and you get your house and a clothing allowance . . .

JOE (*comes over, hand extended*). Don't forget to read Karl Marx, Lee. And if you're ever in the neighbourhood with a toothache look me up. I'll keep an eye out for your by-line.

LEE. Oh, I don't expect a newspaper job – papers are closing all over the place. Drop me a card if you open an office.

JOE. It'll probably be in my girl's father's basement. He promised to dig the floor out deeper so I can stand up . . .

LEE. What about equipment?

JOE. I figure two, three years I'll be able to open, if I can make a down payment on a used drill. Come by, I'll put back those teeth Ohio State knocked out.

LEE. I sure will! So long, Rudy!

RUDY. Oh, you might still be seeing me around next semester.

JOE. You staying on campus?

RUDY. I might for the sake of my root canals. There's a group of physicists taking over one of those abandoned houses on Lawrence Avenue – it's a little dark with all the windows boarded up, but it's rent-free, and if I just take one university course I'm still entitled to the Health Service – could get my canals finished.

LEE. You mean there's a course in the Lit School you haven't taken?

RUDY. Yeah, I just found out about it. 'Roman Band Instruments.'

JOE (*laughs*). You're kiddin'!

RUDY. No, in the Classics Department. 'Roman Band Instruments.' (*Pulls his cheek back.*) See, I've still got three big ones to go on this side. (*Laughter.*) Well, if you really face it, where am I running? Chicago's loaded with anthropologists. Here, the university's like my mother – I've got free rent, wash dishes for my meals, get my teeth fixed, and God knows, I might pick up the paper one morning and there's an ad: 'Help Wanted: Handsome young college graduate, good teeth, must be thoroughly acquainted with Roman band instruments'! (*Laughter.*)

RALPH. Hey, come on, we'll be late! I hope things are better by the time you get out, Lee. I'll keep looking for your by-line anyway.

LEE. No, I doubt it; but I might angle a job on a Mississippi paddleboat.

RUDY. They still run those?

LEE. Yeah, there's a few. I'd like to retrace Mark Twain's voyages.

RUDY. Well, if you run into Huckleberry Finn –

LEE. I'll give him your regards. (*Laughing,* RALPH *and* RUDY *start out.*)

RALPH. Beat Ohio State, kid!

JOE (*alone with* LEE *he gives him a clenched-fist salute*). So long, Lee.

LEE (*returning the salute*). So long, Joe! (*They are gone. Alone,* LEE *mimes pulling on a boat whistle. And quietly, to himself . . .*) Tooot! Tooooot! (*Blackout. Music. Lights emblazon the map at rear, the full breadth of the country appearing. Light on* LEE. *He is greasy, bare to the waist, wiping sweat off his face.*) Dear Mom and Pa. It's not really a job because they don't pay me, but they let me eat in the galley and I sleep on deck. The Mississippi is so beautiful, but sometimes it's frightening. Yesterday we stopped at a little town where they were handing out beans and meat to the hungry. The meat was full of maggots, you could see them wriggling out when the butcher cut into it. Suddenly a man with a gun pointed it at the butcher and forced him to give out the good meat which the government had paid him for, but which he kept for his paying customers. I keep trying to imagine how Mark Twain would deal with a scene like that. I don't understand how people are managing to live; a great many banks are boarded up. And there hasn't been rain for months; even the sky dried out. Every town is full of men sitting on the sidewalks with their backs against the storefronts. Just looking at you, or asleep. It's like a magic spell. I keep trying to find the holes in Marxism but I can't. I just read an article where the salaries of twelve executives in the tobacco business were more than thirty thousand tobacco farmers made. That's why this happened – the workers never made enough to buy back what they produced. The boom of the twenties was a gigantic fake. The rich have simply looted the people. And all President Hoover can say is to have confidence! I've passed fields of corn rotting on the stalks unsold, and sheriffs guarding them while on the roads people fall down from hunger. – There is going to be a revolution, Mama . . . (LEE *goes. Light on* ROSE *entering; she is reading from a letter.*)

ROSE. '. . . You can smell it in the air. I am going to try to find some way to help it happen.' But how is he ever going to become a sportswriter if he's a Communist? (*Three men enter, lower the top of the piano;* ROSE *hesitates, then gathers up her music and softly closes the keyboard cover. The men move the piano and bench out. She stands motionless, her face tired. She walks into darkness. Light up on* JOE. *He carries a large basket of flowers.*)

JOE (*facing audience*). Dear Lee. Sounds great in Mississippi, almost as good as here. I'm writing this in a whorehouse. I come here to get my sanity back. Such as it is. I decided to give myself one more year. After that I'll be too nervous to pick up an instrument. I may be too nervous now, this is my fear. I hope I'm wrong, but I'm thinking that the more trouble people have the less they question things. They're constantly talking to themselves on the IRT platform; they get so involved they even miss trains. Insanity is taking over. It's amazing how many Americans come up behind me and try to feel my ass. Yesterday, apropos of nothing, a small hunchback starts yelling at me, 'You will not find one word about democracy in the Constitution! This is a Christian republic!' Nobody laughed. The Nazi swastika is blooming all over the toopthpaste ads. I keep my nose in the flower basket but the subway smells of fascism. Up on Forty-Ninth Street and Eighth Avenue you can get two very good hot dogs for seven cents. What can that man make on two for seven cents? Suddenly some bright morning I expect to see millions of people pouring out of the buildings and just – I don't know what. Kill each other? Or only the Jews? Or just sit down on the street and cry? (*A bed is pushed on and* ISABEL *enters.* JOE *puts a second pair of pants on.*)

ISABEL. Ain't that uncomfortable, hey? Two pair of pants?

JOE. Gets very cold on the subway platform all day. The wind's like the Gobi Dessert. The only problem is when you run out to pee it takes twice as long.

ISABEL. Sell books too?

JOE. That's for reading. On my way home after work I'm

trying not to forget the English language. All I hear all day is shit, fuck, and piss.

ISABEL (*turning over the book*). It's about families?

JOE. Not exactly. That's by Engels: *The Origins of the Family and the State.*

ISABEL (*heavily impressed, turns a page*). Huh!

JOE (*a sudden thought*). Hey, why don't try to read it? I'd really like your reaction. You see, it's Marxism – says that all our relationships are basically ruled by money.

ISABEL (*nodding – as she well knows*). Oh, right. Yeah.

JOE. . . . No, I didn't mean exactly that way. (*Changes his mind.*) Although, maybe –

ISABEL. It's a whole *book* about that?

JOE. Well, he's trying to change it, you see. With socialism, the girls would all have jobs so they wouldn't have to do this.

ISABEL. But what would the guys do, though?

JOE (*only slightly flustered*). Well . . . they would just have to, ah . . . For instance, if I had money to open my office, I would probably get married very soon.

ISABEL. But I get married guys. (*Brightly.*) And I got two dentists you brought me . . . Bernie and Allan? . . . and they've got offices.

JOE (*troubled*). You don't understand. He shows that underneath our ideals and so on, it's all economies between people. And it shouldn't be.

ISABEL. You mean it should be like . . . love?

JOE (*not exactly, but . . .*). Ah . . . yeah, well, in a way.

ISABEL. Oh! Well, that's nice hey. (*Opening book again.*) I'd like to read this.

JOE. But don't expect a love story; it's basically theoretical anthropology.

ISABEL (*alarmed*). Oh. Well, I probably wouldn't have time. (*Embarrassed, hands him the book.*) But, hey, I meant to tell you – I know a very nice shark, maybe he could lend you for a drill.

JOE. I borrowed too much already. Here, take a carnation.

ISABEL. Oh – thanks, hey – But maybe keep it and sell it.

JOE. No, go ahead. I like the illusion. Here's your buck. (*Gives her a bill, puts on wool cap.*) Maybe next week, huh?

ISABEL. But couldn't you come a little later, hey? I'm still tired so early in the morning.

JOE. I gotta catch the office girls going to work – they like a flower for the desk. And I like you early; you look fresh, gives me an illusion. – Bernie finish the inlay?

ISABEL (*opening her mouth*). Yeah, he polished yesterday.

JOE (*looking in*). Bernie's good. I told you, we were in the same class. Say I said hello if you see him again.

ISABEL. He said he might come after five, said to give you his best.

JOE. Yeah, give him my best, too.

ISABEL. Till you I never had so many dentists. (ROBERTSON *appears.*)

ROBERTSON. I catch myself feeling smug about the tremendous number of extremist crusades that came roaring down the runway, but never took off. Furious, cruel-talking haters of labour, Jews and blacks and foreigners. Sometimes the political air could stink with hate. And worst of all, after two years or so, you knew that no one really had a solution to this crisis . . . none at all; and it bit closer and closer to the bone. (*Light rises on* LEE. *In dungarees, sitting at a counter eating a slice of watermelon.* ISAAC, *the black proprietor, is wiping the counter which he has just pushed on.*)

ISAAC. You been workin' the river long? I ain't seen you before, have I?

LEE. No, this is my first trip down the river, I'm from New York City. – I'm just kind of looking around the country, talking to people.

ISAAC. What you lookin' around *for*?

LEE. Nothing – just trying to figure out what's happening. Ever hear of Mark Twain?

ISAAC. He from around here?

LEE. Well, long time ago, ya. He was a story writer.

ISAAC. Uh, huh. I ain't seen him around here. You ask at the post office?

LEE. No, but I might. I'm kind of surprised you can get fifteen cents a slice down here these days.

ISAAC. Ohhh – white folks *loves* watermelon. Things bad as this up North?

LEE. Probably not quite. – I sure wouldn't want to be one of you people down here . . . 'specially with this Depression.

ISAAC. Mister, if I was to tell you the God's honest truth, the main thing about the Depression is that it finally hit the white people. 'Cause us folks never had nothin' else. (*Sees offstage.*) Well now – here come the big man.

LEE. He trouble?

ISAAC. He's anything he wants to be, mister – he the sheriff. (SHERIFF *enters – holstered gun, boots, badge, broad-brimmed hat, and carrying something wrapped under his arm. He stares silently at* LEE.)

LEE (*nervous half-apology*). I'm off the boat. (*Indicates offstage.*)

SHERIFF. You don't bother me, boy – relax. (*He sits at counter and sets his package down and turns with gravity to* ISAAC. LEE *makes himself unobtrusive and observes in silence.*) Isaac?

ISAAC. Yes sir. (*After a moment . . .*)

SHERIFF. . . . Sit down.

ISAAC. Yes, sir. (*He sits on another stool; he is intensely curious about the* SHERIFF'S *calling on him but not frightened. Since the* SHERIFF *seems to be having trouble starting the conversation:*) Looks like rain.

SHERIFF (*preoccupied*). Mm. – Hard to know.

ISAAC. Yeah . . . always is in Louisiana. – Anything I can do for you, Sheriff?

SHERIFF. Read the papers today?

ISAAC. I couldn't read my name if an air-o-plane wrote it in the sky, Sheriff, you know that.

SHERIFF. My second cousin Allan? The state senator?

ISAAC. Uh huh?

SHERIFF. The governor just appointed him. He's gonna help run the state police.

ISAAC. Uh huh?

SHERIFF. He's comin' down to dinner Friday night over to my house. Bringin' his wife and two daughters. I'm gonna try to talk to Allan about a job on the state police. They still paying the *state* police, see.

ISAAC. Uh huh. Well that be nice, won't it.

SHERIFF. Isaac, I like you to cook me up some of that magical fried chicken around six o'clock, Friday night. Okay? I'll pick it up.

ISAAC (*noncommittal*). Mm.

SHERIFF. That'd be for . . . let's see . . . (*Counts on his fingers.*) . . . eight people. My brother and his wife comin' over too, 'cause I aim to give Allan a little spread there, get him talkin' real good, y'know?

ISAAC. Mm. (*An embarrassed pause.*)

SHERIFF. What's that gonna cost me for eight people, Isaac?

ISAAC (*at once*). Ten dollars.

SHERIFF. Ten.

ISAAC (*with a little commiseration*). That's right, Sheriff.

SHERIFF (*slight pause. Starts to unwrap radio*). Want to show you something here, Isaac. My radio, see?

ISAAC. Uh huh. (*Runs his hand over it.*) Play?

SHERIFF. Sure! Plays real good. I give twenty-nine ninety-five for that two years ago.

ISAAC (*looks in the back of it*). I plug it in?

SHERIFF. Go right ahead, sure. You sure painted this place up real nice. Like a real restaurant. You oughta thank the Lord, Isaac.

ISAAC (*takes out the wire and plugs it in as . . .*). I sure do. The Lord and fried chicken!

SHERIFF. You know the county ain't paid nobody at all in three months now . . .

ISAAC. Yeah, I know. Where you switch it on?

SHERIFF. Just turn the knob. There you are. (*Turns it on.*) They're still payin' the *state* police, see. And I figure if I can get Allan to put me on – (*Radio music. It is very dim.*)

ISAAC. Cain't hardly hear it.

SHERIFF (*angrily*). Hell, Isaac, gotta get the aerial out! (*Untangling a wire at the back of the set*). You give me eight fried chicken dinners and I let you hold this for collateral, okay? Here we go now. (SHERIFF *backs aways stretching out the aerial wire, and* ROOSEVELT'S *voice suddenly comes on strong.* SHERIFF *holds still, the wire held high.* LEE *is absorbed.*)

ROOSEVELT. Clouds of suspicion, tides of ill-will and intolerance gather darkly in many places. In our own land we enjoy, indeed, a fullness of life . . .

SHERIFF. And nice fat chickens, hear? Don't give me any little old scruffy chickens.

ISAAC (*of* ROOSEVELT). Who's that talkin'?

ROOSEVELT. . . . greater than that of most nations. But the rush of modern civilisation itself has raised for us new difficulties, . . .

SHERIFF. Sounds like somebody up North.

ISAAC. Hush! (*To* LEE.) Hey, that's Roosevelt, ain't it?!

LEE. Yes.

ISAAC. Sure! – That's the President!

SHERIFF. How about it, we got a deal? (ISAAC *has his head close to the radio, absorbed.* LEE *comes closer, bends over to listen.*)

ROOSEVELT. . . . new problems which must be solved if we are to preserve to the United States the political and economic freedom for which Washington and Jefferson planned and fought. We seek not merely to make government a mechanical implement, but to give it the vibrant personal character that is the embodiment of human charity. We are poor indeed if this nation cannot afford to lift from every recess of American life the dark fear of the unemployed that they are not needed in the world. We cannot afford to accumulate a deficit in the books of human fortitude. (*With even the* SHERIFF *caught in the speech, its volume slowly fades . . . light starts to go down as* ISAAC *listens, and the* SHERIFF *still holds the wire. During the above,* LEE *has moved from* ISAAC *and* SHERIFF *as a crowd moves on, the unemployed who pause before a welfare worker who hands each a numbered slip of paper, and then continue off.* LEE *is anxiously looking around in a vast empty space. Now* MOE *appears and joins him. He is deeply anxious.*)

LEE. Hi, Pop! Glad you could get here.

MOE. One minute, Lee, before we go in there . . .

LEE. Look, Pa, if it's too embarrassing . . .

MOE. You sure you know what you're doing? . . . because I distinctly read in the paper that anybody wants to work can go direct to WPA and they fix you up with a job.

LEE. Originally, yes, but they changed it now. You can only get a WPA job now if you're on relief.

MOE. I don't understand that . . .

LEE. Well, there's sixteen million unemployed. They haven't got jobs for everybody.

MOE. Then what's Roosevelt been talking about?

LEE. He probably thought things would improve, and they didn't, so now you've got to be destitute to be eligible for WPA.

MOE (*pointing towards the line*). So this is not the WPA.

LEE. I told you, Pa, this is the relief office.

MOE. Like . . . welfare.

LEE. Look, if it embarrasses you –

MOE. Listen, if it has to be done it has to be done. Now let me go over it again. – What do I say?

LEE. You refuse to let me live in the house. We don't get along.

MOE. Why can't you live at home?

LEE. If I live at home, I don't need relief. That's the rule.

MOE. Okay. So I can't stand the sight of you.

LEE. Right.

MOE. So you live with your friend in a rooming house.

LEE. Correct.

MOE. . . . They're gonna believe that?

LEE. Why not? I've got some of my clothes over there.

MOE. All this for twenty-two dollars a week?

LEE (*angering*). What am I going to do? Even old-time newspapermen are out of work. – See, if I can get on the WPA Writers Project, at least I'd get experience if a real job comes along. I've explained this a dozen times, Pa, there's nothing complicated.

MOE (*unsatisfied*). I'm just trying to get used to it. All

right. Let's go. (*They embrace. Then:*) We shouldn't look too friendly, huh?

LEE (*laughs*). That's the idea!

MOE. I don't like you and you can't stand the sight of me.

LEE. That's it! (*Laughs.*)

MOE (*to the air with mock outrage*). So he laughs! (*The crowd of unemployed enters as a row of warehouse-like lamps lowers over the scene and a table and one chair are carried to Centre.* RYAN, *the social worker, enters with case folders. People stand around as in an impromptu relief office. Black and white. Old and young.* MOE *looks around.*)

ROBERTSON. I did a lot of walking in those days. The contrasts were so startling. Along the West side of Manhattan you had eight or ten of the world's greatest ocean liners tied up – I recall the S.S. Manhattan, the Berengaria, the United States – most of them would never sail again. But at the same time they were putting up the Empire State Building, highest in the world. But who would ever rent space in it when there were whole streets and avenues of empty stores? It was incredible to me how long it was lasting. I would never, never have believed we could not recover before this. Whole years were passing, a whole generation was withering in the best years of its life . . . (*The light on him goes out.*)

MOE (*continues*). Well! There's some nice-looking people.

LEE. Sure.

RYAN (*the supervisor, at a desk*). Matthew R. Bush! (*A very dignified man of forty-five rises, crosses, and follows* RYAN *out.*)

MOE. Looks like a butler.

LEE. Probably was.

MOE (*shakes his head mournfully*). Hmm! (*A baby held by* GRACE, *a young woman in the back, cries.* MOE *turns to look, then stares ahead.*) Lee, what'll you do if they give you a pick-and-shovel job?

LEE. I'll take it.

MOE. You'll dig holes in the streets?

LEE. It's no disgrace, Dad.

KAPUSH (*late sixties, Slavonic, moustache, ferocious frustration*). What can you expect from a country that puts a frankfurter on the Supreme Court? Felix the Frankfurter. Look it up.

DUGAN (*from another part of the room*). Get back in the clock, ya cuckoo!

KAPUSH (*turning his body around angrily to face* DUGAN *and jarring a black woman,* IRENE, *sitting next to him*). Who's talkin' to me!

IRENE (*middle-aged black woman*). Hey now, don't mess with me, mister!

DUGAN. Tell him, tell him! (RYAN *rushes in. He is pale, his waistcoat is loaded with pens and pencils, and a sheaf of papers is in his hand. A tired man.*)

RYAN. We gonna have another riot, folks? Is that what we're gonna have? Mr Kapush, I told you three days running now, if you live in Bronx you've got to apply in Bronx.

KAPUSH. It's all right, I'll wait.

RYAN (*as he passes* DUGAN). Leave him alone, will you? He's a little upset in his mind.

DUGAN. He's a fascist. I seen him down Union Square plenty of times. (IRENE *slams her walking stick down on the table.*)

RYAN. Oh, Jesus . . . here we go again.

IRENE. Gettin' on to ten o'clock, Mr Ryan.

RYAN. I've done the best I can, Irene . . .

IRENE. That's what the good lord said when he made the jackass, but he decided to knuckle down and try harder. People been thrown out on the sidewalk, mattresses, pots and pans, and everything else they own. Right on a Hundred and Thirty-Eighth Street. They goin' back in their apartments today or we goin' raise us some real hell.

RYAN. I've got no more appropriations for you till the first of the month and that's it, Irene.

IRENE. Mr Ryan, you ain't talkin' to me, you talkin' to Local Forty-Five of the Workers Alliance, and you know what that mean.

DUGAN (*laughs*). Communist Party.

IRENE. That's right, mister, and they don't mess. So why don't you get on your phone and call Washington. And while you're at it, you can remind Mr Roosevelt that I done swung One Hundred and Thirty-Ninth Street for him in the last election, and if he want it swung again he better get crackin'!

RYAN. Holy Jesus. (*Hurries away, but* LEE *tries to delay him.*)

LEE. I was told to bring my father.

RYAN. What?

LEE. Yesterday. You told me to –

RYAN. Get off my back, will ya? (*He hurries out.*)

DUGAN. This country's gonna end up on the top of the trees throwin' coconuts at each other.

MOE (*quietly to* LEE). I hope I can get out by eleven, I got an appointment with a buyer.

TOLAND (*Daily News open in his hands. He is next to* MOE). Boy, oh boy, looka this – Helen Hayes gonna put on forty pounds to play Victoria Regina.

MOE. Who's that?

TOLAND. Queen of England.

MOE. She was so fat?

TOLAND. Victoria? Horse. I picked up Helen Hayes when I had my cab. Very small girl. And Adolphe Menjou once – he was small, too. I even had Al Smith once, way back before he was governor. He was real small.

MOE. Maybe you had a small cab.

TOLAND. What do you mean? I had a regular Ford.

MOE. You lost it?

TOLAND. What're you gonna do? You can't make it in a cab anymore. The town is walkin'. I paid five hundred dollars, brand-new Ford, including bumpers and a spare. But thank God, at least I got into the housing project. It's nice and reasonable.

MOE. What do you pay?

TOLAND. Nineteen-fifty a month. It sounds like a lot but we got three nice rooms. – Providin' I get a little help here. What's your line?

MOE. I sell on commission right now. I used to have my own business.

TOLAND. Used-ta. Whoever you talk to, 'I used-ta'. If they don't do something, I tell ya, one of these days this used-ta be a country.

KAPUSH (*exploding*). Ignorance, ignorance! People don't know facts. Greatest public library system in the entire world and nobody goes in but Jews.

MOE (*glancing at him*). Ah ha.

LEE. What're you, Iroquois?

DUGAN. He's a fascist. I seen him talking on Union Square.

IRENE. Solidarity, folks, black and white together, that's what we gotta have. Join the Workers Alliance, ten cents a month, and you git yourself some solidarity.

KAPUSH. I challenge anybody to find the word democracy in the Constitution. This is a republic! *Demos* is the Greek word for mob.

DUGAN (*imitating the bird*). *Cuckoo!*

KAPUSH. Come to get my money and the bank is closed up! Four thousand dollars up the flue. Thirteen years in hardware, savin' by the week.

DUGAN. Mental diarrhoea.

KAPUSH. Mobocracy. Gimme, gimme, gimme, all they know.

DUGAN. So what're *you* doing here?

KAPUSH. Roosevelt was sworn in on a Dutch Bible! (*Silence.*) Anybody know that? (*To* IRENE.) Betcha didn't know that, did you?

IRENE. You givin' me a headache, mister . . .

KAPUSH. I got nothin' against coloured. Coloured never took my store away. Here's my bankbook, see that? Bank of the United States. See that? Four-thousand six-hundred and ten dollars and thirty-one cents, right? Who's got that money? Savin' thirteen years, by the week. *Who's got my money?* (*He has got to his feet. His fury has turned the moment silent.* MATTHEW BUSH *enters and sways.* RYAN *enters.*)

RYAN. Arthur Clayton! (CLAYTON *starts towards* RYAN *and indicates* MATTHEW BUSH.)

CLAYTON. I think there's something the matter with – (BUSH *collapses on the floor. For a moment no one moves. Then* IRENE *goes to him, bends over him.*)

IRENE. Hey. Hey, Mister. (LEE *helps him up and sits him in the chair.*)

RYAN (*calling to offstage*). Myrna, call the ambulance! (IRENE *lightly slaps* BUSH'*s cheeks.*)

LEE. You all right?

RYAN (*looking around*). Clayton?

CLAYTON. I'm Clayton.

RYAN (CLAYTON'*s form in his hand*). You're not eligible for relief; you've got furniture and valuables, don't you?

CLAYTON. But nothing I could realize anything on.

RYAN. Why not? – Is this your address? Gramercy Park South?

CLAYTON (*embarrassed*). That doesn't mean a thing. I haven't really eaten in a few days, actually . . .

RYAN. Where do you get that kind of rent?

CLAYTON. I haven't paid my rent in over eight months . . .

RYAN (*starting away*). Forget it, mister, you got valuables and furniture; you can't –

CLAYTON. I'm very good at figures, I was in brokerage. I thought if I could get anything that required . . . say, statistics . . .

IRENE. This man's starvin', Mr Ryan.

RYAN. What're you, a medical doctor now, Irene? I called the ambulance! Now don't start makin' an issue, will you? (*He returns to his desk.* CLAYTON *stands there, uncertain.*)

IRENE. Grace? You got anything in that bottle?

GRACE (*in a rear rank with a baby in her arms, reaches forward with a baby bottle which has an inch of milk on the bottom*). Ain't much left there . . .

IRENE (*handed the bottle, takes off the nipple*). Okay now, open your mouth, mister. (BUSH *gulps the milk.*) There, look at that, see? Man's starvin'!

MOE (*stands, reaching into his pocket*). Here . . . look . . . for God's sake. (*Takes out change and picks out a dime.*) Why don't you send down, get him a bottle of milk?

IRENE (*calls towards the back*). Lucy –

LUCY (*a young girl, coming forward*). Here I am, Irene.

IRENE. Go down the corner, bring a bottle of milk. (MOE *gives* LUCY *the dime and she hurries out.*) And a couple of straws, honey! You in bad shape, Mister – why'd you wait so long to get on relief?

BUSH. Well. I just don't like the idea, you know.

IRENE. Yeah, I know – you're a real bourgeois. Let me tell you something –

BUSH. I'm a chemist.

IRENE. I believe it, too – you so educated you sooner die than say brother. Now lemme tell you people. (*She is addressing the crowd.*) Time has come to say brother. My husband pass away and leave me with three small children. No money, no work – I's about ready to stick my head in the cookin' stove. Then the city marshal come and take my chest of drawers, bed, and table, and leave me sittin' on a old orange crate in the middle of the room. And it come over me, mister, come over me to get mean. And I got real mean. Go down in the street and start yellin' and howlin' like a real mean woman. And the people crowd around the marshal truck and 'fore you know it that marshal turn himself around and go on back downtown empty-handed. And that's when I see it, I see the solidarity, and I start to preach it up and down. 'Cause I got me a stick and when I start poundin' time with this stick, a whole lot of people starts to march, keepin' time. We shall not be moved, yeah, we shall in no wise be disturbed. Some days I goes to court with my briefcase, raise hell with the judges. Ever time I goes into court the cops commence to holler, 'Here comes that old lawyer woman!' But all I got in here is some tore-up newspaper and a bag of cayenne pepper. Case any cop start musclin' me around – that's hot pepper, that's hot cayenne pepper. And if the judge happen to be Catholic I got my rosary layin' in there and I kind of let that crucifix hang out so's they think I'm Catholic too . . .

LUCY (*enters with milk*). Irene!

IRENE. Give it here, Lucy. Now drink it slow, mister.

Slow, slow . . . (BUSH *is drinking in sips. People now go back into themselves, read papers, stare ahead.*)

RYAN. Lee Baum! (LEE *hurries to* MOE.)

LEE. Here! Okay, Dad, let's go. (LEE *and* MOE *go to* RYAN'S *desk.*)

RYAN. This your father?

MOE. Yes.

RYAN (*to* MOE). Where's he living now?

LEE. I don't live at home because –

RYAN. Let *him* answer. Where's he living, Mr Baum?

MOE. Well he . . . he rents a room someplace.

RYAN. You gonna sit there and tell me you won't let him in the house?

MOE (*with great difficulty*). I won't let him, no.

RYAN. You mean you're the kind of man, if he rang the bell and you opened the door and saw him, you wouldn't let him inside?

MOE. Well, naturally, if he just wants to come in the house –

LEE. I don't want to live there –

RYAN. I don't care what *you* want, fella. (*To* MOE.) You will let him into the house, right?

MOE (*stiffening*). . . . I can't stand the sight of him.

RYAN. Why I saw you both sitting here talking together the last two hours.

MOE. We weren't talking . . . We were arguing, fighting! . . .

RYAN. Fighting about what?

MOE (*despite himself growing indignant*). Who can remember? We were fighting, we're always fighting! . . .

RYAN. Look, Mr Baum . . . you're employed, aren't you?

MOE. I'm employed? Sure I'm employed. Here. (*Holds up the folded Times.*) See. Read it yourself. R. H. Macy, right? Ladies' full-length slip, genuine Japanese silk, hand-embroidered with lace top and trimmings, two ninety-eight. My boss makes four cents on these, I make a tenth of a cent. That's how I'm employed!

RYAN. You'll let him in the house. (*He starts to move.*)

MOE. I will not let him in the house! He . . . he don't believe in anything! (LEE *and* RYAN *look at* MOE *in surprise, and* MOE *himself is caught off-balance by his outburst. He goes.* RYAN *glances at* LEE, *stamps a requisition form and hands it to him, convinced.*)

LEE. Thank you. (*Turns front. The welfare clients go, the row of overheard lights flies out, and only the table remains. Light up on* EDIE. *She is at an easel.* LEE *in spotlight. To audience.*) Any girl with an apartment of her own was beautiful. She made thirty-six dollars a week. She was one of the dialogue writers for the *Superman* comic strip. Edie, can I sleep here?

EDIE. Oh, hi, Lee – yeah, sure. Let me finish and I'll put a sheet on the couch. If you have any laundry throw it in the sink. I'm going to wash later. (*He stands behind her as she works.*) This is going to be a terrific sequence.

LEE. It's amazing to me how you can keep your mind on it.

EDIE. Why! Superman is one of the greatest teachers of class consciousness.

LEE. Really?

EDIE. Of course. He stands for justice. You can't have justice under capitalism, so the implications are terrific.

LEE. You're beautiful when you talk about politics, you know that? Your face gets an emanation –

EDIE (*smiling*). Don't be such a bourgeois horse's ass.

LEE. Edie, can I sleep in your bed tonight?

EDIE. Where'd you get an idea like that?

LEE. I'm lonely.

EDIE. Why don't you join the Party, for God's sake?

LEE. Aren't you lonely?

EDIE (*flushing*). I don't have to go to bed with people to be connected to mankind.

LEE. Forget I said that, will you? I'm ashamed of myself.

EDIE. I don't understand how a person who knows Marxism can hold aloof from the struggle. You're lonely because you refuse to be part of history. Why don't you join the Party?

LEE. . . . I guess I don't want to ruin my chances; I want to be a sportswriter.

EDIE. Well maybe you could write for the *Worker* sports page.

LEE. The *Daily Worker* sports page? It's a joke.

EDIE. Then help improve it.

LEE. Tell me the truth. You really think this country can go socialist?

EDIE. Where have you been? We're living in the middle of the greatest leap in class consciousness that's ever happened. Hundreds of people are joining the Party every week! Why are you so goddamn defeatist?

LEE. I was in Flint, Michigan, when the sit-down strikes started. I thought I'd write a feature story, try to sell it. It was a very confusing experience. The solidarity was enough to bring tears to your eyes. But I interviewed about thirty of them afterwards. You ought to talk to them.

EDIE. Well they're still backward. I know that.

LEE. They're not backward, they're normal. Normally anti-Semitic, anti-Negro, and anti-Soviet. They're building unions and that's good, but inside their heads it's full of fascism.

EDIE. How can you say a thing like that?

LEE. I talked to thirty men, Edie, and I found one who even knew what socialism was. There's an openly fascist organisation in Detroit – the Knights of the White Camellia –

EDIE. I know that –

LEE. It's full of auto workers. All I mean is – I'm afraid there isn't going to be time to save this country. I mean – you're afraid too, aren't you? Or are you?

EDIE. You really want my answer?

LEE. I do, yes.

EDIE. Tomorrow we're picketing the Italian consulate; Mussolini's sending Italian troops into the Spanish civil war. Come. Do something. You love Hemingway so much, read what he just said. 'One man alone is no fucking good.' As decadent as he is, even he's learning. If you want to be any good you've got to believe. It really is the final conflict, like the song says. They're fighting it out in Spain and they're going to win; the German workers are going to rise up any day now and destroy Nazism . . .

LEE. Your face gets so beautiful when you –

EDIE. Anyone can be beautiful if what they believe is beautiful. I believe in my comrades. I believe in the Soviet Union. I believe in the victory of the working class here and everywhere, and I believe in the peace that will come to the world when the people take power.

LEE. . . . But what about now, Edie?

EDIE. Now doesn't matter. The future matters! (*She removes her hand from his and limps to her writing table.*) I've got to finish this strip. I'll make up the couch in a minute.

LEE. You're a marvellous girl, Edie. Now that I'm on relief I'll take you out to dinner. – I'll pay, I mean.

EDIE (*smiles*). You are something. Why must you pay for me just because I'm a woman?

LEE. Right. I forgot about that. (*He stands. She works. He saunters up behind her and looks at her work.*) Why don't you have Superman get laid? Or married even?

EDIE. He's too busy. (*She laughs softly as she works, and he suddenly leans down to kiss her, turning her face. She starts to respond, then pushes his hand away.*) What are you doing! (*He looks down at her, nonplussed. She seems about to weep, angry and flying apart.*) I thought you were a serious person! (*She stands.*)

LEE. You suddenly looked so beautiful . . .

EDIE. But you don't want me! Why do you make everything trivial? You have no real faith in anything, do you?

LEE. Must I agree with everything you believe before I can –

EDIE. Yes! It is all one thing. Everything is connected. The same cynicism you look at the auto workers with lets you pretend to have a serious conversation when all you want is to jump into my bed.

LEE. I can't see the connection between the auto workers and –

EDIE. I have to ask you not to sleep here.

LEE. Edie, because I don't go along with all your ideas, is that –

EDIE. I'm asking you to leave. You are not a good person! (*She bursts into tears, gets up, and goes into the dark.* LEE *turns front.*)

LEE. Dear Mother. Greetings from Lake Champlain! I got paid today and I am wallowing in WPA luxury. I bought a wool shirt and a pair of warm gloves – it's already pretty cold up here. But it's so pure up here you can get drunk breathing. The job is really wonderful; we are researching this whole section of New York state for a sort of intimate historical guide which the WPA is doing for every region of the country. I've been interviewing direct descendants of soldiers who were in the Battle of Fort Ticonderoga during the Revolution. They all send their love. Sorry you still miss the piano but as you say no use looking back. See you in a couple of months. Sincerely, Lee. P.S. I assume you're the one who put the ten-dollar bill in my jacket pocket. *Are* things better? Please tell me the truth. (*During the above,* ROSE *has entered and sat at the table shuffling cards. Then enter* GRANDPA, *her niece* LUCILLE, *her sister* FANNY, *and* DORIS, *wearing a bathrobe. They carry chairs, sit around the table and play cards.* GRANDPA *reads his paper.*)

ROSE. You're wearing out your bathrobe, Doris – why don't you ever get dressed?

DORIS. Well, we only live around the corner.

ROSE. You're so young and you hardly leave the block.

DORIS. Sidney really wants me to get my high school diploma!

ROSE. But first you'll have to get dressed.

LEE. Those long Julys in the Brooklyn neighbourhoods! The owlish smell of the attic seeping down the stairs, as the little house baked in the heat. Dreaming at cards they were waiting it out where nothing any longer seemed to move in the streets. And in the back of the mind was always the doorbell – who could it be but a hobo or bill collector? From Coney to Brooklyn Bridge the cards in their thousands snapped in the silences. (LEE *goes.* FANNY *brushes something off her chest as she stares at the cards.*)

ROSE. Concentrate – forget your dandruff for a minute. (*The others laugh.*)

FANNY (*laughing but piqued*). It's not dandruff! It was a thread.

ROSE. *Her* dandruff is threads. (*To* LUCILLE.) Your mother!

LUCILLE. You know what she actually asked me and my sisters to do . . .?

FANNY. What's so terrible!

LUCILLE. To come over and spend the afternoon cleaning her house!

FANNY. What is so wrong? We had the most marvellous times when you were growing up – the four of us just cleaning and cleaning.

ROSE. It's an obsession.

FANNY (*mops her face*). It's really getting like an oven in here, Rose . . .

LUCILLE. I'm going to faint.

ROSE. Don't faint, all the windows are open in the back of the house. We're supposed to be away.

FANNY. But there's no draught. – For Papa's sake . . .

LUCILLE. Why couldn't you be away and you left a window open? . . . Just don't answer the door.

ROSE. I don't want to take the chance. This one is a professional collector, I've seen him do it; if a window's open he tries to listen. They're merciless . . . I sent Stanislaus for lemons, we'll have cold lemonade. Play . . .

FANNY. I can't believe they'd actually put you out, Rose.

ROSE. You can't? Wake up, Fanny, you can't be so sweet anymore – it's a bank – may they choke after the fortune of money we kept in there all those years! Ask them for two hundred dollars now and they . . . (*Tears start to her eyes.*)

FANNY. Rose, dear, come on – something'll happen, you'll see. Moe's got to find something soon, a man so well-known . . .

ROSE. I wouldn't mind so much if we hadn't been so stupid! He builds a marvellous business like that and lets a bunch of idiot brothers suck him dry.

LUCILLE. Couldn't he ask his mother for a little? . . .

ROSE. His mother says there's a Depression going on. Meantime you can go blind from the diamonds on her fingers. Which he gave her! The rottenness of people! – I tell you, the next time I start believing in anybody or anything I hope my tongue is cut out!

DORIS. Maybe Lee should come back and help out?

ROSE. Never! Lee is going to think his own thoughts and face the facts. He's got nothing to learn from us. Let him help himself.

LUCILLE. But to take up Communism –

ROSE. Lucille, what do you know about it? What does anybody know about it? The newspapers? The newspapers said the stock market will never again come down.

LUCILLE. But they're against God, Aunt Rose.

ROSE. I'm overjoyed you got so religious, Lucille, but please for God's sake don't tell me about it again!

FANNY (*rises, starts to leave*). I'll be right down.

ROSE. Now she's going to pee on her finger for luck.

FANNY. All right! So I won't go! (*She returns to her chair.*)

ROSE. So what're we playing, Doris? – cards or statues? (DORIS *sits before her cards, full of confusion.*)

GRANDPA (*putting down his paper*). Why do they need this election?

ROSE. What do you mean, why they need this election?

GRANDPA. But everybody knows Roosevelt is going to

win again. I still think he's too radical, but to go through another election is a terrible waste of money.

ROSE. What are you talking about, Papa – it's four years, they have to have an election.

GRANDPA. Why! – If they decided to make him king . . .

ROSE. King!

FANNY (*pointing at* GRANDPA, *laughing*). Believe me!

GRANDPA. If he was king he wouldn't have to waste all his time making these ridiculous election speeches and maybe he could start to improve things!

ROSE. If I had a stamp I'd write him a letter.

GRANDPA. He could be another Kaiser Franz Joseph. And the whole country would get quiet. Then after he dies you can have all the elections you want.

ROSE (*to* DORIS). Are you playing cards or hatching an egg?

DORIS (*startled*). Oh, it's my turn? (*Turns a card.*) All right; here!

ROSE. Hallelujah. (*She plays a card. It is* LUCILLE'*s turn; she plays.*) Did you lose weight?

LUCILLE. I've been trying. I'm thinking of going back to the carnival. (DORIS *quickly throws an anxious look towards* GRANDPA, *who is oblivious, reading.*)

FANNY (*indicating* GRANDPA *secretively*). You better not mention . . .

LUCILLE. He doesn't have to know, and anyway I would never dance anymore; I'd only assist the magician and tell a few jokes. They're talking about starting up again in Jersey.

ROSE. Herby can't find anything?

LUCILLE. He's going out of his mind, Aunt Rose.

ROSE. Godalmighty. So what's it going to be, Fanny?

FANNY (*feeling rushed, studying her cards*). One second! Just let me figure it out.

ROSE. When they passed around the brains this family was out to lunch. (*She gets up, unnerved, goes to a point, and is halted by . . .*)

FANNY. It's so hot in here I can't think.

ROSE. Play! I can't open the window. I'm not going to face that man again. He has merciless eyes. (STANISLAUS *enters from left – the front door. A middle-aged seaman in T-shirt and dungarees.*) You come in the front door? The mortgage man could come today!

STANISLAUS. I forgot! I didn't see anybody on the street, though. (*Lifts bag of lemons.*) Fresh lemonade coming up on deck. (*He crosses.*) I starched all the napkins. (*He goes.*)

ROSE. Starched all the napkins . . . they're cracking like matzos. I feel like doing a fortune. (*Takes out another deck of cards, lays out a fortune.*)

LUCILLE. I don't know, Aunt Rose, is it so smart to let this man live with you?

DORIS. I would never dare! How can you sleep at night with a strange man in the cellar?

FANNY. Nooo! Stanislaus is a gentleman. (*To* ROSE.) I think he's a little bit a fairy, isn't he?

ROSE. I hope! (*They all laugh.*) For God's sake, Fanny, play the queen of clubs!

FANNY. How did you know I had the queen of clubs!

ROSE. Because I'm smart, I voted for Herbert Hoover. – I see what's been played, dear, so I figure what's left.

FANNY (*to* GRANDPA, *who continues reading*). She's a marvel, she's got Grandma's head.

ROSE. Huh! – Look at this fortune.

FANNY. Here, I'm playing. (*Plays a card.*)

ROSE (*continuing to lay out the fortune*). I always feed them on the porch, but when I hand him a plate of soup he says he wants to wash the windows before he eats. *Before!* That I never heard. I nearly fell over. Go ahead, Doris, it's you.

DORIS (*desperately trying to be quick*). I know just what to do, wait a minute. (*The women freeze, study their cards;* ROSE *now faces front. She is quickly isolated in light.*)

ROSE. When I went to school we had to sit like soldiers, with backs straight and our hands clasped on the desk; things were supposed to be upright. When the navy came up the Hudson River, you cried it was so beautiful. You even cried when they shot the Czar of Russia. He was also beautiful. President Warren Gamaliel Harding, another beauty. Mayor James J. Walker smiled like an angel, what a nose, and tiny feet. Richard Whitney, president of the Stock Exchange, a handsome, upright man. I could name a hundred from the rotogravure! Who could know that these upright handsome men would either turn out to be crooks who would land in jail or ignoramuses? What is left to believe? The bathroom. I lock myself in and hold onto the faucets so I shouldn't scream. At my husband, my mother-in-law, at God knows what until they take me away . . . (*Returning to the fortune and with deep anxiety.*) What the hell did I lay out here? What is this? (*Light returns to normal.*)

DORIS. 'Gray's Elegy in the Country Churchyard.'

ROSE. What?

FANNY (*touching her arm worriedly*). Why don't you lie down, Rose? . . .

ROSE. Lie down . . . why? (*To* DORIS.) What Gray's 'Elegy'? What are you? . . . (STANISLAUS *enters rapidly – wearing a waist-length, white starched waiter's jacket, a tray expertly on his shoulder on which are glasses, and rolled napkins. Rose shows alarmed expression as she lays a card down on the fortune.*)

STANISLAUS. It's a braw bricht moonlicht nicht tonicht – that's Scotch.

FANNY. How does he get those napkins to stand up!

ROSE (*under terrific tension – she tears her gaze from the cards she laid out*). What's the jacket suddenly? (*The women watch her tensely.*)

STANISLAUS. S.S. Manhattan. Captain's steward at your service. (*Salutes.*)

ROSE. Will you stop this nightmare? Take that jacket off. What're you talking about, captain's steward? Who are you?

STANISLAUS. I was captain's personal steward, but they're not sailing the Manhattan anymore. Served J. Pierpont Morgan, John D. Rockefeller, Enrico Caruso, Lionel –

ROSE (*very suspiciously*). Bring in the cookies, please. (*He picks up the pitcher to pour the lemonade.*) Thank you, I'll pour it. Go, please. (*She doesn't look at him; he goes out. In the silence she picks up the pitcher, tilts it, but her hand is shaking and* FANNY *takes the pitcher.*)

FANNY. Rose, dear, come upstairs . . .

ROSE. How does he look to you?

FANNY. Why? He looks very nice.

LUCILLE. He certainly keeps the house beautiful, Aunt Rose, it's like a ship.

ROSE. He's a liar, though; anything comes into his head, he says; what am I believing him for? What the hell got into me? You can tell he's full of shit and he comes to the door, a perfect stranger, and I let him sleep in the cellar!

LUCILLE. Shh! (STANISLAUS *enters with a plate of cookies, in T-shirt again, determinedly . . .*)

ROSE. Listen, Stanislaus . . . (*She stands.*)

STANISLAUS (*he senses his imminent dismissal*). I go down

to the ship chandler store tomorrow, get some special white paint, paint the whole outside the house. I got plenty of credit, don't cost you.

ROSE. I thought it over, you understand?

STANISLAUS (*with a desperate smile*). I borrow big ladder from the hardware store. And I gonna make nice curtains for the cellar windows. Excuse me, gotta clean out icebox. Taste the lemonade, I learn that in Spanish submarine. (*He gets himself out.*)

FANNY. I think he's very sweet, Rose . . . Here . . . (*Offers a glass of lemonade.*)

LUCILLE. Don't worry about that mortgage man, Aunt Rose, it's after five, they don't come after five . . .

ROSE (*caught in her uncertainty*). He seems sweet to you?

GRANDPA (*putting the paper down*). What Lee ought to do . . . Rosie?

ROSE. Hah?

GRANDPA. Lee should go to Russia. (*The sisters and* LUCILLE *turn to him in surprise.*)

ROSE (*incredulous, frightened*). To Russia?

GRANDPA. In Russia they need everything; whereas here, y'see, they don't need anything, so therefore, there's no work.

ROSE (*with an edge of hysteria*). Five minutes ago Roosevelt is too radical, and now you're sending Lee to Russia?

GRANDPA. That's different. Look what it says here . . . a hundred thousand American people applying for jobs in Russia. Look, it says it. So if Lee would go over there and open up a nice chain of clothing stores –

ROSE. Papa! You're such a big anti-Communist . . . And you don't know the government owns everything in Russia?

GRANDPA. Yeah, but not the *stores.*

ROSE. Of course the stores!

GRANDPA. The *stores* they own?

ROSE. Yes!

GRANDPA. Them bastards.

ROSE (*to* LUCILLE). I'll go out of my mind here . . .

DORIS. So who wrote it?

ROSE. Wrote what?

DORIS. 'Gray's Elegy in a Country Churchyard.' It was a fifteen-dollar question on the radio yesterday, but you were out. I ran to call you.

ROSE. Who wrote Gray's 'Elegy in a Country Churchyard'?

DORIS. By the time I got back to the radio it was another question.

ROSE. Doris, darling . . . (*Slowly.*) Gray's 'Elegy in a' – (FANNY *laughs.*) What are you laughing at, do you know?

FANNY (*pleasantly*). How would I know?

LUCILLE. Is it Gray? (ROSE *looks at her, an enormous sadness in her eyes. With a certain timidity.*) Well it says 'Gray's Elegy', right?

DORIS. How could it be Gray? That's the title! (ROSE *is staring ahead in an agony of despair.*)

FANNY. What's the matter, Rose?

DORIS. Well, what'd I say?

FANNY. Rose, what's the matter?

LUCILLE. You all right?

FANNY (*really alarmed – turning* ROSE*'s face to her*). What is the matter! (ROSE *bursts into tears.* FANNY *gets up and embraces her, almost crying herself.*) Oh, Rosie, please . . . don't. It'll get better, something's got to happen . . . (*A sound from the front door – galvanizes them.*)

DORIS (*pointing off left.*). There's some –

ROSE (*her hands flying up in fury*). Sssh! (*Whispering.*) I'll go upstairs. I'm not home. (*Starts right.* MOE *enters.*)

DORIS (*laughing*). It's Uncle Moe!

MOE. What's the excitement?

ROSE (*crossing to him*). Oh, thank God, I thought it was the mortgage man. You're home early. (*He stands watching her.*)

FANNY. Let's go, come on. (*They begin to clear table of tray, lemonade, glasses, etc.*)

MOE (*looking into* ROSE'*s face*). You crying?

LUCILLE. How's it in the city?

ROSE. Go out the back, huh?

MOE. The city is murder.

FANNY. Will you get your bills together? I'm going downtown tomorrow.

ROSE. Take a shower. Why are you so pale?

LUCILLE. Bye-bye, Uncle Moe.

MOE. Bye, girls.

DORIS (*as she goes with* FANNY *and* LUCILLE). I must ask him how he made that lemonade . . . (*They are gone.* MOE *is staring at some vision, quite calmly, but absorbed.*)

ROSE. You . . . sell anything? . . . No, heh? (*He shakes his head negatively – but that is not what he is thinking about.*) Here . . . (*She gets a glass from the table.*) Come drink, it's cold. (*He takes it, but doesn't drink.*)

MOE. You're hysterical every night.

ROSE. No, I'm all right. It's just all so stupid and every once in a while I can't . . . I can't . . . (*She is holding her head.*)

MOE. The thing is . . . You listening to me?

ROSE. What? (*Suddenly aware of her father's pressure on* MOE, *turns and goes quickly to him.*) Go on the back porch, Papa, huh? It's shady there now . . . (*She hands him a glass of lemonade.*)

GRANDPA. But the man'll see me.

ROSE. It's all right, he won't come so late, and Moe is here. Go . . . (GRANDPA *is moving upstage.*) . . . And why don't you put on your other glasses, they're much cooler. (GRANDPA *is gone. She returns to* MOE.) Yes, dear. What. What's going to be?

MOE. We are going to be all right.

ROSE. Why?

MOE. Because we are. So this nervousness every night is unnecessary and I wish to God –

ROSE (*indicating the table and the cards spread out*). It's just a fortune. I . . . I started to do a fortune, and I saw . . . a young man. The death of a young man.

MOE (*struck*). You don't say.

ROSE (*sensing*). Why? (*He turns front, amazed, frightened.*) Why'd you say that!

MOE. Nothing . . .

ROSE. Is Lee? . . .

MOE. Will you cut that out –

ROSE. Tell me!

MOE. I saw a terrible thing on the subway. Somebody jumped in front of a train.

ROSE. Aaaahhh – again! My God! You saw him?

MOE. No, a few minutes before I got there. Seems he was a very young man. One of the policemen was holding a great big basket of flowers. Seems he was trying to sell flowers.

ROSE. I saw it! (*Her spine tingling, pointing down at the cards.*) Look, it's there! I'm going to write to Lee to come home immediately. I want you to put in that you want him home.

MOE. I have nothing for him, Rose; how can I make him come home?

ROSE (*screaming and weeping*). Then go to your mother

and stand up like a man to her . . . instead of this goddamned fool! (*She weeps.*)

MOE (*stung, nearly beaten – not facing her*). This can't . . . it can't go on forever, Rose, a country can't just die! (*She goes on weeping; he cries out in pain.*) Will you stop? I'm trying! Godalmighty, I am trying! (*The doorbell rings. They start with shock, she facing left, he only half-turned toward the sound.* GRANDPA *enters hurrying, pointing left.*)

GRANDPA. Rose –

ROSE. Ssssh! (*The bell rings again.* MOE *presses stiffened fingers against his temple, his eyes averted in humiliation. Whispering.*) God in heaven . . . make him go away! (*The bell rings again.* MOE*'s head is bent, his hand quivering as it grips his forehead.*) Oh, dear God, give our new President the strength, and the wisdom . . . (*Doorbell rings, a little more insistently.*) . . . give Mr Roosevelt the way to help us . . . (*Doorbell.*) Oh, my God, help our dear country . . . and the people! . . . (*The doorbell rings unceasingly now as the lights lower. The sound of a sports crowd. Light on* LEE, *finishing his notes at ringside.* SIDNEY *in a guard's uniform appears. Both are grey-haired. Elements of a fight ring in background.*)

SIDNEY. Good fight tonight, Mr Baum.

LEE. Huh? It was all right.

SIDNEY. Pardon me bothering you, but I enjoy your column a lot.

LEE. Oh? Thanks very much. (*Starts to pass him.*)

SIDNEY (*finally coming out with it*). Hey!

LEE (*surprised by the impertinence*). Huh? (*Recognises him now.*) Sidney! Good God, Sidney!

SIDNEY. Boy, you're some cousin. I'm looking straight at you and no recognito!

LEE. Well I've never seen you in that uniform.

SIDNEY. I'm Chief of Uniformed Security here.

LEE. Great!

SIDNEY. I was surprised you were covering the fight tonight.

LEE. I decided to get back to my column again – Did I hear your mother died?

SIDNEY. Yep, she's gone – I was sorry to hear about Aunt Rose . . . and Moe.

VOICE (*off*). Takin' 'em out, Sidney!

SIDNEY (*calls off*). Yeah, okay. (*Spotlights over the ring go out.*)

LEE. And you are Doris are? . . .

SIDNEY. Oh yeah, we're practically the only ones we know who didn't get divorced. You know who'd love to see you? Remember Lou Charney?

LEE. Charney.

SIDNEY. On the track team, you remember – you and him used to trot to school together every morning.

LEE (*still not sure, but*). Oh yeah, Lou – how is he?

SIDNEY. He's dead – he got killed in Italy in the war . . . but his mother still talks about you and him trotting off together every morning . . .

LEE. Really . . . and who lives in our house?

SIDNEY. Puerto Rican FBI man. Nice people, but they never mow. (*Holds out hand knee-high.*) You knew Georgie Rosen got killed, didn't you?

LEE. Georgie Rosen.

SIDNEY (*holds hand out very low*). Little Georgie – sold you his racing bike, I think.

LEE (*recalling now*). Georgie too!

SIDNEY (*nodding happily*). Plenty of wars on that block.

LEE (*shakes his head*). – You look good, Sidney.

SIDNEY. You too. – It's a different country, though, huh?

LEE. How do you mean?

SIDNEY. I don't know – the attitudes, and all. But I can't help it – I guess I'm hooked on this country – I still look forward! Still keep waiting for the good news! – You probably think I'm crazy . . .

LEE. No, why should I?

SIDNEY (*grasps* LEE'S *arm gratefully*). You're that way too, right?

LEE. . . . I'm afraid so.

SIDNEY. I knew it! – Come on, Lee, let me drop you – I've got a car in the garage. – Can I buy you a drink?

LEE. Great!

SIDNEY. Listen, I'll send you a tape of my last song? – I call it 'A Moon of My Own'. Nice title, you think?

LEE. Yeah, that sounds terrific. (SIDNEY *is vanishing into darkness.*)

SIDNEY. 'A Moon of My Own' – suddenly came to me when I was sitting on the porch . . . (SIDNEY *goes into darkness, but* LEE *remains behind. And light rises, hazy and dim, on* ROSE *at the piano, very softly playing in an abnormally slow tempo that seems to come across a vast distance.* LEE *is in sharp white light.*)

LEE. After all these years I still can't settle with myself about my mother. In her own crazy way she was so much like the country. There was nothing she believed that she didn't also believe the opposite. She'd sit down on the subway next to a black man and in a couple of minutes she had him confiding some very intimate things in his life. Then, maybe a day later – (*Alarmed.*) 'Did you hear! They say the coloured are moving in!' Or she'd lament her fate as a woman: 'I was born twenty years too soon,' she'd say. 'They treated a woman like a cow, fill her up with a baby and lock her in for the rest of her life.' But then she'd warn me, 'Watch out for women – when they're not stupid they're full of deceit.' I'd come home and give her a real bath of radical idealism and she was ready to storm the barricades; by evening she'd fallen in love again with the Prince of Wales. She was so like the country; money obsessed her but what she really longed for was some kind of height where she could stand and see out and around and breathe in the air of her own free life. With all her defeats she believed to the end that the world was meant to be better. – I don't know; all I know for sure whenever I think of her is that I always end up – with this headful of life!

ROSE (*at piano*). Sing! (*He grins, turns quickly to her; she is far off in the distance, hands beckoning to him over the keyboard. As bright light flashes over the cloud-covered continent in the background . . . He walks towards her and lights lower to dark on them both, as* ROBERTSON *appears – in his seventies, with his cane.*)

ROBERTSON. Interviewers always ask the same two questions – could it happen again, is the first. I cannot get myself to believe that we would allow the whole economy to disintegrate again, but of course there is no limit to human stupidity. The second question is whether it was really Roosevelt who saved the country. (*Pause.*) In truth, he was a conservative, traditional man who was driven to the Left by one emergency after another. There were moments when the word Revolution was not regarded as rhetoric. But willy-nilly, the net result of all his floundering, his experimentation, his truth-telling and his dire prevarications – was that the people came to believe that the country actually belonged to them. I'm not at all sure that this was his intention; I'm not even certain exactly how it came to be, but in my opinion – that belief is what saved the United States.

Blackout.

THE ARCHBISHOP'S CEILING

With an Afterword by Christopher Bigsby

CAST

ADRIAN
MAYA
MARCUS
IRINA
SIGMUND

Act One

Some time ago.

The sitting-room in the former residence of the archbishop; a capital in Europe.

Judging by the depth of the casement around the window at Right, the walls must be two feet thick. The room has weight and power, its contents chaotic and sensuous. Decoration is early Baroque.

The ceiling is first seen: in high relief the Four Winds, cheeks swelling, and cherubims, darkened unevenly by soot and age.

Light is from a few lamps of every style, from a contemporary bridge lamp to something that looks like an electrified hookah, but the impression of a dark overcrowded room remains; the walls absorb light.

A grand piano, scarved; a large blue vase on the floor under it.

Unhung paintings, immense and dark, leaning against a wall, heavy gilt frames.

Objects of dull brass not recently polished.

Two or three long dark, carved chests topped with tasselled rose-coloured cushions.

A long vaguely decrepit brown leather couch with billowing cushions; a stately carved armchair, bolsters, oriental camel bags.

A pink velour settee, old picture magazines piled on its foot and underneath – Life, Stern, Europ-aeo . . .

A Bauhaus chair in chrome and black leather on one of the smallish Persian rugs.

A wide ornate rolltop desk, probably out of the Twenties, with a stuffed Falcon or gamebird on its top.

Contemporary books on shelves, local classics in leather.

A sinuous chaise in faded pink.

Layers of chaos.

At Up Right a doorway to the living quarters.

At Left a pair of heavy doors opening on a dimly lit corridor. More chests here, a few piled-up chairs. This corridor leads upstage into darkness (and the unseen stairway down to the front door.) The corridor wall is of large unfaced stones.

ADRIAN *is seated on a couch. He is relaxed, an attitude of waiting, legs crossed, arms spread wide. Now he glances up at the doorway to the living quarters, considers for a moment, then lifts up the couch cushions looking underneath. He stands and goes to a table lamp, tilts it over to look under its base. He looks about again, and peers into the open piano.*

He glances up at the doorway again, then examines the ceiling, his head turned straight up. With another glance at the doorway he proceeds to the window at Right and looks behind the drapes.

MAYA *enters from the living quarters with a coffee pot and two cups on a tray.*

ADRIAN. Tremendous view of the city from up here.

MAYA. Yes.

ADRIAN. Like seeing it from a plane. Or a dream.

He turns and approaches the couch, blows on his hands.

MAYA. Would you like one of his sweaters? I'm sorry there's no firewood.

ADRIAN. It's warm enough. He doesn't heat this whole house, does he?

MAYA. It's impossible – only this and the bedroom. But the rest of it's never used.

ADRIAN. I forgot how gloomy it is in here.

MAYA. It's a hard room to light. Wherever you put a lamp it makes the rest seem darker. I think there are too many unrelated objects – the eye can't rest here.

She laughs, offers a cup; he takes it.

ADRIAN. Thanks, Maya. (*Sitting.*) Am I interrupting something?

MAYA. I never do anything. When did you arrive?

ADRIAN. Yesterday morning. I was in Paris.

MAYA. And how long do you stay?

ADRIAN. Maybe tomorrow night – I'll see.

MAYA. So short!

ADRIAN. I had a sudden yen to come look around again – see some of the fellows. And you.

MAYA. They gave a visa so quickly?

ADRIAN. Took two days.

MAYA. How wonderful to be famous.

ADRIAN. I was surprised I got one at all – I've attacked them, you know.

MAYA. In the *New York Times*.

ADRIAN. Oh, you read it.

MAYA. Last fall, I believe.

ADRIAN. What'd you think of it?

MAYA. It was interesting. I partly don't remember. I was surprised you did journalism.

She sips. He waits; nothing more.

ADRIAN. I wonder if they care what anybody writes about them anymore.

MAYA. Yes, they do – very much, I think. But I really don't know. – How's your wife?

ADRIAN. Ruth? She's good.

MAYA. I liked her. She had a warm heart. I don't like many women.

ADRIAN. You look different.

MAYA. I'm two years older – and three kilos.

ADRIAN. It becomes you.

MAYA. Too fat.

ADRIAN. No . . . *zaftig*. You look creamy. You changed your hairdo.

MAYA. From *Vogue* magazine.

ADRIAN (*laughs*). That so! It's sporty.

MAYA. What brings you back?

ADRIAN. . . . Your speech is a thousand per cent better. More colloquial.

MAYA. I recite aloud from *Vogue* magazine.

ADRIAN. You're kidding.

MAYA. Seriously. Is all I read anymore.

ADRIAN. Oh go on with you.

MAYA. Everything in *Vogue* magazine is true.

ADRIAN. Like the girl in pantyhose leaning on her pink Rolls-Royce.

MAYA. Oh yes, is marvellous. One time there was a completely naked girl in a mink coat. (*She extends her foot.*) and one foot touching the bubble bath. Fantastic imagination.

It is the only modern art that really excites me.

ADRIAN (*laughs*).

MAYA. And their expressions, these girls. Absolutely nothing. Like the goddesses of the Greeks – beautiful, stupid, everlasting. This magazine is classical.

ADRIAN. You're not drinking anymore?

MAYA. Only after nine o'clock.

ADRIAN. Good. You seem more organised.

MAYA. Until nine o'clock.

They laugh. MAYA *sips. Slight pause.* ADRIAN *sips.*

ADRIAN. What's Marcus doing in London?

MAYA. His last novel is coming out there just now.

ADRIAN. That's nice. I hear it was a success here.

MAYA. Very much. – You say very much or . . . ?

ADRIAN. Very much so.

MAYA. Very much so. – What a language!

ADRIAN. You're doing great. You must practise a lot.

MAYA. Only when the English come to visit Marcus, or the Americans. – I have his number in London if you . . .

ADRIAN. I have nothing special to say to him.

Pause.

MAYA. You came back for one day?

ADRIAN. Well, three, really. I was in a symposium in the Sorbonne – about the contemporary novel – and it got so pompous I got a yen to sit down again with writers who had actual troubles. So I thought I'd stop by before I went home.

MAYA. You've seen anyone?

ADRIAN. Yes.

Slight pause.

MAYA (*he had reached for a pack of cigarettes; in the pause she turns to him quickly, to forgive his not elaborating*). . . . It's all right . . .

ADRIAN. I had dinner with Otto and Sigmund, and their

wives.

MAYA (*surprised*). Oh! – You should have called me.

ADRIAN. I tried three times.

MAYA. But Sigmund knows my number.

ADRIAN. You don't live here anymore?

MAYA. Only when Marcus is away. (*She indicates the bedroom doorway.*) He has that tremendous bathtub . . .

ADRIAN. I remember, yes. When'd you break up?

MAYA. I don't remember – eight or nine months, I think. We are friends. Sigmund didn't tell you?

ADRIAN. Nothing. Maybe 'cause his wife was there.

MAYA. Why? I am friends with Elizabeth. So you have a new novel, I suppose.

ADRIAN (*laughs*). You make it sound like I have one every week.

MAYA. I always think you write so easily.

ADRIAN. I always have. But I just abandoned one that I worked on for two years. I'm still trying to get up off the floor. I forgot how easy you are to talk to.

MAYA. But you seem nervous.

ADRIAN. Just sexual tension.

MAYA. You wanted to make love tonight?

ADRIAN. If it came to it, sure. (*He takes her hand.*) In Paris we were in the middle of a discussion of Marxism and surrealism and I suddenly got this blinding vision of the inside of your thigh . . .

She laughs, immensely pleased.

. . . so I'm here.

He leans over and kisses her on the lips. Then he stands.

Incidentally . . . Ruth and I never married, you know.

MAYA (*surprised*). But didn't you call each other . . . ?

ADRIAN. We never did, really, but we never bothered to correct people. It just made it easier to travel and live together.

MAYA. And now?

ADRIAN. We're apart together. I want my own fireplace, but with a valid plane ticket on the mantel.

MAYA. Well that's natural, you're a man.

ADRIAN. In my country I'm a child and a son of a bitch. But I'm toying with the idea of growing up – I may ask her to marry me.

MAYA. Is that necessary?

ADRIAN. You're a smart girl – that's exactly the question.

MAYA. Whether it was necessary.

ADRIAN. Not exactly that – few books are necessary; a writer has to write. It's that it became absurd, suddenly – here I'm laying out motives, characterisations, secret impulses – the whole psychological chess game – when the truth is I'm not sure anymore that I believe in psychology. That anything we think really determines what we're going to do. Or even what we feel. This interest you?

MAYA. You mean anyone can do anything.

ADRIAN. Almost. Damn near. But the point is a little different. Ruth – when we came back from here two years ago – she went into a terrible depression. She'd had them before, but this time she seemed suicidal.

MAYA. Oh my God. Why?

ADRIAN. Who knows? There were so many reasons there was no reason. She went back to psychiatry. Other therapies . . . nothing worked. Finally, they gave her a pill.

Slight pause.

It was miraculous. Turned her completely around. She's full of energy, purpose, optimism. Looks five years younger.

MAYA. A chemical.

ADRIAN. Yes. She didn't have the psychic energy to pull her stockings up. Now they've just made her assistant to the managing editor of her magazine. Does fifty laps a day in the swimming pool – It plugged her in to some . . . some power. And she lit up.

MAYA. She is happy?

ADRIAN. I don't really know – she doesn't talk about her mind anymore, her soul; she talks about what she does. Which is terrific . . .

MAYA. But boring.

ADRIAN. In a way, maybe – but you can't knock it; I really think it saved her life. But what bothers me is something else.

Slight pause.

She knows neither more nor less about herself now than when she was trying to die. The interior landscape has not changed. What has changed is her reaction to power. Before she feared it, now she enjoys it. Before she fled from it, now she seeks it. She got plugged in, and she's come alive.

MAYA. So you have a problem.

ADRIAN. What problem do you think I have?

MAYA. It is unnecessary to write novels anymore.

ADRIAN. God, you're smart – yes. It made me think of Hamlet. Here we are tracking that marvellous maze of his mind, but isn't that slightly ludicrous when one knows that with the right pill his anxiety would dissolve? Christ, he's got everything to live for, heir to the throne, servants, horses – correctly medicated he could have made a deal with the king and married Ophelia. Or Socrates – instead of hemlock, a swig of Lithium and he'd end up the mayor of Athens and live to a hundred. What is lost? Some wisdom, some knowledge found in suffering. But knowledge is power, that's why it's good – so what is wrong with gaining power without having to suffer at all?

MAYA (*with the faintest colour of embarrassment, it seems*). You have some reason to ask me this question?

ADRIAN. Yes.

MAYA. Why?

ADRIAN. You have no pills in this country, but power is very sharply defined here. The government makes it very clear that you must snuggle up to power or you will never be happy.

Slight pause.

I'm wondering what that does to people, Maya. Does it smooth them all out when they know they must all plug-in or their lights go out regardless of what they think, or their personalities?

MAYA. I have never thought of this question. (*She glances at her watch.*) I am having a brandy, will you? (*She stands.*)

ADRIAN (*laughs*). It's nine o'clock?

MAYA. In one minute.

She goes upstage, pours.

ADRIAN. I'd love one; thanks.

MAYA. But I have another mystery.

She carefully pours two glasses. He waits. She brings him one, remains standing.

Cheers.

ADRIAN. Cheers.

They drink.

Wow – that's good.

MAYA. I prefer whisky, but he locks it up when he is away.

She sits apart from him.

I have known intimately so many writers; they all write books condemning people who wish to be successful, and praised, who desire some power in life. But I have never met one writer who did not wish to be praised, and successful . . . (*She is smiling.*) . . . and even powerful. Why do they condemn others who wish the same for themselves?

ADRIAN. Because they understand them so well.

MAYA. For this reason I love *Vogue* magazine.

He laughs.

I am serious. In this magazine everyone is successful. No one has ever apologised because she was beautiful and happy. I believe this magazine.

She knocks back the remains of her drink, stands, goes towards the liquor upstage.

Tell me the truth – why have you come back?

ADRIAN (*slight pause*). You think I could write a book about this country?

She brings down the bottle, fills his glass.

MAYA. No, Adrian.

ADRIAN. I'm too American.

MAYA. No, the Russians cannot either.

She refills her own glass.

A big country cannot understand small possibilities. When it is raining in Moscow, the sun is shining in Tashkent. Terrible snow in New York, but it is a beautiful day in Arizona. In a small country, when it rains it rains everywhere.

She sits beside him.

Why have you come back?

ADRIAN. I've told you.

MAYA. Such a trip – for three days?

ADRIAN. Why not? I'm rich.

MAYA (*she examines his face*). You are writing a book about us.

ADRIAN. I've written it, and abandoned it. I want to write it again.

MAYA. About this country.

ADRIAN. About you.

MAYA. But what do you know about me?

ADRIAN. Practically nothing. But something in me knows

everything.

MAYA. I am astonished.

ADRIAN. My visa's good through the week – I'll stay if we could spend a lot of time together. Could we? It'd mean a lot to me.

An instant. She get up, goes to a drawer and takes out a new pack of cigarettes.

I promise nobody'll recognise you – the character is blonde and very tall and has a flat chest. What do you say?

MAYA. But why?

ADRIAN. I've become obsessed with this place, it's like some Jerusalem for me.

MAYA. But we are of no consequence . . .

ADRIAN. Neither is Jerusalem, but it always has to be saved. Let me stay here with you till Friday. When is Marcus coming back?

MAYA. I never know – not till spring, probably. Is he also in your book?

ADRIAN. In a way. Don't be mad, I swear you won't be recognised.

MAYA. You want me to talk about him?

ADRIAN. I'd like to understand him, that's all.

MAYA. For example?

ADRIAN. Well . . . let's see. You know, I've run into Marcus in three or four countries the past five years; had long talks together, but when I go over them in my mind I realise he's never said anything at all about himself. I like him, always glad to see him, but he's a total blank. For instance, how does he manage to get a house like this?

MAYA. But why not?

ADRIAN. It belongs to the government, doesn't it?

MAYA. It is the same way he gets everything – his trips abroad, his English suits, his girls . . .

ADRIAN. How?

MAYA. He assumes he deserves them.

ADRIAN. But his money – he seems to have quite a lot.

MAYA (*shrugs, underplaying the fact*). He sells his father's books from time to time. He had a medieval collection . . .

ADRIAN. They never confiscate such things?

MAYA. Perhaps they haven't thought of it. You are the only person I know who thinks everything in a Socialist country is rational.

ADRIAN. In other words, Marcus is a bit of an operator.

MAYA. Marcus? Marcus is above all naive.

ADRIAN. Naive! You don't mean that.

MAYA. No one but a naive man spends six years in prison, Adrian.

ADRIAN. But in that period they were arresting everybody, weren't they?

MAYA. By no means everybody. Marcus is rather a brave man.

ADRIAN. Huh! I had him all wrong. What do you say, let me bring my bag over.

MAYA. You have your book with you?

ADRIAN. No, it's home.

She seems sceptical.

. . . Why would I carry it with me?

She stares at him with the faintest smile.

What's happening?

MAYA. I don't know – what do you think?

She gets up and cradling her glass walks thoughtfully to another seat and sits. He gets up and comes to her.

ADRIAN. What is it?

She shakes her head. She seems overwhelmed by some wider sadness. His tone now is uncertain.

Maya?

MAYA. You've been talking to Allison Wolfe?

ADRIAN. I've talked to him, yes.

She stands, moves, comes to a halt.

MAYA. He is still telling that story?

ADRIAN (*slight pause*). I didn't believe him, Maya.

MAYA. He's a vile gossip.

ADRIAN. He's a writer, all writers are gossips.

MAYA. He is a vile man.

ADRIAN. I didn't believe him.

MAYA. What did he say to you?

ADRIAN. Why go into it?

MAYA. I want to know. Please.

ADRIAN. It was ridiculous, I know that. Allison has a puritan imagination.

MAYA. Tell me what he said.

ADRIAN (*slight pause*). Well . . . that you and Marcus . . . look, it's so stupid . . .

MAYA. That we have orgies here?

ADRIAN. . . . Yes.

MAYA. And we bring in young girls?

He is silent.

Adrian?

ADRIAN. That this house is bugged. And you bring in girls to compromise writers with the government.

Pause.

MAYA. You'd better go, I believe.

He is silent for a moment, observing her. She is full.

I'm tired anyway . . . I was just going to bed when you called.

ADRIAN. Maya, if I believed it, would I have talked as I have in here?

MAYA (*smiling*). I don't know, Adrian – would you? Anyway, you have your passport. Why not?

ADRIAN. You know I understand the situation too well to believe Allison. Resistance is impossible anymore. I know the government's got the intellectuals in its pocket, and the few who aren't have stomach ulcers.

He comes to her, takes her hand.

I *was* nervous when I came in but it was sexual tension – I knew we'd be alone.

Her suspicion remains; she slips her hand out of his.

. . . All right, I did think of it. But that's inevitable, isn't it?

MAYA. Yes, of course.

She moves away again.

ADRIAN. It's hard for anyone to know what to believe in this country, you can understand that.

MAYA. Yes.

She sits, lonely.

ADRIAN (*sits beside her*). Forgive me, will you?

MAYA. It is terrible.

ADRIAN. What do you say we forget it?

She looks at him with uncertainty.

What are you doing now?

MAYA (*slight pause. She stares front for a moment, then taking a breath as though resolving to carry on, her tone brightens*). I write for the radio.

ADRIAN. No plays anymore?

MAYA. I can't work that hard anymore.

ADRIAN. They wouldn't put them on?

MAYA. Oh, they would – I was never political, Adrian.

ADRIAN. You were, my first time . . .

MAYA. Well everybody was in those days. But it wasn't really politics.

ADRIAN. What then?

MAYA. I don't know – some sort of illusion that we could be Communists without having enemies. It was a childishness, dancing around the Maypole. It could never last, life is not like that.

ADRIAN. What do you write?

MAYA. I broadcast little anecdotes; amusing things I notice on the streets, the trams. I am on once a week; they have me on Saturday mornings for breakfast. What is it you want to know?

ADRIAN. I'm not interviewing you, Maya.

MAYA (*she stands suddenly, between anger and fear*). Why have you come?

ADRIAN (*stands*). I've told you, Maya – I thought maybe I could grab hold of the feeling again.

MAYA. Of what?

ADRIAN. This country, this situation. It escapes me the minute I cross the border. It's like some goddamned demon that only lives here.

MAYA. But we are only people, what is so strange?

ADRIAN. I'll give you an example – it's an hour from Paris here; we sit down to dinner last night in a restaurant and two plainclothesmen take the next table. It was blatant. Not the slightest attempt to disguise that they were there to intimidate Sigmund and Otto. They kept staring straight at them.

MAYA. But why did he take you to a restaurant? Elizabeth could have given you dinner.

ADRIAN. . . . I don't understand.

MAYA. But Sigmund knows that will happen if he walks about with a famous American writer.

ADRIAN. You're not justifying it . . . ?

MAYA. I have not been appointed to justify or condemn anything. (*She laughs.*) And neither has Sigmund. He is an artist, a very great writer, and that is what he should be doing.

ADRIAN. I can't believe what I'm hearing, Maya.

MAYA (*laughs*). But you must, Adrian. You really must believe it.

ADRIAN. You mean it's perfectly all right for two cops to be . . .

MAYA. But that is their *business*. But it is not Sigmund's business to be taunting the government. Do you go about trying to infuriate your CIA, your FBI?

He is silent.

Of course not. You stay home and write your books. Just as the Russian writers stay home and write theirs . . .

ADRIAN. But Sigmund isn't permitted to write his books . . .

MAYA. My God – don't you understand *anything*?

The sudden force of her outburst is mystifying to him. He looks at her, perplexed. She gathers herself.

I'm very tired, Adrian. Perhaps we can meet again before you leave.

ADRIAN. Okay. (*He looks about.*) I forgot where I put my coat . . .

MAYA. I hung it inside.

She goes upstage and out through the doorway. ADRIAN, *his face taut, looks around at the room, up at the ceiling. She returns, hands him the coat.*

You know your way back to the hotel?

ADRIAN. I'll find it.

He extends his hand, she takes it.

I'm not as simple as I seem, Maya.

MAYA. I'm sorry I got excited.

ADRIAN. I understand – you don't want him taking risks.

MAYA. Why should he? Especially when things are improving all the time anyway.

ADRIAN. They aren't arresting anybody . . .

MAYA. Of course not. Sigmund just can't get himself to admit it so he does these stupid things. One can live as peacefully as anywhere.

ADRIAN (*putting on his coat*). Still, it's not every country that writers keep a novel manuscript behind their fireplace.

MAYA (*stiffening*). Goodnight.

ADRIAN (*he sees her cooled look . . . slight pause*). Goodnight, Maya.

He crosses the room to the double doors at Left, and as he opens one . . .

MAYA. Adrian?

He turns in the doorway.

You didn't really mean that, I hope.

He is silent. She turns to him.

No one keeps manuscripts behind a fireplace anymore. You know that.

ADRIAN (*looks at her for a moment, and with irony*). . . . Right.

He stands there, hand on the doorhandle, looking down at the floor, considering. He smiles, turning back to her.

Funny how life imitates art; the melodrama kept flattening out my characterisations. It's an interesting problem – whether it matters who anyone is or what anyone thinks, when all that counts anymore – is power.

He goes brusquely into the corridor, walks upstage into darkness. She hesitates then rushes out, closing the door behind her, and calls up the corridor.

MAYA (*a suppressed call*). Adrian? (*She waits.*) Adrian!

He reappears from the darkness and stands shaking his head, angry and appalled. She has stiffened herself against her confession.

We can talk out here, it is only in the apartment.

ADRIAN. Jesus Christ, Maya.

MAYA. I want you to come inside for a moment – you should not have mentioned Sigmund's manuscript . . .

ADRIAN (*stunned, a look of disgust – adopting her muffled tone*). Maya . . . how can you do this?

MAYA (*with an indignant note*). They never knew he has written a novel, how dare you mention it! Did he give it to you?

ADRIAN. My head is spinning, what the hell is this . . . ?

MAYA. Did he give it to you?

ADRIAN (*a flare of open anger*). How can I tell you anything . . . ?

MAYA. Come inside. Say that you have sent it to Paris. Come . . .

She starts for the door.

ADRIAN. How the hell would I send it to Paris?

MAYA. They'll be searching his house now, they'll destroy it! You must say that you sent it today with some friend of yours.

She pulls him by the sleeve.

ADRIAN (*freeing himself*). Wait a minute – you mean they were taping us in bed?

MAYA. I don't know. I don't know when it was installed. Please . . . simply say that you have sent the manuscript to Paris. Come.

She grasps the door handle.

ADRIAN (*stepping back from the door*). That's a crime.

She turns to him with a contemptuous look.

Well it is, isn't it? Anyway, I didn't say it was his book.

MAYA. It was obviously him. Say you have sent it out! You must!

She opens the door instantly, enters the room, and speaking in a relaxed, normal tone . . .

Perhaps you'd better stay until the rain lets up. I might go to bed, but why don't you make yourself comfortable?

ADRIAN (*he hesitates in the corridor, then enters the room. He stands there in silence, glancing about*). . . . All right. Thanks.

He stands there silent, in his fear.

MAYA. Yes?

ADRIAN. Incidentally.

He breaks off. A long hiatus. He is internally positioning himself to the situation.

. . . that manuscript I mentioned.

MAYA. Yes?

ADRIAN. It's in Paris by now. I . . . gave it to a friend who was leaving this morning.

MAYA. Oh?

ADRIAN. Yes.

Slight pause. It occurs to him suddenly . . .

A girl.

MAYA (*as though amused*). You already have girls here?

ADRIAN (*starting to grin*). Well not really – she's a cousin of mine. Actually, a second cousin. Just happened to meet her on the street. All right if I have another brandy?

MAYA. Of course.

He pours.

ADRIAN. I'll be going in a minute.

He sits in his coat on the edge of a chair with his glass.

Just let me digest this. This drink, I mean.

She sits on the edge of another chair a distance away.

Quite an atmosphere in this house. I never realised it before.

MAYA. It's so old. Sixteenth century, I think.

ADRIAN. It's so alive – once you're aware of it.

MAYA. They built very well in those days.

ADRIAN (*directly to her*). Incredible. I really didn't believe it.

MAYA. Please go.

ADRIAN. In one minute. Did I dream it or did it belong to the archbishop?

MAYA. It was his residence.

ADRIAN (*looks up to the ceiling*). That explains the cherubims . . . (*He looks at his drink.*) . . . and the antonyms.

She stands.

I'm going. This is . . . (*He looks around.*) . . . this is what

I never got into my book – this doubleness. This density with angels hovering overhead. Like power always with you in a room. Like God, in a way. Just tell me – do you ever get where you've forgotten it?

MAYA. I don't really live here anymore.

ADRIAN. Why? You found this style oppressive?

MAYA. I don't hear the rain. Please.

ADRIAN (*stands facing her*). I'm not sure I should but I'm filling up with sympathy. I'm sorry as hell, Maya.

She is silent.

I could hire a car – let's meet for lunch and take a drive in the country.

MAYA. All right. I'll pick you up at the hotel. (*She starts past him toward the doors.*)

ADRIAN (*he takes her hand as she passes*). Thirty seconds. Please. I want to chat. Just to hear myself. (*Moving her to a chair.*) Half a minute . . . just in case you don't show up.

MAYA (*sitting*). Of course I will.

ADRIAN (*clings to her hand, kneebends before her*). I've never asked you before – you ever been married?

She laughs.

ADRIAN. Come on, give me a chat. Were you?

MAYA. Never, no.

ADRIAN. And what were your people – middle class?

MAYA. Workers. They died of flu in the war.

ADRIAN. Who brought you up?

MAYA. The nuns.

ADRIAN (*stands; looks around*). . . . Is it always like a performance? Like we're quoting ourselves?

MAYA (*she stands*). Goodnight.

She goes and opens a door.

ADRIAN. My God – you poor girl.

He takes her into his arms and kisses her.

Maybe I should say – in all fairness – (*Leaving her, he ad-*

dresses the ceiling.) that the city looks much cleaner than my last time. And there's much more stuff in the shops. And the girls have shaved their legs. In fact – (*He turns to her – she is smiling.*) this is the truth – I met my dentist in the hotel this morning. He's crazy about this country! (*With a wild underlay of laughter.*) Can't get over the way he can walk the streets any hour of the night, which is impossible in New York. Said he'd never felt so relaxed and free in his whole life! And at that very instant, Sigmund and Otto walked into the lobby and he congratulated them on having such a fine up-and-coming little civilisation!

He suddenly yells at the top of his lungs.

Forgive me, I scream in New York, sometimes.

She is half-smiling, alert to him; he comes to the open doorway and grasps her hands.

Goodnight. And if I never see you again . . .

MAYA. I'll be there, why not?

ADRIAN. How do I know? But just in case – I want you to know that I'll never forget you in that real short skirt you wore last time, and the moment when you slung one leg over the arm of the chair. You have a sublime sluttishness, Maya – don't be mad, it's a gift when it's sublime.

She laughs.

How marvellous to see you laugh – come, walk me downstairs.

He pulls her through the doorway.

MAYA. It's too cold out here . . .

ADRIAN (*shuts the door to the room, draws her away from it*). For old times' sake . . .

MAYA. We'll talk tomorrow.

ADRIAN (*with a wild smile, excited eyes*). You're a government agent?

MAYA. What can I say? Will you believe anything?

ADRIAN (*on the verge of laughter*). My spine is tingling. In my book, Maya – I may as well tell you, I've been struggling with my sanity the last ten minutes – in my book I made you an agent who screws all the writers and blackmails them so they'll give up fighting the government. And I abandoned it because I finally decided it was too melodramatic, the characters got lost in the plot. I invented it and I didn't believe it; and I'm standing here looking at you and *I still don't believe it*!

MAYA. Why should you?

ADRIAN (*instantly, pointing into her face*). That's what you say in the book! (*He grasps her hand passionately in both of his.*) Maya, listen – you've got to help me. I believe in your goodness. I don't care what you've done, I still believe that deep inside you're a rebel and you hate this goddamned government. You've got to tell me – I'll stay through the week – we'll talk, and you're going to tell me what goes on in your body, in your head in this situation.

MAYA. . . . Wait a minute . . .

ADRIAN (*kissing her hands*). Maya, you've made me believe in my book!

She suddenly turns her head. He does. Then he sees her apprehension.

ADRIAN. You expecting somebody?

Voices are heard now from below. She is listening.

Maya?

MAYA (*mystified*). Perhaps some friends of Marcus.

ADRIAN. He gives out the key?

MAYA. Go, please. Goodnight.

She enters the room. He follows her in.

ADRIAN. You need any help?

A MAN *and* WOMAN *appear from upstage darkness in the corridor.*

MAYA. No – no, I am not afraid . . . (*She moves him to the door.*)

ADRIAN. I'll be glad to stay . . .

He turns, sees the man, who is just approaching the door, a valise in his hand, wearing a raincoat.

For Christ's sake – it's Marcus!

MARCUS *is older, fifty-eight. He puts down his valise, spreads out his arms.*

MARCUS. Adrian!

Laughter. A GIRL, *beautiful, very young, stands a step behind him as he and* ADRIAN *embrace.*

MAYA (*within the room*). Marcus?

MARCUS (*entering the room*). You're here, Maya! This is marvellous.

He gives her a peck. The GIRL *enters, stands there looking around.*

(*To* ADRIAN.) A friend of yours is parking my car, he'll be delighted to see you.

ADRIAN. Friend of *mine*?

MARCUS. Sigmund.

MAYA. Sigmund?

ADRIAN. Sigmund's *here*?

MARCUS. He's coming up for a drink. We ran into each other at the airport. (*To* MAYA.) Is there food? (*to* ADRIAN.) You'll stay, won't you? I'll call some people, we can have a party.

ADRIAN. Party? (*Flustered, glances at* MAYA.) Well . . . yeah, great!

An understanding outburst of laughter between him and MARCUS.

MAYA. There's only some ham. I'm going home.

She turns to go upstage to the bedroom.

MARCUS (*instantly*). Oh no, Maya! – You mustn't. I was going to call you first thing . . . (*Recalling.*) Wait, I have something for you.

He hurriedly zips open a pocket of his valise, takes out a pair of shoes in tissue.

I had an hour in Frankfurt. Look, dear . . .

He unwraps the tissue. Her face lights. She half unwillingly takes them.

MAYA. Oh my God.

MARCUS *laughs. She kicks off a shoe and tries one on.*

MARCUS. Right size?

IRINA (*as* MAYA *puts on the other shoe*). Highly beautiful.

MAYA *takes a few steps watching her feet, then goes to* MARCUS *and gives him a kiss, then looks into his eyes with a faint smile, her longing and hatred.*

MARCUS (*taking out folds of money*). Here, darling . . . ask Mrs Andrus to prepare something, will you? (*Handing her money.*) Let's have an evening. (*He starts her toward the bedroom door upstage.*) But come and put something on, it's raining. (*And comes face to face with the* GIRL.) Oh, excuse me – this is Irina . . .

MAYA *barely nods, and goes back to pick up her other shoes.*

ADRIAN. I'll go along with you, Maya – (*He reaches for his coat.*)

MARCUS. No, it's only down the street. Irina, this is my good friend, Maya.

IRINA. 'Aloo.

MAYA *silently shakes her hand.*

MARCUS. And here is Adrian Wallach. Very important American writer.

MAYA *exits upstage.*

ADRIAN. How do you do?

IRINA. 'Aloo. I see you Danemark.

ADRIAN. She's going to see me in Denmark?

MARCUS. She's Danish. But she speaks a little English.

IRINA (*with forefinger and thumb barely separated – to* ADRIAN).

Very small.

ADRIAN. When do you want to meet in Denmark?

MAYA *enters putting on a raincoat.*

MAYA. Sausages?

MARCUS. And maybe some cheese and bread and some fruit. I'll open wine.

IRINA. I see your book.

ADRIAN (*suddenly – as* MAYA *goes for the door*). Wait! – I'll walk her there . . .

MAYA *hesitates at the door.*

MARCUS (*grasping* ADRIAN'*s arm, laughing*). No-no-no, you are our guest; please, it's only two doors down. Maya doesn't mind.

MAYA *starts out to the door.* SIGMUND *appears in the corridor. A heavy man shaking out his raincoat. He is in his late forties. She halts before the doorway.*

MAYA (*questioningly; but with a unique respect*). Sigmund.

SIGMUND. Maya.

He kisses the palm of her hand. For a moment they stand facing each other.

MARCUS. Look who we have here, Sigmund!

MAYA *exits up the corridor as* SIGMUND *enters the room.*

SIGMUND. Oh – my friend!

He embraces ADRIAN, *laughing, patting his back.*

ADRIAN. How's it going, Sigmund? (*Grasping* SIGMUND'*s hand.*) What a terrific surprise! How's your cold, did you take my pills?

SIGMUND. Yes, thank you. I take pills, vodka, brandy, whisky – now I have only headache. (*With a nod to* IRINA.) Grüss Gött.

MARCUS *goes and opens a chest, brings bottles and glasses to the marble table.*

IRINA. *Grüss Gött.*

ADRIAN. Oh, you speak German?

IRINA (*with the gesture*). Very small.

MARCUS. Come, help yourselves. (*Taking a key ring out of his valise.*) I have whisky for you, Adrian.

ADRIAN. I'll drink brandy, how about you, Sigmund?

SIGMUND. For me whisky.

MARCUS (*taking out an address book*). I'll call a couple of people, all right?

ADRIAN. *Girls*!

SIGMUND *sits downstage, takes out a cigarette.*

MARCUS. If you feel like it.

ADRIAN (*glancing at* SIGMUND *who is lighting up*). Maybe better just us.

MARCUS. Sigmund likes a group. (*He picks up his valise.*)

SIGMUND. What you like.

ADRIAN. (*To* MARCUS). Well okay.

MARCUS (*pointing upstage to* IRINA). Loo?

IRINA. Oh ya!

He holds her by the waist carrying the valise in his free hand, as they move upstage he says to SIGMUND.) We can talk in the bedroom in a little while.

He exits with IRINA.

ADRIAN. That's a nice piece of Danish.

SIGMUND *draws on his cigarette.* ADRIAN *gets beside him and taps his shoulder;* SIGMUND *turns up to him.* ADRIAN *points to ceiling, then to his own ear.*

Capish?

SIGMUND *turns front, expressionless.*

SIGMUND. The police have confiscated my manuscript.

ADRIAN (*his hand flies out to grip* SIGMUND's *shoulder*). No! Oh Jesus – when?

SIGMUND. Now. Tonight.

ADRIAN (*glancing quickly around*). He had a record player ...

SIGMUND (*a contemptuous wave toward the ceiling*). No – I don't care.

ADRIAN. The last fifteen-twenty minutes you mean?

SIGMUND. Tonight. They have take it away.

ADRIAN. My God, Sigmund . . .

SIGMUND *turns to him.*

I mentioned something to Maya, but I had no idea it was really . . .

Breaks off, pointing to the ceiling.

SIGMUND. When, you told Maya?

ADRIAN. In the last fifteen minutes or so.

SIGMUND. No – they came earlier – around six o'clock.

ADRIAN. Nearly stopped my heart . . .

SIGMUND. No, I believe they find out for different reason.

ADRIAN. Why?

SIGMUND. I was so happy. (*Pause.*)

ADRIAN. So they figured you'd finished the book?

SIGMUND. I think so. I worked five years on this novel.

ADRIAN. How would they know you were happy?

SIGMUND (*pause. With a certain projection*). In this city, a man my age who is happy, attract attention.

ADRIAN. . . . Listen. When I leave tomorrow you can give . . .

He stops himself, glances upstage to the bedroom doorway, taking out a notebook and pencil. As he writes . . . speaking in a tone of forced relaxation . . .

Before I leave you've got to give me a tour of the Old Roman bath . . .

He shows the page to SIGMUND *who reads it and looks up at him.*

SIGMUND *shakes his head negatively.*

ADRIAN (*horrified*). They've got the only . . . ?

SIGMUND *nods positively and turns away.*

ADRIAN (*appalled*). Sigmund – why?

SIGMUND. I thought would be safer with . . . (*He holds up a single finger.*)

Pause. ADRIAN *keeps shaking his head.*

ADRIAN (*sotto*). What are you doing here?

SIGMUND. I met him in the airport by accident.

ADRIAN. What were you doing at the airport?

SIGMUND. To tell my wife. She works there.

ADRIAN. I thought she was a chemist.

SIGMUND. She is wife to me – they don't permit her to be chemist. She clean the floor, the windows in the airport.

ADRIAN. Oh my God, Sigmund . . . (*Pause.*) Is there anything you can do?

SIGMUND. I try.

ADRIAN. Try what?

SIGMUND *thumbs upstage.*

Could he?

SIGMUND *throws up his chin – tremendous influence.*

Would he?

SIGMUND *holding a telephone to his mouth, then indicates the bedroom doorway.*

Really? To help?

SIGMUND. Is possible.

ADRIAN. Can you figure him out?

SIGMUND *extends a hand and rocks it, an expression of uncertainty on his face.*

ADRIAN. And Maya?

SIGMUND (*for a moment he makes no answer*). Woman is always complicated.

ADRIAN. You know that they . . . lie a lot.

SIGMUND. Yes.

Slight pause. He looks now directly into ADRIAN's *eyes.*

Sometimes not.

ADRIAN. You don't think it's time to seriously consider . . . (*He spreads his arms wide like a plane, lifting them forward in a take-off – then points in a gesture of flight.*) What I mentioned at dinner?

SIGMUND *emphatically nods 'No', while pointing downward – he'll remain here.*

ADRIAN. When we leave here I'd like to discuss whether there's really any point in that anymore.

SIGMUND *turns to him.*

I don't know if it was in your papers, but there's a hearing problem all over the world. Especially among the young. Rock music, traffic – modern life is too loud for the human ear – you understand me. The subtler sounds don't get through much anymore.

SIGMUND *faces front, expressionless.*

On top of that there's a widespread tendency in New York, Paris, London, for people to concentrate almost exclusively on shopping.

SIGMUND. I have no illusion.

ADRIAN. I hope not – shopping and entertainment. Sigmund?

SIGMUND *turns to him, and he points into his face, then makes a wide gesture to take in the room, the situation.*

Not entertaining. Not on anybody's mind in those cities.

SIGMUND. I know.

ADRIAN. Boring.

SIGMUND. Yes.

ADRIAN. Same old thing. It's the wrong style.

SIGMUND. I know.

ADRIAN. I meant what I said last night; I'd be happy to support – (*He points at* SIGMUND *who glances at him.*) until a connection is made with a university. (*He points to himself.*) Guarantee that.

SIGMUND *nods negatively and spreads both hands – he will stay here.*

We can talk about it later. I'm going to ask you why. I don't understand the point anymore. Not after this.

SIGMUND. You would also if it was your country.

ADRIAN. I doubt it. I would protect my talent. I saw a movie once where they bricked up a man in a wall.

MARCUS *enters in a robe, opening a whisky bottle.*

MARCUS. A few friends may turn up. (*He sets the whisky bottle on the marble table. To* ADRIAN.) Will you excuse us for a few minutes? Sigmund? (*He indicates the bedroom.*)

SIGMUND. I have told him.

MARCUS *turns to* ADRIAN *with a certain embarrassment.*

ADRIAN. They wouldn't destroy it, would they?

MARCUS *seems suddenly put-upon, and unable to answer.*

Do you know?

MARCUS (*with a gesture toward the bedroom; to* SIGMUND). Shall we?

SIGMUND (*standing*). I would like Adrian to hear.

ADRIAN (*to* MARCUS). Unless you don't feel . . .

MARCUS (*unwillingly*). No – if he wishes, I have no objection.

SIGMUND *sits.*

ADRIAN. If there's anything I can do you'll tell me, will you?

MARCUS (*to* SIGMUND). Does Maya know?

SIGMUND. She was going out.

MARCUS. I suppose she might as well. (*As a muted hope for alliance.*) But it won't help her getting excited.

SIGMUND. She will be calm, Maya is not foolish.

ADRIAN. Maybe we ought to get into it, Marcus – they wouldn't destroy the book, would they?

MARCUS (*a fragile laugh*). That's only one of several questions, Adrian – the first thing is to gather our thoughts. – Let me get your drink. (*He stands.*)

ADRIAN. I can wait with the drink, why don't we get into it?

MARCUS. All right. (*He sits again.*)

ADRIAN. Marcus?

MARCUS *turns to him. He points to the ceiling.*

I know.

MARCUS *removes his gaze from* ADRIAN, *a certain mixture*

of embarrassment and resentment in his face.
Which doesn't mean I've drawn any conclusions about anyone. I mean that sincerely.

MARCUS. You understand, Adrian, that the scene here is not as uncomplicated as it may look from outside. You must believe me.

ADRIAN. I have no doubt about that, Marcus. But at the same time I wouldn't want to mislead you . . . (*He glances upwards.*) . . . or anyone else. If that book is destroyed or not returned to him – for whatever it's worth I intend to publicise what I believe is an act of barbarism. This is not some kind of an issue for me – this man is my brother.

Slight pause. MARCUS *is motionless. Then he turns to* ADRIAN *and gestures to him to continue speaking, to amplify.* ADRIAN *looks atonished.* MARCUS *repeats the gesture even more imperatively.*

For example . . . I've always refused to peddle my books on television but there's at least two national network shows would be glad to have me, and for this I'd go on.

He stops; MARCUS *gestures to continue.*

Just telling the story of this evening would be hot news from coast to coast – including Washington, D.C. where some congressmen could easily decide we shouldn't sign any more trade bills with this country. And so on and so forth.

MARCUS. It was brandy, wasn't it?

ADRIAN (*still amazed*). . . Thanks, yes.

MARCUS *goes up to the drinks.* ADRIAN *catches* SIGMUND's *eye but the latter turns forward thoughtfully.* IRINA *enters, heading for the drinks.* MARCUS *brings* ADRIAN *a brandy as she makes herself a drink. In the continuing silence,* MARCUS *returns to the drink table, makes a whisky and takes it down to* SIGMUND. *Then . . .*

ADRIAN (*toward her, upstage*). So how's everything in Denmark?

IRINA (*pleasant laugh*). No-no, not everything.

ADRIAN (*thumbing to the ceiling – to* SIGMUND). *That* ought to keep them busy for a while.

MARCUS *chuckles, sits with his own drink.*

MARCUS. Cheers.

ADRIAN. Cheers.

SIGMUND. Cheers.

They drink. IRINA *brings a drink, sits on the floor beside* MARCUS.

MARCUS. Have you been to London this time?

ADRIAN (*slight pause. He glances toward* SIGMUND. *Then* . . .). No. How was London?

MARCUS. It's difficult there. It seems to be an endless strike.

ADRIAN (*waits a moment*). Yes.

He decides to continue.

Last time there my British publisher had emphysema and none of the elevators were working. I never heard so many Englishmen talking about a dictatorship before.

MARCUS. They probably have come to the end of it there. It's too bad, but why should evolution spare the English?

ADRIAN. Evolution toward what – Fascism?

MARCUS. Or the Arabs taking over more of the economy.

ADRIAN. I can see the bubble pipes in the House of Commons.

Laughter.

The Honorable Member from Damascus.

Laughter. It dies. ADRIAN *thumbs toward* SIGMUND *and then to the ceiling – addressing* MARCUS.

If they decide to give an answer, would it be tonight?

MARCUS (*turns up his palms . . . then . . .*) Relax, Adrian.

He drinks.

Please.

ADRIAN (*swallows a glassful of brandy*). This stuff really

spins the wheels. (*He inhales.*)

MARCUS. It comes from the mountains.

ADRIAN. I feel like I'm on one.

MARCUS. What's New York like now?

ADRIAN. New York? New York is another room in hell. (*Looking up.*) Of course not as architecturally ornate. In fact, a ceiling like this in New York – I can't imagine it lasting so long without some half-crooked writer climbing up and chopping holes in those cherubim.

MARCUS. The ceiling is nearly four hundred years old, you know.

ADRIAN. That makes it less frightful?

MARCUS. In a sense, maybe – for us it has some reassuring associations. When it was made, this city was the cultural capital of Europe – the world, really, this side of China. A lot of art, science, philosophy poured from this place.

ADRIAN. Painful.

MARCUS (*a conceding shrug*). But on the other hand, the government spends a lot keeping these in repair. It doesn't do to forget that, you know.

SIGMUND. That is true. They are repairing all the angels. It is very good to be an angel in our country.

MARCUS *smiles.*

Yes, we shall have the most perfect angels in the whole world.

MARCUS *laughs.*

But I believe perhaps every government is loving very much the angels, no, Adrian?

ADRIAN. Oh, no doubt about it. But six months under this particular kind of art and I'd be ready to cut my throat or somebody else's. What do you say we go to a bar, Marcus?

MARCUS (*to* SIGMUND). *Ezlatchu stau?*

SIGMUND (*he sighs, then nods*). *Ezlatchu.*

ADRIAN (*to* MARCUS). Where does that put us?

MARCUS. He doesn't mind staying till we've had something to eat. Afterwards, perhaps.

Pause. Silence.

ADRIAN. Let me in on it, Marcus – are we waiting for something?

MARCUS. No-no, I just thought we'd eat before we talked.

ADRIAN. Oh. All right.

IRINA (*patting her stomach*). I to sandwich?

MARCUS (*patting her head like a child's, laughing*). Maya is bringing very soon.

ADRIAN. She's as sweet as sugar, Marcus, where'd you find her?

MARCUS. Her husband is the head of Danish programming for the BBC. *There's* Maya.

He crosses to the corridor door.

ADRIAN. What does he do, loan her out?

MARCUS (*laughs*). No-no, she just wanted to see the country.

He exits into the corridor.

SIGMUND. And Marcus will show her every inch.

ADRIAN (*bursts out laughing*). Oh Sigmund, Sigmund – what a century! (*Sotto.*) What the hell is happening?

Men's shouting voices below, MAYA *yelling loudly.* MARCUS *instantly breaks into a run, disappears up the corridor.* ADRIAN *and* SIGMUND *listen. The shouting continues.* SIGMUND *gets up, goes and listens at the door.*

ADRIAN. What is it?

SIGMUND *opens the door, goes into the corridor, listens.*

Who are they?

A door is heard slamming below, silencing the shouts. Pause.

Sigmund?

SIGMUND *comes back into the room.*

What was it?

SIGMUND. Drunken men. They want to see the traitor to the motherland. Enemy of the working class.

He sits. Pause.

ADRIAN. . . . Come to my hotel.

SIGMUND. Is not possible. Be calm.

ADRIAN. How'd they know you were here?

SIGMUND *shrugs, then indicates the ceiling.*

They'd call out hoodlums?

SIGMUND *turns up his palms, shrugs.*

MARCUS *and* MAYA *appear up the corridor. She carries a large tray covered with a white cloth. He has a handkerchief to his cheekbone. He opens the door for her.* IRINA *stands and clears the marble table for the tray.* MARCUS *crosses to the Upstage Right doorway and exits.*

SIGMUND *stands.* MAYA *faces him across the room. Long pause.*

What happened?

MAYA (*with a gesture toward the food*). Come, poet.

SIGMUND *watches her for a moment more, then goes up to the food. She is staring excitedly into his face.*

The dark meat is goose.

SIGMUND *turns from her to the food.*

Adrian?

ADRIAN. I'm not hungry. Thanks.

MAYA (*she takes the plate from* SIGMUND *and loads it heavily*). Beer?

SIGMUND. I have whisky. You changed your haircut?

MAYA. From *Vogue* magazine. You like it?

SIGMUND. Very.

MAYA (*touching his face*). Very much, you say.

SIGMUND. Very, very much.

He returns to his chair with a loaded plate, sits and proceeds to eat in silence.

She pours herself a brandy, sits near him.

MAYA (*to* ADRIAN *as she watches* SIGMUND *admiringly*). He comes from the peasants, you know. That is why he is so beautiful. And he is sly. Like a snake.

Slight pause.

SIGMUND *eats.*

What have you done now? (*Indicates below.*) Why have they come?

SIGMUND *pauses in his eating, not looking at her.*

ADRIAN (*after the pause*). The cops took his manuscript tonight.

She inhales sharply with a gasp, nearly crying out. SIGMUND *continues to eat. She goes to him, embraces his head, mouth pressed to his hair.*

He draws her hands down, apparently warding off her emotion and continues eating. She moves and sits further away from him, staring ahead, alarmed and angry. MARCUS *enters from the bedroom, a bandage stuck to his cheekbone.*

MARCUS (*to* ADRIAN). Have you taken something?

ADRIAN. Not just yet, thanks.

MAYA *rises to confront* MARCUS *but, refusing her look, he passes her, a fixed smile on his face, picks up his drink from the marble table and comes downstage and stands. First he, then* ADRIAN, *then* MAYA *turn and watch* SIGMUND *eating. He eats thoroughly.* IRINA *is also eating, off by herself. Pause.*

MARCUS *goes to his chair, sits and lights a cigarette.* ADRIAN *watches him.*

It's like some kind of continuous crime.

MAYA. You are so rich, Adrian, so famous – why do you make such boring remarks?

ADRIAN. Because I am a bore.

MARCUS. Oh now, Maya . . .

MAYA (*sharply, to* MARCUS). Where is it not a continuous crime?

SIGMUND. It is the truth. (*To* ADRIAN.) Just so, yes. It is a continuous crime.

MAYA (*to the three*). Stupid. Like children. Stupid!

MARCUS. Sssh – take something to eat, dear . . .

ADRIAN. Why are we stupid?

Ignoring his question she goes up to the table, takes a goose wing and bites into it. Then she comes down and stands eating. After a moment . . .

MARCUS. It's wonderful to see you again, Adrian – what brought you back?

MAYA. He has been talking to Allison Wolfe.

MARCUS (*smiling – to* ADRIAN). Oh, to Allison.

ADRIAN. Yes.

MARCUS. Is he still going around with that story?

MAYA. Yes.

MARCUS (*slight pause*). Adrian . . . you know, I'm sure, that this house has been a sort of gathering place for writers for many years now. And they've always brought their girlfriends, and quite often met girls here they didn't know before. Our first literary magazine after the war was practically published from this room.

ADRIAN. I know that, Marcus.

MARCUS. Allison happened to be here one night, a month or so ago, when there was a good bit of screwing going on.

ADRIAN. Sorry I missed it.

MARCUS. It *was* fairly spectacular. But believe me – it was a purely spontaneous outburst of good spirits. Totally unexpected, it was just one of those things that happens with enough brandy.

ADRIAN *laughs.*

What I think happened is that – you see, we had a novelist here who was about to emigrate; to put it bluntly, he is paranoid. I can't blame him – he hasn't been able to publish here since the government changed. And I am one of the people he blamed, as though I had anything to say about who is or isn't to be published. But the fact that I live decently and can travel proved to him that I have some secret power with the higher echelons – in effect, that I am some sort of agent.

ADRIAN. Those are understandable suspicions, Marcus.

MARCUS (*with a light laugh*). But why!

MAYA. It is marvellous, Adrian, how understandable everything is for you.

ADRIAN. I didn't say that at all, Maya; I know practically nothing about Marcus so I could hardly be making an accusation, could I?

MARCUS. Of course not. It's only that the whole idea is so appalling.

ADRIAN. Well, I apologise. But it's so underwater here an outsider is bound to imagine all sorts of nightmares.

MAYA. You have no nightmares in America?

ADRIAN. You know me better than that, Maya – of course we have them, but they're different.

IRINA (*revolving her finger*). Is music?

MARCUS. In a moment, dear.

MAYA. I really must say, Adrian – when you came here the other times it was the Vietnam war, I believe. Did anyone in this country blame you personally for it?

ADRIAN. No, they didn't. But it's not the same thing, Maya.

MAYA. It never is, is it?

ADRIAN. I was arrested twice for protesting the war. Not that that means too much – we had lawyers to defend us and the networks had it all over the country the next day. So there's no comparison, and maybe I know it better than most people. And that's why I'm not interested in blaming anyone here. This is impossible, Marcus, why don't we find a restaurant, I'm beginning to sound like an idiot.

MARCUS. We can't now, I've invited . . .

ADRIAN. Then why don't you meet us somewhere. Sigmund? What do you say, Maya – where's a good place?

MARCUS. Not tonight, Adrian.

ADRIAN *turns to him, catching a certain obscure decision.* MARCUS *addresses* SIGMUND.

I took the liberty of asking Alexandra to stop by.

SIGMUND *turns his head to him, surprised.* MAYA *turns to* MARCUS *from upstage, the plate in her hand.*

(*To* MAYA.) I thought he ought to talk to her. (*To* SIGMUND.) I hope you won't mind.

MAYA (*turns to* SIGMUND, *and with a certain surprise*). You will talk with Alexandra?

SIGMUND *is silent.*

IRINA (*revolving her finger*). Jazz?

MARCUS. In a moment, dear.

SIGMUND. She is coming?

MARCUS. She said she'd try. I think she will. (*To* ADRIAN.) she is a great admirer of Sigmund's.

MAYA *comes down to* ADRIAN *with a plate. She is watching* SIGMUND *who is facing front.*

MAYA. I think you should have asked if he agrees.

MARCUS. I don't see the harm. She can just join us for a drink, if nothing more.

ADRIAN (*accepting the plate*). Thanks. She a writer?

MAYA. Her father is the Minister of Interior. (*Pointing at the ceiling.*)

He is in charge . . .

ADRIAN. Oh! I see.

He turns to watch SIGMUND *who is facing front.*

MARCUS. She writes poetry.

MAYA. Yes. (*Glances anxiously to* SIGMUND.) Tremendous . . . (*She spreads her arms.*). . . *long* poems.

She takes a glass and drinks deeply.

MARCUS (*on the verge of sharpness*).

Nevertheless, I think she has a certain talent.

MAYA. Yes. You think she has a certain talent, Sigmund?

MARCUS. Now Maya . . .

He reaches out and lifts the glass out of her hand.

MAYA. Each year, you see, Adrian – since her father was appointed, this woman's poetry is more and more admired by more and more of our writers. A few years ago only a handful appreciated her, but now practically everybody calls her a master. (*Proudly.*) Excepting for Sigmund – until now, anyway.

She takes the glass from where MARCUS *placed it.*

SIGMUND (*a pause*). She is not to my taste, (*He hesitates.*) but perhaps she is a good poet.

MAYA (*slight pause*). But she has very thick legs.

MARCUS *turns to her.*

But that must be said, Marcus . . . (*She laughs.*) We are not yet obliged to overlook a fact of nature. Please say she has thick legs.

MARCUS. I have no interest in her legs.

MAYA. Sigmund, my darling – surely you will say she . . .

MARCUS. Stop that, Maya . . .

MAYA (*suddenly, at the top of her voice*). It is important! (*She turns to* SIGMUND.)

SIGMUND. She has thick legs, yes.

MAYA. Yes. (*She presses his head to her hip.*) Some truths will not change, and certain people, for all our sakes, are appointed never to forget them. How do the Jews say? – If I forget thee, O Jerusalem, may I cut off my hand . . . ? (*To* IRINA.) You want jazz?

IRINA (*starts to rise, happily*). Jazz!

MAYA (*helping her up*). Come, you poor girl, we have hundreds . . . I mean he does. (*She laughs.*) My God, Marcus, how long I lived here. (*She laughs, nearly weeping.*) I'm going crazy . . .

SIGMUND (*stands*). I must walk. I have eaten too much. (*He buttons his jacket.*)

ADRIAN (*indicating below*). What about those men?

SIGMUND *beckons* ADRIAN *toward the doorway Left. He moves toward the left door, which he opens as* ADRIAN *stands, starts after him, then halts and turns with uncertainty to* MARCUS *and* MAYA *who look on without expression.* ADRIAN *goes out, shutting the door.* SIGMUND *is standing in the corridor.*

MAYA. (*to* IRINA). Come, we have everything. (*She goes and opens an overhead cabinet revealing hundreds of records.*) From Paris, London, New York, Rio . . . you like Conga?

IRINA *reads the labels.* MAYA *turns her head toward the corridor.* MARCUS *now turns as well.*

SIGMUND. Do you understand?

ADRIAN. No.

SIGMUND. I am to be arrested.

ADRIAN. How do you know that?

SIGMUND. Alexandra is the daughter of . . .

ADRIAN. I know – the Minister of . . .

SIGMUND. Marcus would never imagine I would meet with this woman otherwise.

ADRIAN. Why? What's she about?

SIGMUND. She is collecting the dead for her father. She arrange for writers to go before the television, and apologise for the government. Mea Culpa – to kissing their ass.

Slight pause.

ADRIAN. I think you've got to leave the country, Sigmund.

MAYA *crosses the room.*

SIGMUND. Is impossible. We cannot discuss it.

MAYA *enters the corridor, closing the door behind her.*

MAYA. Get out.

SIGMUND (*he comes to her, takes her hand gently*). I must talk to Adrian.

MAYA. Get out, get out! (*To* ADRIAN.) He must leave the country. (*To* SIGMUND.) Finish with it! Tell Marcus.

SIGMUND (*turns her to the door, a hand on her back. He opens the door for her*). Please, Maya.

(*She enters the room glancing back at him in terror. He shuts the door.*)

IRINA (*holding out a record*). Play?

MAYA looks to MARCUS who turns away. Then she goes and uncovers a record player, turns it on, sets the record on it. During the following the music plays, a jazz piece or Conga. First IRINA dances by herself, then gets MARCUS up and dances with him. MAYA sits, drinking.

Pause.

SIGMUND. You have a pistol?

ADRIAN. . . . A pistol?

SIGMUND. Yes.

ADRIAN. No. Of course not. (*Pause.*) How could I carry a pistol on an airplane?

SIGMUND. Why not? He has one in his valise. I saw it.

Pause.

ADRIAN. What good would a pistol do?

Pause.

SIGMUND. . . . It is very difficult to get pistol in this country.

ADRIAN. This is unreal, Sigmund, you can't be thinking of a . . .

SIGMUND. If you will engage him in conversation, I will excuse myself to the bathroom. He has put his valise in the bedroom. I will take it from the valise.

ADRIAN. And do what with it?

SIGMUND. I will keep it, and he will tell them that I have it. In this case they will not arrest me.

ADRIAN. But why not?

SIGMUND. They will avoid at the present time to shoot me.

ADRIAN. . . . And I'm to do . . . what am I to . . . ?

SIGMUND. It is nothing; you must only engage him when I am excusing myself to the bathroom. Come . . .

ADRIAN. Let me catch my breath, will you? . . . It's unreal to me, Sigmund, I can't believe you have to do this.

SIGMUND. It is not dangerous, believe me.

ADRIAN. Not for me, but I have a passport. – Then this is why Marcus came back?

SIGMUND. I don't know. He has many friend in the government, but . . . I don't know why.

ADRIAN. He's an agent.

SIGMUND. Is possible not.

ADRIAN. Then what is he?

SIGMUND. Marcus is Marcus.

ADRIAN. Please, explain to me. I've got to understand before I go in there.

SIGMUND. It is very complicated between us.

ADRIAN. Like what? Maya?

SIGMUND. Maya also. (*Slight pause.*) When I was young writer, Marcus was the most famous novelist in our country. In Stalin time he has six years in prison. He cannot write. I was not in prison. When he has returned I am very popular, but he was forgotten. It is tragic story.

ADRIAN. You mean he's envious of you.

SIGMUND. This is natural.

ADRIAN. But didn't you say he's protected you . . .

SIGMUND. Yes, of course. Marcus is very complicated man.

ADRIAN. But with all that influence, why can't you sit down and maybe he can think of something for you.

SIGMUND. He has thought of something – he has thought of Alexandra.

ADRIAN. You mean he's trying to destroy you.

SIGMUND. No. Is possible he believes he is trying to help me.

ADRIAN. But subconsciously . . .

SIGMUND. Yes. Come, we must go back.

ADRIAN. Just one more minute. You're convinced he's not an agent.

SIGMUND. My opinion, no.

ADRIAN. But how does he get all these privileges?

SIGMUND. Marcus is lazy. Likewise, he is speaking French, English, German – five-six language. When the foreign writers are coming, he is very gentleman, he makes amusing salon, he is showing the castles, the restaurants, introduce beautiful girls. When these writers return home they say is no bad problem in this civilised country. He makes very nice impression, and for this they permit him to be lazy. Is not necessary to be agent.

ADRIAN. You don't think it's possible that he learned they were going to arrest you, and came back to help you?

SIGMUND *looks at him, surprised.*

That makes as much sense as anything else, Sigmund. Could he have simply wanted to do something decent? Maybe I'm being naive, but if he wanted your back broken his best bet would be just to sit tight in London and let it happen.

SIGMUND *is silent.*

And as for calling Alexandra – maybe he figured your only chance *is* actually to make peace with the government.

SIGMUND *is silent.*

You grab that gun and you foreclose everything – you're an outlaw. Is it really impossible to sit down with Marcus, man to man? I mean you're pinning everything on an interpretation, aren't you?

SIGMUND. I know Marcus.

ADRIAN. Sigmund – every conversation I've ever had with him about this country, he's gone out of his way to praise you – your talent and you personally. I can't believe I was taken in, he genuinely admires your guts, your resistance. Let me call him out here.

SIGMUND *turns, uncertain but alarmed.*

What's to lose? Maybe there's a string he can pull, let's

put *his* feet to the fire. Because he's all over Europe lamenting conditions here, he's a big liberal in Europe. I've seen him get girls with those lamentations. Let me call him on it.

SIGMUND (*a blossoming suspicion in the corners of his eyes*). I will never make speech on the television . . .

ADRIAN (*alarmed*). For Christ's sake, Sigmund, you don't imagine *I* would want that. (*Exploding.*) This is a quagmire, a fucking asylum! . . . But I'm not helping out with any guns. It's suicide, you'll have to do that alone.

He goes to the door.

SIGMUND. Adrian?

ADRIAN. I'm sorry, Sigmund, but that's the way I feel.

SIGMUND. I want my manuscript, if you wish to talk to Marcus, I have nothing to object . . . on this basis.

ADRIAN *looks at him, unsatisfied, angry. He turns and flings the door open, enters the room.*

ADRIAN. Marcus? Can I see you minute?

MARCUS. Of course. What is it?

ADRIAN. Out here, please . . . if you don't mind?

MARCUS *crosses the room and enters the corridor.* ADRIAN *shuts the door.*

SIGMUND *avoids* MARCUS'*s eyes, stands waiting.* MARCUS *turns to* ADRIAN *as he shuts the door.*

MARCUS. Yes?

MAYA *opens the door, enters the corridor, shuts it behind her.* MARCUS *turns up his robe collar.*

ADRIAN (*breaks into an embarrassed grin*). I'm not sure what to say or not say . . . I'm more of a stranger than I'd thought, Marcus . . .

MARCUS. We're all strangers in this situation – nobody ever learns how to deal with it.

ADRIAN. . . . I take it you have some contacts with the government.

MARCUS. Many of us do; it's a small country.

ADRIAN. I think they ought to know that ah . . . (*He glances to* SIGMUND, *but* SIGMUND *is not facing in his direction.*) if he's to be arrested, he'll – resist.

MAYA *turns quickly to* SIGMUND, *alarm in her face.*

MARCUS. I don't understand – (*To* SIGMUND, *with a faintly embarrassed grin.*) Why couldn't you have said that to me?

SIGMUND, *bereft of an immediate answer, starts to turn to him.*

Well, it doesn't matter. (*He is flushed. Turning back to* ADRIAN.) Yes?

ADRIAN. What I thought was, that . . .

MARCUS. Of course, if we're talking about some – violent gesture, they will advertise it as the final proof he is insane. Which is what they've claimed all along. But what was your thought?

ADRIAN. I have the feeling that the inevitable is being accepted. They act and you react. I'd like to sit down, the four of us, and see if we can come up with some out that nobody's ever thought of before.

MARCUS. Certainly. But it's a waste of time if you think you can change their programme.

ADRIAN. Which is what, exactly.

MARCUS. Obviously – to drive him out of the country. Failing that, to make it impossible for him to function.

ADRIAN. And you think?

MARCUS. There's no question in my mind – he must emigrate. They've taken the work of his last five years, what more do you want?

ADRIAN. There's no one at all you could approach?

MARCUS. With what? What can I offer that they need?

ADRIAN. Like what, for example?

MARCUS. Well, if he agreed to emigrate, conceivably they might let go of the manuscript. – Providing, of course, that it isn't too politically inflammatory. But that could be dealt with, I think – they badly want him gone.

ADRIAN. There's no one up there who could be made to understand that if they ignored him he would simply be another novelist . . .

MARCUS (*laughing lightly*). But will he ignore *them*? How is it possible? This whole country is inside his skin – that is his greatness – They have a right to be terrified.

ADRIAN. Supposing there were a copy of the manuscript.

MARCUS. But there isn't, so it's pointless talking about it.

ADRIAN. But if there were.

MARCUS. It might have been a consideration.

ADRIAN. . . . If they knew it would be published abroad.

MARCUS. It might slow them down, yes. But they know Sigmund's personality.

ADRIAN. How do you mean?

MARCUS. He's not about to trust another person with his fate – it's a pity; they'd never have found it in this house in a hundred years. The cellar's endless, the gallery upstairs full of junk – to me, this is the saddest part of all. If it had made a splash abroad it might have held their hand for six months, perhaps longer. (*With a regretful glance at* SIGMUND.) But . . . so it goes.

Pause. He blows on his hands.

It's awfully cold out here, come inside . . .

He starts for the door.

ADRIAN. There's a copy in Paris.

MAYA *and* SIGMUND *turn swiftly to him.*

MARCUS. . . . In Paris.

ADRIAN. I sent it off this morning.

MARCUS. *This* morning?

ADRIAN. I ran into a cousin of mine; had no idea she was here. She took it with her to Gallimard – they're my publishers.

MARCUS (*a broken smile emerges; he is filling with a swirl of colours, glancing first at* MAYA, *then at* SIGMUND, *then back to* ADRIAN). Well then . . . that much is solved.

He goes to the door.

ADRIAN. They should be told, don't you think?

MARCUS (*he stands at the door, his hand on the knob. Finally he turns to all of them*). How terrible. (*Slight pause. To* MAYA *and* SIGMUND.) *Such* contempt. (*Slight pause.*) Why? . . . Can you tell me?

They avoid his gaze. He turns to ADRIAN.

There's no plane to Paris today. Monday, Wednesday and Friday. This is Tuesday, Adrian.

SIGMUND. I did not ask him to say that.

MARCUS. But perfectly willing to stand there and hope I'd believe it.

ADRIAN. I'm sorry, Marcus . . .

MARCUS (*laughing*). But Adrian, I couldn't care less.

MAYA (*moving to him*). Help him.

MARCUS. Absolutely not. I am finished with it. No one will ever manipulate me, I will not be in that position.

MAYA. He is a stupid man, he understands nothing!

ADRIAN. Now hold it a second . . .

MAYA. Get out of here!

ADRIAN. Just hold it a second, Goddammit! I'm out of my depth, Marcus, but I've apologised. I'm sorry. But you have to believe it was solely my invention, Sigmund has absolute faith in you.

SIGMUND. You can forgive him, Marcus – he tells you the truth; he believes you are my friend, he said this to me a moment ago.

ADRIAN. I feel he's drowning, Marcus, it was just something to grab for. (*He holds out his hand.*) Forgive me, it just popped out of my mouth.

MARCUS (*silently clasps his hand for an instant, and lets go. To*

SIGMUND *and* MAYA *especially*). Come inside. We'll talk.

ADRIAN (*as* MARCUS *turns to the door*). . . . Marcus?

MARCUS *turns to him. He is barely able to continue.*

Don't you think – it would be wiser – a bar, or something?

MARCUS. I'm expecting Alexandra.

ADRIAN. Could you leave a note on the door? But it's up to you and Sigmund. (*To* SIGMUND.) What do you think?

SIGMUND (*hesitates*). It is for Marcus to decide – (*He looks at* MARCUS.) – it is his house.

MARCUS *expressionless, stands silent.*

MAYA. Darling . . . (*delicately.*) . . . it will endure a thousand years. (MARCUS *looks at her.*) . . . I've read it. It is all we ever lived. They must not, must not touch it. Whatever humiliation, whatever is necessary for this book, yes. More than he himself, more than any human being – this book they cannot harm. – Francesco's is still open. (*She turns to* ADRIAN.) But I must say to you, Adrian – nothing has ever been found in there. Or in this house. We have looked everywhere.

ADRIAN. It's entirely up to Marcus. (*To* MARCUS.) You feel it's all right to talk in there?

Long pause.

MARCUS (*his resentment*). I think Maya has answered that question, don't you?

ADRIAN. Okay. Then you're not sure.

MARCUS. But you are, apparently.

ADRIAN (*slight pause. To* SIGMUND). I think I ought to leave.

SIGMUND. No-no . . .

ADRIAN. I think I'm only complicating it for you –

SIGMUND. I insist you stay . . .

ADRIAN (*laughs nervously, his arm touching* SIGMUND'*s shoulder*). I'm underwater, kid, I can't operate when I'm drowning. (*Without pausing, to* MARCUS.) I don't understand why you're offended.

MARCUS. But the question has been answered once. There has never been any proof of an installation here. But when so many writers congregate here I've had to assume there might be something. The fact is, I have always warned people to be careful what they say in there – but only to be on the safe side. Is that enough?

SIGMUND. Come! (*To* MARCUS, *heartily, as he begins to press* ADRIAN *towards the door.*) Now I will have one big whisky . . .

MARCUS *laughs, starting for the door.*

ADRIAN (*separating himself from* SIGMUND). I'll see you tomorrow, Sigmund.

Silence. They go still.

This is all your marbles, kid. It's too important for anyone to be standing on his dignity. I think I'm missing some of the overtones. (*To* MARCUS.) but all I know is that if it were me I'd feel a lot better if I could hear you say what you just said – but in there.

MARCUS. What *I* said?

ADRIAN (*slight pause*). . . . That you've always warned people that the government might be listening, in that room.

SIGMUND. Is not necessary . . .

ADRIAN. I think it . . .

SIGMUND. Absolutely not! – Please . . .

He presses ADRIAN *toward the door, and stretching his hand out to* MARCUS. . .

Come, Marcus, please.

SIGMUND *leads the way into the room, followed by* ADRIAN, *then* MARCUS *and* MAYA. *For an instant they are all awkwardly standing there. Then, pressing his hand against his stomach . . .*

Excuse me one moment.

He goes up toward the bedroom doorway.

ADRIAN (*suddenly alerted. He starts after* SIGMUND). Sigmund . . .

But SIGMUND *is gone. He is openly conflicted about rushing after him . . .*

MAYA. What is it?

ADRIAN (*blurting, in body-shock*). Level with him. Marcus . . . this is your Hemingway, your Faulkner, for Christ's sake – help him!

SIGMUND *enters from bedroom, a pistol in his hand.* IRINA, *seeing it, strides away from him in fright.*

SIGMUND (*to* MARCUS). Forgive me. I must have it. (*He puts it in his pocket*).

IRINA (*pointing at his pocket*). Shoot?

SIGMUND. No-no. We are all friend. *Alle gute Freunde hier.*

IRINA. Ah.

She turns questioningly to MARCUS. *Then* ADRIAN, MAYA *and* SIGMUND. *A pause.*

ADRIAN. Marcus?

MARCUS, *at centre, turns front, anger mounting in his face.* MAYA *goes and shuts off the record player. Then she turns to him, waiting.*

Will you say it? In here? Please?

Curtain.

Act Two

Positions the same. A tableau, MARCUS *at centre, all waiting for him to speak. Finally he moves, glances at* SIGMUND.

MARCUS. They are preparing a trial for you.

MAYA (*clapping her hands together, crying out*). Marcus!

She starts toward him but he walks from her, turning away in impatience. She halts.

When?

MARCUS *is silent, downing his resentment.*

Do you know when?

MARCUS. I think within the month.

MAYA (*turning to* SIGMUND). My God, my God.

SIGMUND (*after a moment*). And Otto and Peter?

MARCUS. I don't know about them.

He goes in the silence to his chair, sits. A pause.

ADRIAN. What would they charge him with?

MARCUS. . . . Fantastic. Break off a trip, fly across Europe, and now I'm asked – what am I asked? – to justify myself? Is that it?

Unable to answer, ADRIAN *evades his eyes, then glances to* SIGMUND *for aid; but* SIGMUND *is facing front and now walks to a chair and sits.*

MAYA (*to* MARCUS). No-no, Dear . . . (*Of* SIGMUND.) It's a shock for him . . .

MARCUS (*rejecting her apology he glances at* ADRIAN). . . . Section 19, I'd imagine. Slandering the state.

ADRIAN. On what grounds?

MARCUS. He's been sending out some devastating letters to the European press; this last one to the United Nations – have you read that?

ADRIAN. Just now in Paris, yes.

MARCUS. What'd you think of it?

ADRIAN (*with a cautious glance at* SIGMUND). It was pretty hot, I guess – What's the penalty for that?

MARCUS. A year. Two, three, five – who knows?

Slight pause.

MAYA. It was good of you to return, dear.

MARCUS *does not respond. She invites* SIGMUND's *gratitude.*

... Sigmund?

SIGMUND (*he waits an instant*). Yes. Thank you, Marcus. (MARCUS *remains looking front.*) It is definite?

MARCUS. I think it is. And it will affect every writer in the country, if it's allowed to happen.

SIGMUND. How do you know this?

Slight pause.

MARCUS. My publisher had a press reception for me day before yesterday – for my book. A fellow from our London embassy turned up. We chatted for a moment, then I forgot about him, but in the street afterwards, he was suddenly beside me ... we shared a cab.

Slight pause. He turns directly to SIGMUND.

He said he was from the Embassy Press Section.

SIGMUND. Police.

MARCUS (*he lowers his eyes in admission*). He was ... quite violent ... his way of speaking.

SIGMUND. About me.

Slight pause.

MARCUS. I haven't heard that kind of language ... since ... the old days. 'You are making a mistake,' he said, 'if you think we need tolerate this scum any longer ...'

MAYA. My God, my God ...

MARCUS. 'You can do your friend a favour,' he said, 'and tell him to get out this month or he will eat his own shit for five or six years.'

MAYA *weeps.*

'And as far as a protest in the West, he can wrap it in bacon fat and shove it up his ass.' Pounded the seat with his fist. Bloodshot eyes. I thought he was going to hit me for a moment there . . . it was quite an act.

ADRIAN. An act?

MARCUS. Well he wasn't speaking for himself, of course.

Slight pause.

I started a letter, but I know your feelings about leaving – I felt we had to talk about it face to face.

SIGMUND. Please.

MARCUS (*he hesitates, then turns to* ADRIAN). Are you here as a journalist?

ADRIAN. God, no – I just thought I'd stop by . . .

MAYA. He has written a novel about us.

MARCUS (*unguarded*). About us? Really . . . !

ADRIAN. Well not literally . . .

MARCUS. When is it coming out?

ADRIAN. It won't. I've abandoned it.

MARCUS. Oh! That's too bad. Why?

ADRIAN. I'm not here to write about you, Marcus . . . honestly. MARCUS *nods, unconvinced. To* SIGMUND *as well.*) I'll leave now if you think I'm in the way . . .

SIGMUND *doesn't react.*

MARCUS. It's all right.

Slight pause.

But if you decide to write something about us . . .

ADRIAN. I've no intention . . .

MARCUS (*smiling*). You never know. We have a tactical disagreement, Sigmund and I. To me, it's really a question of having had different experiences – although there are only seven or eight years between us; things that he finds intolerable are actually – from another viewpoint – improvements over the past . . .

ADRIAN (*indicating* MAYA). I only found out today you were

in prison . . .

MARCUS. A camp, actually – we dug coal.

ADRIAN. Six years.

MARCUS. And four months.

ADRIAN. What for?

MARCUS. It's one of those stories which, although long, is not interesting. (*He laughs.*) The point is simple, in any case – We happen to occupy a . . . strategic zone, really – between two hostile ways of life. And no government here is free to do what it would like to do. But some intelligent, sympathetic people are up there now who weren't around in the old times, and to challenge these people, to even insult them is to indulge in a sort of fantasy . . .

SIGMUND (*pointing to the ceiling*). Marcus, this is reality?

MARCUS. Let me finish . . .

SIGMUND. But is very important – who is fantastic?

He laughs.

We are some sort of characters in a poem which they are writing; is not my poem, is their poem . . . and I do not like this poem, it makes me crazy!

He laughs.

ADRIAN. I understand what he means, though . . .

SIGMUND. I not! I am sorry. Excuse me, Marcus – please continue.

MARCUS (*slight pause*). They ought not be forced into political trials again . . .

SIGMUND. *I* am forcing . . . ?

MARCUS. May I finish? It will mean a commitment which they will have to carry through, willingly or not. And that can only mean turning out the lights for all of us, and for a long time to come. It mustn't be allowed to happen, Sigmund. And it need not happen. (*Slight pause.*) I think you have to get out. For all our sakes.

With an ironic shake of his head, SIGMUND *makes a long*

exhale.

MARCUS. . . . I've called Alexandra because I think you need a line of communication now. If only to stall things for a time, or whatever you . . .

SIGMUND (*toward* MAYA). I must now communicate with *Alexandra.*

MARCUS. She adores your work, whatever you think of her.

SIGMUND *gives him a sarcastic glance.*

This splendid isolation has to end, Sigmund – it was never real and now it's impossible.

SIGMUND (*shakes his head*). I will wait for her. – I may wait?

MARCUS. I certainly hope you will. (*Slight pause.*) I only ask you to keep in mind that this goes beyond your personal feelings about leaving . . .

SIGMUND. I have never acted for personal feelings.

MARCUS (*insistently*). You've been swept away now and then – that United Nations letter could change nothing except enrage them . . .

SIGMUND. I may not also be enraged?

MAYA. Don't argue about it, please . . .

SIGMUND (*smiling to her*). Perhaps is time we argue . . .

MAYA. Sigmund, we are all too old to be right!

She picks up a glass.

MARCUS. Are you getting drunk?

MAYA. No, I am getting sorry. Is no one to be sorry? I am sorry for both of you. I am sorry for Socialism. I am sorry for Marx and Engels and Lenin – (*She shouts to the air.*) I am sorry! (*To* IRINA, *irritably.*) Don't be frightened. (*She pours a drink.*)

A pause.

ADRIAN. I'd like to take back what I asked you before, Marcus.

MARCUS. How can I know what is in this room? How ludicrous can you get?

ADRIAN. I agree. I wouldn't be willing to answer that question in my house either.

SIGMUND. But would not be necessary to ask such question in your house.

ADRIAN. Oh, don't kid yourself . . .

MARCUS. The FBI is everywhere . . .

ADRIAN. Not everywhere, but they get around. The difference with us is that it's illegal.

SIGMUND. *Vive la différence.*

MARCUS. Provided you catch them.

ADRIAN (*laughs*). Right.

He catches SIGMUND'*s dissatisfaction with him.*

I'm not saying it's the same . . .

SIGMUND (*turns away from* ADRIAN *to* MAYA). Please, Maya, a whisky.

MAYA (*eagerly*). Yes!

She goes up to the drink table. Silence. She pours a drink, brings it to SIGMUND.

ADRIAN. Did this woman say what time she . . . ?

MARCUS. She's at some embassy dinner. As soon as she can break away. Shouldn't be long. (*Slight pause. Indicating* SIGMUND'*s pocket.*) Give me that thing, will you?

SIGMUND *does not respond.*

ADRIAN. Go ahead, Sigmund.

SIGMUND. I . . . keep for few minutes. (*He drinks. A pause.*)

ADRIAN. I'm exhausted. (*He hangs his head and shakes it.*)

MAYA. You drink too fast.

ADRIAN. No . . . it's the whole thing – it suddenly hit me. (*He squeezes his eyes.*) Mind if I lie down?

MARCUS (*gesturing toward the couch*). Of course.

ADRIAN *goes to the couch.*

What's *your* feeling?

ADRIAN. He's got to get out, I've told him that. (*Lying down.*) They're doing great, what do they need literature for? It's a pain in the ass. (*He throws an arm over his eyes, sighs.*) Christ . . . it's unbelievable. An hour from the Sorbonne.

MAYA (*a long pause; she sits between* SIGMUND *and* MAYA, *glancing uncomfortably from one to the other*). It was raining in London?

MARCUS. No, surprisingly warm. – How's your tooth?

MAYA (*pointing to a front tooth, showing him*). They saved it.

MARCUS. Good. He painted the bathroom.

MAYA. Yes, he came, finally. I paid him. The rest of the money is in the desk.

MARCUS. Thanks, dear. Looks very nice.

Slight pause.

MAYA (*she leans her elbow on her knee, her chin on her fist, she observes her leg, then glances at* MARCUS). My bird died on Sunday.

MARCUS. Really? Lulu?

MAYA. Yes. I finally found out, though – she was a male. (*To* SIGMUND.) And all these years I called him Lulu!

SIGMUND. I can give you one of my rabbits.

MAYA. Oh my God, no rabbits. (*She sighs.*) No birds, no cats, no dogs . . . Nothing, nothing anymore.

She drinks. A pause.

ADRIAN (*from the couch*). You ever get mail from your programme?

MAYA. Oh very much. Mostly for recipes, sometimes I teach them to cook.

SIGMUND. She is very comical. She is marvellous actress.

ADRIAN. It's not a political . . . ?

MAYA. No! It's too early in the morning. I hate politics . . . boring, boring, always the same . . . You know something? You are both very handsome.

They both look at her and laugh softly.

You too, Adrian.

She looks at her glass.

And this is wonderful whisky.

ADRIAN. Not too much, dear.

MAYA. No-no.

She gets up with her glass, moves toward the window at Right.

There was such a marvellous line – that English poet, what was his name? Very famous . . . you published him in the first or second issue, I think . . . 'The world . . .'

She presses her forehead – MARCUS *observes her and she sees him.*

I'm not drunk, it's only so long ago. Oh yes! 'The world needs a wash and a week's rest.'

ADRIAN. Auden.

MAYA. Auden, yes! – a wash and week's rest – what a wonderful solution.

ADRIAN. Yeah – last one into the Ganges is a rotten egg.

They laugh.

MARCUS. Every now and then you sound like Brooklyn.

ADRIAN. That's because I come from Philadelphia. How do you know about Brooklyn?

MARCUS. I was in the American Army.

ADRIAN (*amazed, sits up*). How do you come to the American Army?

MAYA. He was sergeant.

MARCUS. I enlisted in London – we had to get out when the Nazis came. I was translator and interpreter for General McBride, First Army Intelligence.

ADRIAN. Isn't that funny? – every once in a while you come into a kind of – focus, that's very familiar. I've never understood it.

MARCUS. I was in almost three years.

ADRIAN. Huh! (*He laughs.*) I don't know why I'm so glad to hear it . . .

MARCUS. Well, you can place me now – we all want that.

ADRIAN. I guess so. What'd she mean, that you published Auden?

MAYA. Marcus was the editor of the magazine, until they closed it.

ADRIAN (*toward* SIGMUND). I didn't know that.

SIGMUND. Very good editor – Marcus was first editor who accept to publish my story.

MAYA. If it had been in English – or even French or Spanish – our magazine would have been as famous as the *New Yorker*.

MARCUS (*modestly*). Well . . .

MAYA (*to* MARCUS). In my opinion it was better . . . (*To* ADRIAN.) But our language even God doesn't read. People would stand on line in the street downstairs, like for bread. People from factories, soldiers from the army, professors . . . It was like some sort of Bible, every week a new prophecy. Pity you missed it . . .

It was like living on a ship – every morning there was a different island.

MARCUS (*to* SIGMUND – *a gesture of communication*). Elizabeth didn't look well, is she all right?

SIGMUND. She was very angry tonight. She is sometimes foolish.

Slight pause.

MAYA. Could he live, in America?

ADRIAN. I'm sure he could. Universities'd be honoured to have him.

SIGMUND. I am speaking English like six years-old child.

ADRIAN. Faculty wives'll be overjoyed to correct you. You'd be a big hit – with all that hair.

SIGMUND (*laughs dryly*). You are not going to Algeria?

MARCUS. On Friday.

ADRIAN. What's in Algeria?

MARCUS. There's a writers' congress – they've asked me to go.

ADRIAN. Communist countries?

MARCUS. Yes. But it's a big one – Arabs, Africans, Latin Americans . . . the lot.

SIGMUND. The French?

MARCUS. Some French, yes – Italians, too, I think.

ADRIAN. What do you do at those things?

MAYA (*admiringly*). He represents our country – he lies on the beach with a gin and tonic.

MARCUS (*laughs*). It's too cold for the beach now. (*To* ADRIAN.) They're basically ideological discussions.

SIGMUND. Boring, no?

MARCUS. Agony. But there are some interesting people, sometimes.

SIGMUND. You can speak of us there?

MARCUS (*turns to him, silent, unable to answer*). No?

MARCUS. We're not on the agenda.

MAYA. It's difficult, dear . . .

SIGMUND. But perhaps privately – to the Italian comrades? . . . French? Perhaps they would be interested for my manuscript.

MARCUS *nods positively, but turns up his palms – he'll do what he can.*

(*With the slightest edge of sarcasm.*)

You will see, perhaps.

He chucks his head, closes his eyes with his face stretched upward, his hand tapping frustratedly on his chair arm, his foot beating.

So-so-so-so.

MARCUS (*looking front*). The important thing . . . is to be useful.

SIGMUND (*flatly, without irony*). Yes, always. (*Slight pause.*) Thank you, that you have returned for this, I am grateful.

MARCUS. Whatever you decide, it ought to be soon. Once they move to prosecute . . .

SIGMUND. Yes. I have still some questions – we can take a walk later, perhaps.

MARCUS. All right. I've told you all I know . . .

SIGMUND. . . . About ourselves.

MARCUS (*surprised*). Oh. All right.

Pause.

MAYA. How handsome you all are! I must say . . .

MARCUS *laughs – she persists.*

Really, it's unusual for writers. (*Suddenly to* IRINA.) And she is so lovely . . . *Du bist sehr schöne.*

IRINA. *Danke.*

MAYA (*to* MARCUS). Isn't she very young?

MARCUS (*shrugs.*) We only met two days ago.

MAYA (*touching his hair*). How marvellous. You are like God, darling – you can always create new people. (*She laughs, and with sudden energy . . .*) Play something, Sigmund . . . ! (*She goes to* SIGMUND *to get him up.*)

Come . . .

SIGMUND. No-no-no . . .

MAYA (*she suddenly bends and kisses the top of his head. Her eyes fill with tears*). Don't keep that thing . . . (*She reaches for his pocket; he takes her hand and pats it, looking up at her. She stares down at him.*) The day he walked in here for the first time . . . (*Glancing at* MARCUS.) Do you remember? The snow was half a metre high on his hat – I thought he was a peasant selling potatoes, he bowed the snow all over my typewriter. (*Glancing at* ADRIAN.) And he takes out this lump of paper – it was rolled up like a bomb. A story full of colours, like a painting; this boy from the beet fields – a writer! It was a miracle – such prose from a field of beets. That morning – for half an hour – I believed Socialism. For half an hour I . . .

MARCUS (*cutting her off*). What brings you back, Adrian?

The telephone rings in the bedroom.

Probably for you.

MAYA. For me? (*Going toward the bedroom.*) I can't imagine . . . (*She exits.*)

ADRIAN. I don't really know why I came. There's always been something here that I . . .

IRINA (*getting up, pointing to the piano*). I may?

MARCUS. Certainly . . . please.

IRINA *sits at the piano.*

SIGMUND. I think you will write your book again.

ADRIAN. I doubt it – there's a kind of music here that escapes me. I really don't think I dig you people.

IRINA (*testing the piano, she runs a scale; it is badly out of tune and she makes a face, turning to* MARCUS). Ach . . .

MARCUS (*apologising*). I'm sorry, it's too old to be tuned anymore . . . but go ahead . . .

MAYA *enters.*

MAYA. There's no one – they cut off.

SIGMUND *turns completely around to her, alerted.*

MAYA (*to him, reassuringly*). I'm sure they'll call back . . . it was an accident. Good! You play?

IRINA *launches into a fast 'Bei Meir Bist Du Schön', the strings whining . . .*

MAYA. Marvellous! Jitterbug! (*She breaks into a jitterbug with her glass in one hand, lifting her skirt . . .*

Come on, Adrian . . . !

She starts for ADRIAN, *but* IRINA *stops playing and stands up pushing her fingers into her ears.*

IRINA. Is too, too . . .

MAYA. No, play, play . . .

IRINA (*refusing, laughing, as she descends onto the carpet beside* MARCUS, *shutting her ears*). Please, please, please . . .

MARCUS (*patting* IRINA). I believe she's done concerts . . . serious music.

He looks at his watch – then to SIGMUND.

You're not going outside with that thing, are you?

SIGMUND *glances at him.*

It's absurd.

MAYA. It must be the Americans – ever since they started building that hotel the phones keep ringing.

ADRIAN. What hotel?

MAYA. The Hilton . . . three blocks from here. It's disarranged the telephones.

MARCUS. I'd love to read your novel – do you have it with you?

ADRIAN. It's no good.

MARCUS. That's surprising – what's the problem?

ADRIAN (*sits up*). Well . . . I started out with a bizarre, exotic quality. People sort of embalmed in a society of amber. But the longer it got, the less unique it became. I finally wondered if the idea of unfreedom can be sustained in the mind.

MARCUS. You relied on that.

ADRIAN. Yes. But I had to keep injecting melodramatic reminders. The brain tires of unfreedom. It's like a bad back – you simply learn to avoid making certain movements . . . like . . . whatever's in this ceiling; or if nothing is; we still have to live, and talk, and the rest of it. I really thought I knew, but I saw that I didn't; it's been an education tonight. I'd love to ask you something, Marcus – why do you carry a gun?

MARCUS. I don't, normally. I was planning a trip into the mountains in Algeria – still pretty rough up there in places.

He looks at his watch.

MAYA. He fought a battle in Mexico last year. In the Chiappas. Like a cowboy.

MARCUS. Not really – no one was hurt.

ADRIAN. What the hell do you go to those places for?

MARCUS. It interests me – where there is no law, people alone with their customs. I started out to be an anthropologist.

ADRIAN. What happened?

MARCUS. The Nazis, the war. You were too young, I guess.

ADRIAN. I was in the army in the fifties, but after Korea and before Vietnam.

MARCUS. You're a lucky generation, you missed everything.

ADRIAN. I wonder sometimes. History came at us like a rumour. We were never really there.

MARCUS. Is that why you come here?

ADRIAN. Might be part of it. We're always smelling the smoke but we're never quite sure who the devil really is. Drives us nuts.

MARCUS. You don't like ambiguity.

ADRIAN. Oh sure – providing it's clear. (*He laughs.*) Or maybe it's always clearer in somebody else's country.

MARCUS. I was just about to say – the first time I came to America – a few years after the war . . .

ADRIAN. . . . You're not an American citizen, are you?

MARCUS. Very nearly, but I had a little . . . ambiguity with your Immigration Department. (*He smiles.*)

ADRIAN. You came from the wrong country.

MARCUS. No – it was the right country when I boarded ship for New York. But the Communists took over here while I was on the high seas. A Mr Donahue, Immigration Inspector, Port of New York did not approve. He put me in a cage.

ADRIAN. Why!

MARCUS. Suspicion I was a Red agent. Actually, I'd come on an invitation to lecture at Syracuse University – I'd published my first two – or it may have been three novels in Paris by then. I phoned the university – from my cage – and they were appalled – but no one lifted a finger, of course, and I was shipped back to Europe. It was terribly unambiguous, Adrian – you were a Fascist country, to me. I was wrong, of course, but so it appeared. Anyway, I decided to come home and have a look here – I stepped off the train directly into the arms of our police.

ADRIAN. As an American spy.

MARCUS (*laughs*). What else?

ADRIAN (*nodding*). I got ya, Marcus.

MARCUS. Yes. (*Slight pause.*) But it's better now.

ADRIAN *glances at* SIGMUND.

It has been, anyway. But one has to be of the generation that can remember. Otherwise, it's as you say – a sort of rumour that has no reality – excepting for oneself.

SIGMUND *drinks deeply from his glass. Slight pause.*

ADRIAN (*stands, and from behind* SIGMUND *looks down at him for an instant*).

She's sure to come, huh?

MARCUS. I'm sure she will.

ADRIAN (*strolls to the window at Right, stretching his back and arms. He looks out of the window*). It's starting to snow. (*Slight pause.*) God, it's a beautiful city. (*He lingers there for a moment, then walks, his hands thrust into his back pockets.*) What do you suppose would happen if I went to the Minister of the Interior tonight? – If I lost my mind and knocked on his door and raised hell about this?

MARCUS *turns to him, eyebrows raised.*

I'm serious.

MARCUS. Well . . . What happened when you tried to reason with Johnson or Nixon during Vietnam?

ADRIAN. Right. But of course we could go into the streets, which you can't . . .

SIGMUND. Why not?

ADRIAN (*surprised*). With all their tanks here?

SIGMUND. Yes, even so. (*Pause.*) Is only a question of the fantasy. In this country we have not Las Vegas. The

American knows very well is almost impossible to winning money from this slot machine. But he is enjoying to experience hope. He is paying for the hope. For us, is inconceivable. Before such a machine we would experience only despair. For this reason we do not go into the street.

ADRIAN. You're more realistic about power . . .

SIGMUND. This is mistake, Adrian, we are not realistic. We also believe we can escaping power – by telling lies. For this reason, I think you have difficulty to write about us. You cannot imagine how fantastically we lie.

MARCUS. I don't think we're any worse than others . . .

SIGMUND. Oh certainly, yes – but perhaps is not exactly lying because we do not expect to deceive anyone; the professor lies to the student, the student to the professor – but each knows the other is lying. We must lie, it is our only freedom. To lie is our slot machine – we know we cannot win but it gives us the feeling of hope. Is like a serious play, which no one really believes but the technique is admirable. Our country is now a theatre, where no one is permitted to walk out, and everyone is obliged to applaud.

MARCUS. That is a marvellous description, Sigmund – of the whole world.

SIGMUND. No, I must object – when Adrian speaks to me it is always his personal opinion. But with us, is impossible to speaking so simply, we must always making theatre.

MARCUS. I've been as plain as I know how to be. What is it you don't believe?

SIGMUND (*laughs*). But that is the problem in the theatre – I believe everything but I am convinced of nothing.

MAYA. It's enough.

SIGMUND. Excuse me, Maya – for me is not enough; if I am waking up in New York one morning, I must have concrete reason, not fantastic reason.

MAYA. Darling, they've taken your book . . .

SIGMUND (*with sudden force*). But is my country – is this reason to leave my country!

MAYA. There are people who love you enough to want to keep you from prison. What is fantastic about that?

SIGMUND (*turns to* MARCUS – *with a smile*). You are loving me, Marcus?

MARCUS *overwhelmed by resentment, turns to* SIGMUND, *silent*.

Then we have not this reason. (*Slight pause.*) Therefore . . . perhaps you have come back for different reason.

MARCUS. I came back to prevent a calamity, a disaster for all of us . . .

SIGMUND. Yes, but is also for them a calamity. If I am in prison the whole world will know they are gangster. This is not intelligent – my book are published in nine country. For them is also disaster.

MARCUS. So this fellow in London? These threats? They're not serious?

SIGMUND. I am sure they wish me to believe so, therefore is very serious.

MARCUS. You don't believe a word I've told you, do you? There was no man at all in London; that conversation never happened? There'll be no arrest? No trial?

SIGMUND (*pause*). I think not.

MARCUS. Then give me back my pistol.

SIGMUND *does not move.* MARCUS *holds out his hand.*

Give it to me, you're in no danger; I've invented the whole thing.

SIGMUND *is motionless.*

Are you simply a thief? Why are you keeping it?

SIGMUND *is silent.*

MAYA. Marcus . . .

MARCUS. I insist he answer me . . . (*To* SIGMUND.) Why are you keeping that pistol? (*He laughs.*) But of course you know perfectly well I've told you the truth; it was just too good an opportunity to cover me with your contempt . . . in her eyes, (*Pointing toward* ADRIAN.) and the eyes of the world.

ADRIAN. Now, Marcus, I had no intention . . .

MARCUS. Oh come now, Adrian, he's been writing this story for you all evening! *New York Times* feature on Socialist decadence.

ADRIAN. Now wait a minute . . .

MARCUS. But it's so obvious . . . !

ADRIAN. Wait a minute, will you? He has a right to be uneasy.

MARCUS. No more than I do, and for quite the same reason.

ADRIAN. Why!

MARCUS (*laughs*). To whom am *I* talking, Adrian – the *New York Times*, or your novel, or you?

ADRIAN. For Christ's sake, are you serious?

MARCUS (*laughs*). Why not? You may turn out to be as dangerous to me as he believes I am to him. Yes!

ADRIAN *looks astonished.*

Why is it any more absurd? Especially after that last piece of yours, which you'll pardon me, was stuffed with the most primitive misunderstandings of what it means to live in this country. You haven't a clue, Adrian – you'll forgive me, but I have to say that. So I'm entitled to a bit of uneasiness.

ADRIAN. Marcus, are you asking me to account for myself?

MARCUS. By no means, but why must I?

MAYA. Why don't we all go to the playground and swing with the other children?

MARCUS (*laughs*). Very good, yes.

MAYA (*to* ADRIAN). Why is he so complicated? They allow him this house to store his father's library. These books earn hard currency. To sell them he must have a passport.

MARCUS. Oh, he knows all that, dear – it's hopeless; when did the facts ever change a conviction? It doesn't matter. (*He looks at his watch.*)

ADRIAN. It does, though. It's a terrible thing. It's maddening.

MARCUS (*denigrating*). Well . . .

ADRIAN. It is, you know it is. Christ, you're such old friends, you're writers . . . I never understood the sadness in this country, but I swear, I think it's . . .

MARCUS. Oh, come off it, Adrian – what country isn't sad?

ADRIAN. I think you've accepted something.

MARCUS. And you haven't?

ADRIAN. Goddammit, Marcus, we can still speak for ourselves! And not for some . . . (*He breaks off.*)

MARCUS. Some what?

ADRIAN (*walks away*). . . . Well, never mind.

MARCUS. I've spoken for no one but myself here, Adrian. If there seems to be some . . . unspoken interest . . . well, there is, of course. I am interested in seeing that this country does not fall back into darkness. And if he must sacrifice something for that, I think he should. That's plain enough, isn't it?

ADRIAN. I guess the question is . . . how you feel about that yourself.

MARCUS (*laughs*). But I feel terribly about it. I think it's dreadful. I think there's no question he is our best living writer. Must I go on, or is that enough?

Silence.

What change can feelings make? It is a situation which I can tell you – *no one wants* . . . no one. If I flew into an orgasm of self-revelation here it might seem more candid, but it would change nothing . . . (except possibly to multiply the confusion).

MAYA (*to* ADRIAN). I think you were saying the same thing

before . . . Tell him.

MARCUS. What?

ADRIAN. Whether it matters anymore, what anyone feels . . . about anything. Whether we're not just some sort of . . . filament that only lights up when it's plugged into whatever power there is.

MAYA. It's interesting.

MARCUS. I don't know – it seems rather childish. When was a man ever conceivable apart from society? Unless you're looking for the angel who wrote each of our blessed names in his book of gold. The collective giveth and the collective taketh away – beyond that . . .

He looks to the ceiling.

was never anything but a sentimental metaphor; a god which now is simply a form of art. Whose style may still move us, but there was never any mercy in that plaster. The only difference now, it seems to me, is that we've ceased to expect any.

ADRIAN. I know one reason I came. I know it's an awkward question, but – those tanks bivouacked out there in the countryside . . . do they figure at all in your minds?

MAYA. Do you write *every minute*?

ADRIAN. Well, do they? (*To* MARCUS.) Are they part of your lives at all?

MARCUS. I don't really know . . .

ADRIAN. Maya? It interests me.

MAYA. It's such a long time, now. And you don't see them unless you drive out there . . .

MARCUS. It's hard to say.

ADRIAN (*of* SIGMUND). Why do you suppose he can't stop thinking about them? I bet there isn't an hour a day when they don't cross his mind.

MAYA. Because he is a genius. When he enters the tram the conductor refuses to accept his fare. In the grocery store they give him the best oranges. The usher bows in the theatre when she shows him to his seat.

She goes to SIGMUND, *touches his hair.*

He is our Sigmund. He is loved, he creates our memories. Therefore, it is only a question of time when he will create the departure of these tanks, and they will go home. And then we shall all be ourselves, with nothing overhead but the sky, and he will turn into a monument standing in the park.

Her eyes fill with tears, she turns up his face.

Go, darling. Please. There is nothing left for you.

SIGMUND (*touches her face*). Something, perhaps. We shall see.

MAYA *moves Right to the window, sips a drink.*

IRINA (*with a swimming gesture to* MARCUS). I am bathing?

MARCUS. Yes, of course – come, I'll get you a towel. (*He starts to rise.*)

MAYA (*looking out of the window*). She'd better wait a little – I used all the hot water. (*With a laugh, to* SIGMUND.) I came tonight to take a bath!

MARCUS *laughs.*

ADRIAN. Marcus, when they arrested you . . .

MAYA (*suddenly*). Will you stop writing, for Christ's sake! Isn't there something else to talk about?

MARCUS. Why not? – if he's interested?

MAYA. Are we some sick fish in a tank! (*To* ADRIAN.) Stop it! (*She get up, goes to the drink table.*) What the hell do you expect people to *do*? What *is* it?

MARCUS. You've had enough, dear . . .

MAYA (*pouring*). I have not had enough, dear. (*She suddenly slams the glass down on the table.*) Fuck all this diplomacy! (*At* ADRIAN.) You're in no position to judge anybody! We have nothing to be ashamed of!

MARCUS (*turning away in disgust*). Oh for God's sake . . .

MAYA. You know what he brought when he came to me? A bottle of milk!

Perplexed, MARCUS *turns to her.*

I wake up and he's in the kitchen, drinking *milk*!

She waits before MARCUS, *awaiting his reaction.*

A grown man!

MARCUS (*to calm her*). Well, they drink a lot of it in the States.

MAYA (*quietly, seeking to explain*). He smelled like a baby, all night.

MARCUS (*stands*). I'll make you some coffee . . .

He starts past her, but she stops him with her hand on his arm, frightened and remorseful. She kisses him.

MAYA. I'm going home. (*She takes his hand, tries to lead him toward* SIGMUND *with imperative force.*) Come, be his friend . . . you are friends, darling . . .

The telephone in the bedroom rings. She turns up to the entrance in surprise.

Goddamn that Hilton!

She starts towards the bedroom, but as the telephone rings again, MARCUS *goes up and exits into the bedroom. She comes to* SIGMUND.

Darling . . . (*She points up to the ceiling – speaking softly in desperation.*) I really don't think there is anything there. I would never do that to you, you know that. I think it was only to make himself interesting – he can't write anymore; it left him . . . (*In anguish.*) . . . it left him!

SIGMUND. I know.

MAYA. He loves you, he loves you, darling . . . ! (*Gripping her head.*) My God, I'm sick . . .

She starts upstage as MARCUS *enters. He has a stunned look. She halts, seeing him, looks at him questioningly.* SIGMUND *turns to look at him, and* ADRIAN. *After a moment . . .*

MARCUS (*turning to* SIGMUND *with a gesture inviting him to go* to the phone.

It's Alexandra.

SIGMUND *does not move.*

. . . she wishes to speak to you.

SIGMUND *stands, confounded by* MARCUS's *look, and goes out into the bedroom.* MARCUS *remains there, staring.*

MAYA. What?

MARCUS *is silent, staring.*

ADRIAN. Something happen?

MARCUS *crosses the stage and descends into his chair, his face transfixed by some enigma.*

MAYA (*in fright . . . starting up toward the bedroom.*) Sigmund . . . !

SIGMUND *enters, halts, shakes his head uttering an almost soundless laugh, his eyes alive to something incredible.*

MARCUS. They're returning his manuscript.

MAYA *claps her hands together, then crosses herself, her face between explosive joy and some terror, rigid, sobered.*

ADRIAN (*grabs* SIGMUND *by the shoulders*). Is it true?

MARCUS. She may be able to bring it when she comes.

ADRIAN. Sigmund!

He kisses him. They look at each other and laugh.

SIGMUND (*half-smiling*). You believe it?

ADRIAN (*takes aback*). Don't you?

SIGMUND (*laughs*). I don't know! (*He walks, dumbfounded.*) . . . Yes, I suppose I believe. (*He suddenly laughs.*) Why not! They have made me ridiculous, therefore I must believe it.

MARCUS. Well, the main thing is, you . . .

SIGMUND. Yes, that is the main thing. I must call Elizabeth . . . (*He starts to the bedroom, but looks at his watch.*) No . . . she will not yet be home.

ADRIAN (*to all*). What could it mean? (*He laughs, seeing* SIGMUND.) You look punchy. (*He grabs him.*) Wake up! –

you got it back! . . . Listen, come to Paris with me . . . with the boy and Elizabeth. We'll get you a visa – you can be in New York in ten days. We'll go to my publisher, I'll break his arm, we'll get you a tremendous advance and you're on your way.

SIGMUND (*laughing*). Wait, wait . . .

ADRIAN. Say yes! Come on! You can waste the rest of your life in this goddamned country. Jesus, why can't they steal it again tomorrow? – (*To the ceiling:*) I didn't mean that about the country. But it's infuriating – they play you like a yo-yo.

SIGMUND (*sits; an aura of irony on his voice*). So, Maya . . . you are immortal again.

ADRIAN. Is *she* that character?

MAYA. Of course.

ADRIAN. She sounded terrific.

MAYA. She is the best woman he has ever written – fantastic, complicated personality. (*To* SIGMUND.) What is there to keep you now? It is enough, no?

IRINA. Is good?

MARCUS (*patting her*). Yes, very good.

SIGMUND. She is so lucky – she understands nothing. We also understand nothing – but for us is not lucky.

MAYA. We should go to Francesco's later – we should have a party.

SIGMUND (*turns to her with a faint smile*). It is strange, eh? We have such good news and we are sad.

MARCUS. It isn't sadness.

SIGMUND. Perhaps only some sort of humiliation. (*He shakes his head.*) We must admire them – they are very intelligent – they can even create unhappiness with good news.

ADRIAN (*to* MARCUS). What do you suppose happened?

MARCUS. I've no idea.

ADRIAN. It seems like a gesture of some kind. Is it?

MARCUS. I haven't the foggiest.

ADRIAN. Could it be that I was here?

MARCUS. Who knows? Of course they would like to make peace with him, it's a gesture in that sense.

SIGMUND *looks across at him.*

I think you ought to consider it that way.

SIGMUND. It is their contempt; they are laughing.

MARCUS. Not necessarily – Some of them have great respect for you.

SIGMUND. No-no, they are laughing.

MAYA. Why are you such children?

SIGMUND *turns to her.*

It is not respect and it is not contempt – it is nothing.

ADRIAN. But it must mean something.

MAYA. Why? They have the power to take it and the power to give it back.

ADRIAN. Well that's a meaning.

MAYA. You didn't know that before? When it rains you get wet – that is not exactly meaningful. (*To the three.*) There's nothing to say; it is a terrible embarrassment for geniuses but there is simply no possible comment to be made.

SIGMUND. How is in Shakespeare? – 'We are like flies to little boys, they kill us for their sport.'

MAYA. They are not killing you at all. Not at all.

SIGMUND. Why are you angry with me? I am not obliged to ask why something happens?

MAYA. Because you can live happily and you don't want to.

ADRIAN. It's not so simple.

MAYA. But for you it is! You are so rich, Adrian, you live so well – why must he be heroic?

ADRIAN. I've never told him to . . .

MAYA. Then tell him to get out! Be simple, be clear to him . . .

ADRIAN. I've been very clear to him . . .

MAYA. Good! (*To* SIGMUND.) So the three of us are of the same opinion, you see? Let's have a party at Francesco's . . . call Elizabeth . . . a farewell party. All right?

He looks up at her.

It is all finished, darling!

He smiles, shaking his head. She is frightened and angry.

What? What is it? What more can be said?

SIGMUND (*with a certain laughter*). Is like some sort of theatre, no? Very bad theatre – our emotions have no connection with the event. Myself also – I *must* speak, darling – I do not understand myself. I must confess, I have feeling of gratitude; *before* they have stolen my book I was never grateful. *Now* I am grateful – (*His laughter vanishes.*) I cannot accept such confusion, Maya, is very bad for my mentality. I must speak! I think we must all speak now!

He ends looking at MARCUS; *his anger is open.*

MARCUS. What can I tell you? I know nothing.

SIGMUND. I am sure not, but we can speculate, perhaps? (*To* MAYA.) Please, darling – sit; we must wait for Alexandra, we have nothing to do. Please, Adrian – sit down . . . I have some idea . . .

ADRIAN *sits.* SIGMUND *continues to* MAYA.

. . . which I would like to discuss before I leave my country.

MAYA *sits slowly, apprehensively. He turns to* MARCUS, *adopting a quiet, calm air.*

Is possible, Marcus – there was some sort of mistake? Perhaps only one police commander has made this decision for himself – to stealing my book? Perhaps the government was also surprised?

MARCUS *considers in silence.*

SIGMUND. I am interested your opinion. *I* think so, perhaps – no?

MARCUS. Do you know if they were the Security Police?

SIGMUND. Yes, Security Police.

MARCUS. *They* might, I suppose.

SIGMUND. I think so. But in this case . . . this fellow in London taxi – is possible he was also speaking for himself?

MARCUS. I can't believe that.

SIGMUND. But if he was speaking for government . . . such terrible thing against me – why have they chosen to returning my manuscript? I think is not logical, no?

MARCUS. . . . Unless they had second thoughts, and felt it would make it easier for you to leave.

SIGMUND. Yes. That is very strong idea.

ADRIAN. I think that's it.

SIGMUND. Very good, yes. But at same time, if have manuscript – you do not object that I . . . ?

MARCUS. Go ahead – it's simply that I know no more than . . .

SIGMUND. You understand is very important to me . . . I must understand why I am leaving.

MARCUS. Of course. Go ahead.

SIGMUND (*slight pause*). If I have manuscript, I must probably conclude is *not* dangerous for me here, no? I must believe is only some particular antagonistic enemy who wish me to go out. Is possible?

MARCUS. What can I tell you?

SIGMUND (*with nearly an outcry through his furious control*). But you know you are sad! I am sad, Maya is sad – if was some sort of mistake . . . why we are not happy?

MAYA *gets up and strides towards the bedroom.*

Maya?

MAYA (*hardly turning back*). I'm going home . . .

SIGMUND (*leaps up and intercepts her*). No-no, – we must have celebration! (*He grips her hands.*)

MAYA. Let me go!

SIGMUND. No! We have tremendous good news, we must

have correct emotion!

MAYA (*wrenching her hands free, pointing at his pocket*). Give me that thing. . . . Give it to me!

SIGMUND. My God – I had forgotten it. (*He takes out the pistol, looks at it.*)

MAYA. Please. Sigmund. Please . . . !

SIGMUND. I have crazy idea . . .

MAYA (*weeping*). Sigmund . . .

SIGMUND (*moving toward the piano*). One time very long ago, I have read in American detective story . . . that criminal has placed revolver inside piano.

He sets the pistol on the strings, and comes around to the bench.

Then someone is playing very fortissimo . . . something like Beethoven . . . (*Raising his hands over the keyboard.*) . . . and he is firing the pistol.

ADRIAN. What the hell are you doing?

SIGMUND (*smashes his hands down on the keyboard*). Ha! Is not true.

ADRIAN (*stands*). What the hell are you doing?

SIGMUND. Wait! I have idea . . . (*He reaches over, takes out the pistol and cocks it.*)

MAYA. Marcus!

SIGMUND (*replacing the cocked pistol in the piano*). Now we shall see . . .

ADRIAN (*rushing* MAYA *away from the piano*). Watch out!

SIGMUND (*crashes his hands down – the gun explodes, the strings reverberating.*) Is true! (*Reaching in and taking out the revolver.*) My God, I am so happy . . . (*Holding up the revolver.*) The truth is alive in our country, Marcus!

He comes and sits near MARCUS.

Is unmistakable, no? – when something is true?

He looks at the pistol, puts it in his pocket. MARCUS *turns to him only now.* MAYA *suddenly weeps, sobbing, and makes for the bedroom.*

I cannot permit you to leave, Maya! (*She halts, turning to him in terror.*)

I must insist, darling – is most important evening of my life and I understand nothing. Why do you weep, why do you go? If I am ridiculous I must understand why! Please . . . sit. Perhaps you can say something.

She sits, a distance from him and MARCUS. ADRIAN *remains standing, catching his breath; he leans his head on his hand, as though caught by a rush of sadness and he shakes his head incredulously, glancing at* MARCUS.

MARCUS. What is it? What *is* it!

SIGMUND. This fellow . . . this fellow in taxi who has threatened me – what was his name?

MARCUS. I don't recall, I only heard it once. Granitz, I think. Or Grodnitz. But I'm sure he didn't know you.

SIGMUND. Grodnitz.

MARCUS. . . . Or Granitz.

ADRIAN. You know him?

SIGMUND. . . . No. (*Slight pause.*) No Granitz. No Grodnitz. (*Slight pause. He takes the pistol out of his pocket, looks at it in his hand, then turns again to* MARCUS.)

He exists? Or is imaginary man?

MARCUS *is silent.*

Was *ever* discussion of trial for me? Or is imaginary trial?

MARCUS *is silent.* SIGMUND *looks at the pistol again, then stretching over to* MARCUS *he places it in his hand.*

I believe I have no danger, at the moment.

Slight pause. A long pause. No one dares do more than glance at MARCUS *whose face is filled with his fury. The pause lengthens.* SIGMUND *looks at his watch.*

I will try to call Elizabeth.

MARCUS. The sole function of every other writer is to wish he were you.

SIGMUND *stands, looks to* MAYA, *who avoids his eyes. He*

exits into the bedroom. After a moment . . .

ADRIAN (*sotto, to assuage* MARCUS). He's terribly scared . . .

MARCUS (*slight pause. Like a final verdict*). I couldn't care less. (*He looks at his watch.*)

ADRIAN (*silent for a moment*). For what it's worth . . . I know he has tremendous feeling for you.

MARCUS. For his monument. To build his monument he has to prove that everyone else is a coward or corrupt. My mistake was to offer him my help – it's a menace to his lonely grandeur. No one is permitted anything but selfishness. He's insane.

ADRIAN. Oh come on . . .

MARCUS. He's paranoid – these letters to the foreign press are for nothing but to bring on another confrontation – it was too peaceful; they were threatening him with tolerance. He must find evil or he can't be good.

MAYA. Let's not talk about it anymore . . .

MARCUS. I exist too, Maya! I am not dancing around that megalomania again. (*Slight pause.*)

ADRIAN. I can't blame you, but I wish you wouldn't cut out on him yet. Look, I'll stay through the week, maybe I can convince him. Does he have a week?

MARCUS (*slowly turns to* ADRIAN). How would I know?

ADRIAN. All I meant was whether you . . .

MARCUS. I won't have anymore of this, Adrian!

Slight pause.

ADRIAN. I believe you – I've told him to get out.

MARCUS. No you haven't; you've insinuated.

ADRIAN. Christ's sake, you've heard me say . . .

MARCUS. I *have* heard you.

They are facing each other. Slight pause.

You don't believe me, Adrian . . . not really.

ADRIAN *can't answer.*

MARCUS. So it's all over. It's the end of him. – I've been there. He will smash his head against the walls, and the rest of us will pay for his grandeur.

Slight pause. ADRIAN *turns front in his conflict.* SIGMUND *enters.* MARCUS *turns away.*

MAYA (*with a tonal attempt at cheerfulness*). Did you reach her? Elizabeth?

SIGMUND. She is very happy. (*To* MARCUS.) She send you her greetings – she is grateful.

Slight pause.

I also.

MARCUS *half-turns toward him.* SIGMUND *says no more, goes to his chair and sits.*

ADRIAN. Sigmund? (SIGMUND *glances at him.*) Do you trust me?

SIGMUND *is silent.*

I'm convinced he's told you the truth.

SIGMUND *is silent.*

In all the times we've talked about you, he's never shown anything but a wide-open pride in you, and your work. He's with you. You have to believe that.

SIGMUND *turns, stares at* MARCUS*'s profile for a moment. Then looks at* MAYA. *She ultimately turns slightly away. He looks down at the floor.*

SIGMUND. I am afraid; that is all. I think I will not be able to write in some other country.

ADRIAN. Oh, that's impossible . . .

SIGMUND. I am not cosmopolitan writer, I am provincial writer. I believe I must hear my language every day, I must walk in these particular streets. I think in New York I will have only some terrible silence. Is like old tree – it is difficult to moving old tree, they most probably die.

ADRIAN. But if they lock you up . . .

SIGMUND. Yes, but that is my fate; I must accept my fate.

But to run away because of some sort of rumour – I have only some rumour, no? How will I support this silence that I have brought on myself? This is terrible idea, no? How I can accept to be so ridiculous? Therefore, is reasonable, I believe – that I must absolutely understand who is speaking to me.

ADRIAN (*slight pause, a hesitation*). I'm going to level with you, Sigmund – I think you're being far too . . .

SIGMUND (*a frustrated outburst*). I am not crazy, Adrian!

All turn to him, fear in their faces. He spreads his arms, with an upward glance.

Who is commanding me? Who is this voice? *Who is speaking to me?*

MAYA. They.

An instant's silence; she seems ashamed to look directly at SIGMUND. *She gestures almost imperceptibly upward.*

It is there.

MARCUS (*in protest*). Maya!

MAYA. Why not! (*To* SIGMUND). They have heard it all.

MARCUS (*to* SIGMUND *and* ADRIAN). It isn't true, there's nothing.

MAYA (*persisting, to* SIGMUND). He has risked everything . . . for you. God knows what will happen for what has been said here.

MARCUS (*to* SIGMUND). There's nothing . . . she can't know . . . (*To* MAYA.) You can't know that . . .

MAYA (*her eyes to the ceiling*). Who else have we been speaking to all evening! (*To them all.*) Who does not believe it? (*To* MARCUS.) It is his life, darling – we must begin to say what we believe. Somewhere, we must begin!

Pause. She sits a distance from SIGMUND; *only after a moment does she turn to face him as she fights down her shame and her fear of him.*

SIGMUND. So.

MAYA (*downing her shame*). Just so, yes. You must go.

SIGMUND. For your sake.

MAYA. Yes.

MARCUS (*softly, facing front*). It isn't true.

MAYA. And yours. For all of us.

SIGMUND. You must . . . deliver me? My departure?

MAYA *stiffens. She cannot speak.*

SIGMUND. For your programme? His passport . . . ?

ADRIAN. Sigmund, it's enough . . .

MAYA. He had no need to return, except he loves you. There was no need. That is also true.

SIGMUND (*his head clamped in his hands*). My God . . . Maya.

Pause.

(*To* MARCUS.) They brought you back to make sure my departure?

ADRIAN (*aborting the violence coming*). Come on, Sigmund, it's enough . . .

SIGMUND (*trying to laugh*). But she is not some sort of whore! I have many years with this woman . . . !

ADRIAN. What more do you *want*!

MARCUS. Her humiliation; she's not yet on her knees to him. We are now to take our places, you see, at the foot of the cross, as he floats upward through the plaster on the wings of his immortal contempt. We lack remorse, it spoils the picture.

He glares, smiling at SIGMUND *who seems on the verge of springing at him.*

ADRIAN (*to* SIGMUND). Forget it, Sigmund – come on . . . (*To* MARCUS.) Maybe you ought to call that Alexandra woman.

MARCUS. She'll be along.

Silence. The moment expands. SIGMUND *stares front, gripping his lower face.* ADRIAN *is glancing at him with apprehension.* MAYA *is looking at no one.*

SIGMUND (*to* MAYA). You can say nothing to me?

MAYA (*slight pause*). You know my feeling.

SIGMUND. I, not. I know your name. Who is this woman?

MARCUS. Don't play that game with him.

SIGMUND. It is a game?

ADRIAN. Come on, fellas . . .

SIGMUND (*irritated, to* ADRIAN). Is interesting to me. (*To* MARCUS.) What is your game? What did you mean?

MARCUS. It's called Power. Or Moral Monopoly. The winner takes all the justifications. When you write this, Adrian, I hope you include the fact that they refused him a visa for many years and he was terribly indignant – the right to leave was sacred to civilisation. Now he has that right and it's an insult. You can draw your own conclusions.

SIGMUND. And what is the conclusion?

MARCUS. You are a moral blackmailer. We have all humoured you, Sigmund, out of some misplaced sense of responsibility to our literature. Or maybe it's only our terror of vanishing altogether. We aren't the Russians – after you and Otto and Peter there aren't a handful to keep the breath of life in this language. We have taken all the responsibility and left you all the freedom to call us morally bankrupt. But now you're free to go, so the responsibility moves to you. Now it's yours. All yours. We have done what was possible; now you will do what is necessary, or turn out our lights. And that is where it stands.

SIGMUND (*slight pause*). This is all?

MARCUS *is silent.*

ADRIAN. What more can be said, Sigmund? What can they give you? It's pointless.

SIGMUND (*turns to* MAYA). What you can give me, Maya? (*She is silent.*) There is nothing? I am only some sort of . . . comical Jesus Christ? Is only my egotism? This is all?

In silence, MAYA *turns to face him.*

You understand what I ask you?

MAYA. Yes.

SIGMUND. You cannot? (*Slight pause. Then he glances toward* MARCUS.) After so many years . . . so many conversations . . . so many hope and disaster – you can only speak for them?

He gestures toward the ceiling.

Is terrible, no? Why we have lived?

ADRIAN (*to cut off his mounting anger*). Sigmund . . .

SIGMUND (*swiftly, his eyes blazing*). Why have you come here? What do you want in this country?

ADRIAN (*astonished*). What the hell are you . . . ?

SIGMUND. You are scientist observing the specimens – this whore? This clever fellow making business with these gangsters?

ADRIAN. For Christ's sake, Sigmund, what can I do!

SIGMUND. They are killing us, Adrian – they have destroyed my friends! You are free man, (*With a gesture toward the ceiling.*) why you are obliged to be clever? – Why do you come here, Adrian?

MAYA. To save his book.

ADRIAN. That's a lie!

MAYA. But it's exactly what you told me an hour ago. (*She stands, and to both* SIGMUND *and* ADRIAN.) What is the sin? He has come for his profit, to rescue two years' work, to make more money . . .

ADRIAN. That's a goddamned lie!

MAYA. And for friendship! Oh yes – his love for you. I believe it! Like ours. Absolutely like ours! Is love not love because there is some profit in it? Who speaks only for his heart? And yes, I speak to them now – this moment, this very moment to them, that they may have mercy on my programme, on his passport. Always to them, in some part to them for my profit – here and everywhere in this world! Just as you do.

SIGMUND. I speak for Sigmund.

MAYA. Only Sigmund? Then why can't you speak for Sigmund in America? Because you will not have them in America to hate! And if you cannot hate you cannot write and you will not be Sigmund anymore, but another lousy refugee ordering his chicken soup in broken English – and where is the profit in that? They are your theme, your life, your partner in this dance that cannot stop, or you will die of silence! (*She moves toward him . . . and tenderly.*) They are in you, darling. And if you stay . . . it is also for your profit . . . as it is for ours to tell you to go. Who can speak for himself alone?

A heavy brass knocker is heard from below.

SIGMUND *lifts his eyes to the ceiling.*

MARCUS *stands, faces* SIGMUND *who now turns to him. Silence.*

SIGMUND. Tell her, please . . . is impossible . . . any transaction. Only to return my property.

MAYA (*with an abjectness, a terror, taking his hand and kissing it*). Darling . . . For my sake. For this little life that I have made . . .

MARCUS (*with anger, disgust*). Stop it! (*He turns to* SIGMUND.) For your monument. For the bowing ushers in the theatre. For the power . . . the power to bring down everyone.

SIGMUND (*spreads his hands, looks up at the ceiling*). I don't know. (*He turns to* MARCUS.) But I will never leave. Never.

Another knock is heard. MARCUS, *his face set, goes out and up the corridor.* SIGMUND *turns to* MAYA. *She walks away, her face expressionless, and stands at the window staring out.*

Forgive me, Maya.

She doesn't turn to him. He looks to ADRIAN.

Is quite simple. We are ridiculous people now. And when we try to escape it, we are ridiculous too.

ADRIAN. No.

SIGMUND. I think so. But we cannot help ourselves. I must give you . . . certain letters, I wish to keep them . . . before you leave. (*Sitting.*) I have one some years ago from Malraux. Very elegant. *French*, you know? Also Julia Ilyesh, Hungarian . . . very wise fellow. Heinrich Böll, Germany, one letter. Kobo Abe, Japan – he also. Saul Bellow. Also Cortazar, Brazil . . .

Slight pause.

My God, eh? So many writers! Like snow . . . like forest . . . these enormous trees everywhere on the earth. Marvellous.

Slight pause. A welling up in him. He suddenly cries out to MAYA *across the stage.*

Maya! Forgive me . . .

He hurries to her.

I cannot help it.

MAYA. I know. (*She turns to him, reaches out and touches his face.*) Thank you.

SIGMUND (*surprised, he is motionless for an instant, then pulls her into his arms, and holding her face*). Oh, my God! Thank you, Maya.

The voices of MARCUS *and* ALEXANDRA *are heard approaching from the darkness up the corridor. The three of them turn toward the door.*

IRINA (*revolving her finger, to* MAYA). Now, music?

Curtain.

Afterword

When the ballroom of the Mayflower Hotel on Connecticut Avenue, Washington, was redecorated in 1983 the painters and plasterers found twenty-eight hidden microphones. The Mayflower, for long popular with politicians, diplomats and businessmen, had been turned into a kind of permanent theatre by the FBI, or whatever other agency was interested in the alchemical transformation of knowledge into power. Scarcely a shock in a country which had experienced the cynical corruptions of Watergate, it was nonetheless a reminder of the fragile and suspect nature of the real. Those who had once been dismissed as hopelessly paranoid could now claim to have been the most rational of social analysts, for the politicians and their agents had seemingly conspired to corrupt not only the political process but also our sense of reality. When the insane run the asylum who can we trust to define the nature of sanity?

The Archbishop's Ceiling is set in eastern Europe but the pressure of a quarter of a century of illegal surveillance at home can be felt behind what appears at first to be a political drama in which one man, a writer called Sigmund, comes to embody a sense of resistance to the apparatus of the state. At a time when power asserts its presumptive rights he chooses to stay and fight when he could leave – indeed when his exile is the price of his survival as an artist. But, like much else in the play, this is misleading. What appears to be a purely political play slowly reveals itself as a study of metaphysics, a debate about the nature of reality and the problematic status of morality in a world whose certainties dissolve so easily into mere performance.

A group of people assemble in the down-at-heel splendour of a one-time Archbishop's palace: Adrian is an American novelist whose reasons for travelling east are deeply ambiguous; Maya, a one-time poet and actress, who, like her companion, Marcus – also a novelist – may or may not be in league with the authorities. These are joined by Sigmund, a dissident novelist, under pressure to leave for the West. They meet in the conviction – never fully confirmed – that they are overheard by microphones concealed in the room's ornate ceiling. In other words they are turned into actors and their lives into theatre; but there is, finally, no evidence for the existence of the audience before whom they take themselves to be performing. There is no stable reality. They exist in a factitious world. And just as they inhabit the fictions of the state so they, as writers, counter with their own fictions. But in an existence in which performance becomes a personal and political necessity how can morality be constructed? And beyond the psychological, social and political questions which the play raises is a metaphysical anxiety. The Archbishop's palace has fallen into disuse as a religious building. The baroque decorations are now lost in the gloom. Where once human life was charged with significance by the conviction that we acted out our dramas in the eye of God, for whom all actions had meaning and every gesture was a cipher to be decided in terms of grace or damnation, now the suspicion is that He has withdrawn. The eye that saw, the ears that heard are now no longer there.

But there is a paradox – no less on the political than the metaphysical plane – for to believe that there is a hidden audience may be to be turned into an actor but to doubt that presence is in some way to be drained of significance, no matter how arbitrary that significance may be. To be bugged is to be violated but it is also to have one's existence confirmed and one's meaning attested. Willing submission to invisible powers is understandable even if it threatens our identity for the alternative is not only freedom but abandonment. And what meaning can we ascribe to a freedom which is exercised out of the sight of man and god? A courageous act publicly performed perhaps requires rather less courage than one done in a privacy which drains it of its social meaning. The empty auditorium has terrors scarcely less affecting than one filled with those who judge as well as observe.

Taken together, *The Archbishop's Ceiling* and his two one act plays, *Some Kind of Love Story* and *Elegy for a Lady* (published by Methuen under the composite title *Two Way Mirror*) constitute a major new phase in the career of America's leading playwright. But the break is not as radical as it may appear. In fact, behind the moral concerns, the social and political urgencies of his earlier work, there was always a fascination with the problematic status of the real. He argued for what seemed to be the manifest values of a classic American liberalism and a native existentialism in a world in which those principles were under extreme pressure. The myth of independence remained as did the language of social responsibility and the assertion of a cohesive national purpose, but the reality was otherwise. It was not merely that liberal values had deferred to a new materialism, that the independent spirit was threatened by the physical conditions and social coercions of modern American society, but that public myths now exerted an authority which threatened the individual at his or her core. Thus, in *Death of a Salesman*, Willy Loman is finally unable to separate reality from appearance. He is an actor incapable of distinguishing identity from role. As Miller said, he believed that the stars projected on the clouds from the rooftops were real stars. *The Crucible*, in turn, is at base a debate about the nature of the real and about those who claim the right to define it as much as it is a drama of moral responsibility. In *After the Fall*, *Incident at Vichy* and *Playing for Time* Miller tried to understand and analyse the terrible fictions of the Third Reich which quite literally rendered down the grace and complexity of the human sensibility. Thus his present concern with life as theatre, with the coercive power of private and public fictions, with the nature of the real and with the necessity to reconstruct a moral world in the ethical void left by the death of God – or those gods we have invented in order to give ourselves significance – is a natural extension of his earlier plays. But the urgency is now more apparent, the dislocations more threatening, the mood more apocalyptic, the moral certainties under greater pressure.

And if, finally, we do inhabit a world of competing fictions in which our central task is perhaps no longer to learn to distinguish the true from the false but to generate fictions which assert rather than deny human values then the role of the artist becomes central. In a sense we all summon the world into existence and coerce others onto a stage which we have set. This is the tension behind personal relationships. Projected onto a national scale this becomes potentially more lethal. The writer thus seeks to intervene but can only do so on the level of the imagination – an imagination for which the world is so much raw material, his *mise en scène*. The necessity to do so remains but it must be an inherently ambiguous enterprise, touched with guilt and characterised by a profound anxiety.

The American writer, Adrian, who comes to the Archbishop's palace does so less out of feelings of solidarity than because he seeks absolution, for the fact is that he has included Maya as a character in his fiction (she is to be a character in his new novel) just as the state tries to incorporate the individual into its fictions. The play is thus in a sense a contemplation of the ethics of writing no less than a consideration of the morality of social being. Marcus seems the writer turned betrayer, a mere apparatchik. And yet, in the Archbishop's palace, there are no certainties; there is no touchstone of veracity, no proof of sincerity and authenticity. Indeed that is the essence of the play. But the need to make some moral stand survives, the compulsion to assert the significance of identity and to acknowledge a responsibility beyond the seif. How that is to be achieved in a world of fictions, in which action is turned into theatre and ethics into aesthetics, is only one of the questions posed by this complex but moving play.

CHRISTOPHER BIGSBY

TWO-WAY MIRROR

A double-bill of

Elegy for a Lady

and

Some Kind of Love Story

With an Afterword by Christopher Bigsby

Author's Note

The stories and characters of this pair of plays are unrelated to one another but in different ways both works are passionate voyages through the masks of illusion to an ultimate reality. In *Some Kind of Love Story* it is social reality and the corruption of justice which a delusionary woman both conceals and unveils. The search in *Elegy for a Lady* is for the shape and meaning of a sexual relationship that is being brought to a close by a lover's probable death. In both the unreal is an agony to be striven against and, at the same time, accepted as life's condition.

A.M.

Some Kind of Love Story, in tandem with *Elegy for a Lady,* was presented by the Long Wharf Theater in New Haven, Connecticut, in November, 1982 under the omnibus title of *2 by A.M*. The production was directed by the author, with Christine Lahti and Charles Cioffi appearing in both plays. The sets were by Hugh Landwehr; costumes were by Bill Walker and the lighting was by Ronald Wallace.

The British première of *Two-Way Mirror* was at the Young Vic, London in January 1989. The production was directed by David Thacker, and starred Helen Mirren and Bob Peck. The decor was by Bob Crowley; lighting by Paul Denby and sound by Dick Crabbe.

ELEGY FOR A LADY

It isn't always clear exactly where one stands in psychic space when grief passes up through the body into the mind. To be at once the observer and observed is a split awareness that most people know; but what of the grieved-for stranger, the other who is 'not-me'? – Doesn't it sometimes seem as though he or she is not merely outside oneself but also within and seeing outward through one's own eyes at the same time that he or she is being seen?

There is an anguish, based on desire impossible to realize, that is so unrequited, and therefore so intense, that it tends to fuse all people into one person in a so-to-speak spectral unity, a personification which seems to reflect and clarify these longings and may even reply to them when in the ordinary world of 'I' and 'You' they cannot even be spoken aloud. Nor is this really so strange when one recalls how much of each of us is imagined by the other, how we create one another even as we actually speak and actually touch.

A.M.

CAST

MAN
PROPRIETRESS

Music: it has a fine, distant fragility, a simple theme, repeated – like unresolved grief.

The MAN *appears in a single beam of light, facing the audience. He is hatless, dressed in a well-fitted overcoat and tweed suit.*

He stares as though lost in thought, slightly bent forward, perhaps to concentrate better. He is deep into himself, unaware for the moment of his surroundings.

Light rises behind him, gradually dawning across the stage, reveals aspects of what slowly turns out to be a boutique. The shop consists of its elements without the walls, the fragments seeming to be suspended in space.

A sweater is draped over a bust, a necklace on another bust, a garter on an upturned plastic thigh, a watch on an upturned arm, a knitted cap and muffler on a plastic head. Some of these stand on elements of the countershape, others seem to hang in air.

As the light rises to normal level the MAN *moves into the boutique. And now, among the displays a* WOMAN *is discovered standing, motionless, looking off at an angle in passive thought. She is wearing a white silk blouse and a light beige skirt and high heeled shoes. The* MAN *moves from object to object and pauses to look into the display case in the counter where jewellery is kept. As he nears her, he halts, staring into her profile. Music dies.*

MAN. Can you help me?

PROPRIETRESS (*turns now to look into his eyes*). Yes?

MAN. Do you have anything for a dying woman?

PROPRIETRESS (*startled, she waits a moment for him to continue and then looks about, trying to imagine*). Well, let me see . . .

He waits another instant, then resumes his search, examining a pair of gloves, a blouse.

May I ask you if . . . ?

She breaks off when he does not respond or turn to her. Finally, he does.

MAN. Excuse me?

PROPRIETRESS. I was just wondering if you meant that she was actually . . .

MAN. By the end of the month or so. Apparently.

PROPRIETRESS (*seeking hope*). . . . But it isn't sure.

MAN. I think *she's* sure. But I haven't talked to any doctors or anything like that . . .

PROPRIETRESS. And it's . . ?

MAN (*cutting in*). So it seems, yes.

PROPRIETRESS (*helpless personal involvement*). Ah.

MAN (*forcing out the words*). . . . I assume you were going to say cancer.

The PROPRIETRESS *nods with a slight inhale of air. Now she glances around at her stock with a new sense of urgency.*

I started to send flowers, but flowers seem so . . . funereal.

PROPRIETRESS. Not necessarily. Some spring flowers?

MAN. What's a spring flower? – daisies?

PROPRIETRESS. Or daffodils. There's a shop two blocks down – Faynton's.

MAN (*considers*). I passed there twice. But I couldn't decide if it should be a bunch of flowers or a plant.

PROPRIETRESS. Well, either would be . . .

MAN. Except that a bunch would fade, wouldn't they? – in a few days?

PROPRIETRESS. But a plant would last. For years, sometimes.

MAN. But there's a suggestion of irony in that. Isn't there?

PROPRIETRESS (*thinks*). Cut flowers, then.

MAN. They don't last at all, though, and she'd have to watch them withering away every morning . . .

PROPRIETRESS. Yes.

Slight pause. He resumes looking at things, handles a bracelet . . . half asking . . .

She is not an older woman.

MAN. She just turned thirty . . . a couple of months ago.

The PROPRIETRESS *inhales sharply.*

I've never really bought her anything. It struck me this afternoon. Nothing important.

PROPRIETRESS (*delicately*). You've known each other very . . .

MAN (*grieving*). That's always hard to remember exactly. I can never figure out whether we met two winters ago or three. (*A little laugh which she joins.*) – She never can either . . . but we've never been able to stay on the subject long enough . . . in fact, on any subject – Except one.

PROPRIETRESS *laughs softly and he joins her for an instant.*

I'm married.

PROPRIETRESS (*nods*). Yes.

MAN. And a lot older, of course.

PROPRIETRESS. Oh, Well that's not always a . . . (*She does not finish.*)

MAN. No, but it is in most cases. (*He glances around again.*) I tried to think of a book. But after all the reading I've done nothing occurs to me.

PROPRIETRESS. She is not religious.

MAN. No – Although we never talked about religion. I don't

know whether to try to concentrate her mind or distract it. Everything I can think to send her seems ironical; every book seems either too sad or too comical; I can't think of anything that won't increase the pain of it.

PROPRIETRESS. Perhaps you're being too tender. Nothing you could send would be as terrible as what she knows.

He considers this, nods slightly.

People do make a kind of peace with it.

MAN. No; I think in her case the alarm never stops ringing; living is all she ever thought about – She won't answer the phone anymore. She doesn't return my calls for days, a week sometimes. I think, well, maybe she wants me – you know – to disappear, but then she does call back and always makes an excuse for not having called earlier. And she seems so desperate for me to believe her that I forget my resentment and I try to offer to help again and she backs away again . . . and I end up not seeing her for weeks again. (*Slight pause.*) I even wonder sometimes if she's simply trying to tell me there's somebody else. I can't figure out her signal.

PROPRIETRESS. Yes. But then again it might simply be that she . . .

MAN. That's right . . .

PROPRIETRESS. . . . Finds it unbearable to be cheated of someone she loves . . .

MAN. I'm so glad to hear you say that! – it's possible . . . (*With relief, deeper intimacy.*) Sometimes, you know, we're on the phone and suddenly she excuses herself – and there's silence for a whole minute or two. And then she comes back on with a fresh and forward-looking attitude and her voice clear. But a couple of times she's cut out a split second too late, and I hear the rush of sobbing before she can clap her hand to the receiver. And it just burns my mind – and then when she comes back on so optimistically I'm in a terrible conflict; should I insist on talking about the reality, or should I pretend to sort of swim along beside her?

PROPRIETRESS. She's in a hospital.

MAN. Not yet – Although, frankly, I'm not really sure. She's never home anymore. I know that. Unless she's stopped answering her phone altogether. – Even before this happened she would do that; but she's on the phone practically all day in her work so it is understandable. Not that I'm ruling out that she might have been staying elsewhere occasionally. – But of course I've no right to make any demands on her. Or even ask any questions. – What does this sound like to you?

PROPRIETRESS. It sounds like you'd simply like to thank her.

Music resumes behind his speech.

MAN (*with a slight surprise*). Say! That's exactly right, yes! . . . I'd simply like to thank her. I'm so glad it sounds that way.

PROPRIETRESS. Well . . . why not just *do* that?

MAN (*anguished*). But how can I without implying that she's coming to the end . . . ? (*He breaks off.*)

PROPRIETRESS. But she's *said* she's . . . ?

MAN. Not really in so many words; she just . . . as I told you . . . breaks up on the phone or . . .

Music dies away.

PROPRIETRESS (*with anguish now*). Then why are you so sure she's . . . ?

MAN. Because they're evidently operating on her in about ten days. And she won't tell me which hospital.

PROPRIETRESS. . . . When you say evidently . . .

MAN. Well. I know she's had this growth, and there was a pain for awhile – about last summer – but then it passed and she was told it was almost certainly benign. But . . .

(*He goes silent; stares at the* PROPRIETRESS.) Amazing.

PROPRIETRESS. Yes?

MAN. I've never mentioned her at all to anyone. And she has never let on about me. I know that . . . and we have close mutual friends who have no idea. And here I walk in and tell you everything, as though . . . (*From an engaging chuckle the breath seems to suddenly go out of him and he sits weakly on a stool, struggling against helplessness.*)

Music resumes.

PROPRIETRESS. Yes?

He makes an attempt to resume looking around the store but it fails.

When you passed here earlier today . . .

MAN (*with great relief*). Yes, that's right, I remember that! You saw me then . . .

PROPRIETRESS. You stared at the window for a very long time.

MAN. I was trying to think of something for her.

Music resumes.

PROPRIETRESS. Yes, I could see you imagining; it moved me deeply – for her sake.

MAN. It's amazing how absolutely nothing is right. I've been all over this part of town. But every single thing makes some kind of statement that is simply . . . not right.

PROPRIETRESS. I'm sure you're going to think of something.

MAN. I hope so!

PROPRIETRESS. Oh I'm sure!

MAN. It's partly, I think, that I don't know what I want to say because I'm not sure what I have a right to say – I mean someone my age ought to be past these feelings. – (*With sudden revulsion.*) I go on as though there's all the time in the world . . . ! (*He stands, quickened, looking at the goods again.*) That kerchief is beautiful.

PROPRIETRESS. It's silk. Paris. (*She unfurls it for him.*)

MAN. Lovely. How would you wear it?

PROPRIETRESS. Any way. Like this . . (*She drapes it over her shoulders.*)

MAN. Hm.

PROPRIETRESS. Or even as a bandanna. (*She wraps it over her hair.*)

MAN. But she wouldn't do that indoors.

PROPRIETRESS. Well . . . she *could*.

MAN. No. I'm afraid it could taunt her.

PROPRIETRESS (*putting it back on her shoulders*). Well, then – in bed, like this.

MAN (*tempted*). It is the right shade. – You have her colouring, you know; – I can't get over it, walking in off the street like this and blabbing away.

PROPRIETRESS. A thing like that builds up; you never know who you'll suddenly be telling it to.

MAN. Except that you have a look in your eye.

PROPRIETRESS (*smiling*). What kind of look?

MAN (*returns her smile*). You're seeing me. (*Of the scarf, definitely now.*) That isn't right. (*She slips it off. He moves, looking about.*) . . . I think it's also that you're just about her age.

PROPRIETRESS. Why would that matter?

MAN. Someone older usually forgets what thirty was really like.

PROPRIETRESS. But you remember?

MAN. I didn't used to – thirty is far back down the road for me; but when I'm with her it all flows back at the touch of her skin. I feel like a Hindu recalling a former life.

PROPRIETRESS. And what is thirty like?

Music resumes.

MAN. Thirty is an emergency. Thirty is the top of the ridge from where you can see down both sides – the sun and the shadow, your youth and your dying in the same glance. It's the last year to believe that your life can radically change anymore. And now she's caught on that ridge, unable to move. – God . . . (*A surge of anguish.*) . . . how *pleased* with herself she'd gotten lately! – her ambitions and plans really working out . . . (*With a half-proud, half-embarrassed grin.*) although tough too – she can snap your head back with a harsh truth, sometimes. But I don't mind, because all it is is her wide-open desire to live and win. (*He glances around at the objects.*). So it's hard to think of something that won't suggest the end of all that . . . and those eyes closing.

Music dies away.

PROPRIETRESS. I have a kind of warm negligee. That one up there.

MAN (*looks up, studies it for a moment*). But mightn't that look like something after you've had a baby?

PROPRIETRESS. Not necessarily.

MAN. Yes. Like when they stroll around the hospital corridors afterwards . . . If she's very sick she'd have to be in a hospital gown, wouldn't she?

PROPRIETRESS (*sharply, like a personal rebellion*). But *everybody* doesn't die of it! Not *every* case!

MAN (*explosively*). But she weeps on the phone! I *heard* it!

PROPRIETRESS (*a personal outcry*). Well the thought of disfigurement is terrible, isn't it? (*She turns away, pressing her abdomen. Pause.*) You ought to write, and simply thank her.

MAN (*asking . . .*). But that *has* to sound like a goodbye!

PROPRIETRESS. You sound as though you never had a single intimate talk!

MAN. Oh yes, but not about . . . negative things, somehow.

PROPRIETRESS. You met only for pleasure.

MAN. Yes. But it was also that we both knew there was

nowhere it could go. Not at my age. So things tend to float pretty much on the surface . . .

PROPRIETRESS (*smiling*). Still, the point does come . . .

MAN. Surprisingly, yes . . .

PROPRIETRESS. When it begins to be an effort to keep it uncommitted . . .

MAN. Yes, there's a kind of contradiction . . .

PROPRIETRESS. – To care and simultaneously not-care . . .

MAN. You can't find a breakthrough – it's like a fish falling in love with the sun; once he breaks water he can't breathe! – So maybe the whole thing really doesn't amount to anything very much. (*Pause.*)

PROPRIETRESS (*she re-folds a sweater he had opened up*). But you don't always look like this, do you?

MAN. How?

PROPRIETRESS. In pain.

MAN. I guess I'm still unable to understand what she means to me. – I've never felt this way about a death. Even my mother's and father's . . . there has always been some unwelcome, tiny feeling of release; an obligation removed. But in her case, I feel I'm being pulled under myself and suffocated.

The PROPRIETRESS *takes a deeper breath of air and runs a hand down her neck.*

What else do you have that might . . . ? (*He halts as he starts once again to look around at the merchandise.*) . . . Wait! I know – a bed jacket! That's the kind of neutral – healthy people wear them too!

PROPRIETRESS. I haven't any.

MAN. Nothing at all?

PROPRIETRESS. You might try the department stores.

MAN (*greatly relieved*). I will. I think that's what I want. A bed jacket doesn't necessarily *say* anything, you see?

PROPRIETRESS. That's true, there is something non-committal about a bed jacket. Try Saks.

MAN. Yes. Thanks very much. – I never dreamed I'd have such a conversation! (*He starts to button up. With embarrassment* . . .) It really amazes me . . . coming in here like this . . .

PROPRIETRESS. I have an electric kettle if you'd care for a cup of tea.

MAN. . . . Thanks, I wouldn't mind, thanks very much . . . I simply can't get over it, . . . I had no idea all this was in me.

She goes behind the counter, throws a switch; he sits at the counter again.

Are you the owner here? (*He opens his coat again.*)

PROPRIETRESS (*nods, affirmatively, then* . . .). You know, it may be a case of a woman who's simply terrified of an operation, that's all. – I'm that way.

MAN (*thinks, trying to visualise – then* . . .). No, I think it would take a lot more to panic her like this. She's not an hysterical person, except once a month for a few hours, maybe.

PROPRIETRESS. She tends to objectify her situation.

MAN. That's it.

PROPRIETRESS. Sees herself.

MAN. Yes.

PROPRIETRESS. From a distance.

MAN. Yes, she has guts; really cool nerve right up to the moment she flies to pieces.

PROPRIETRESS. She's had to control because she's alone.

MAN. Yes; so something like this must be like opening a shower curtain and a wild animal jumps out.

PROPRIETRESS. She was never married.

MAN. Never. (*He begins to stare off and smile.*)

PROPRIETRESS. Something about her couldn't be. – Unless

to you?

MAN (*joyfully*). She has a marvellous, throaty, almost vulgar laugh; it can bend her forward and she even slaps her thigh like a hick comedian . . .

The PROPRIETRESS *begins laughing.*

And gets so helpless she hangs on my arm and nearly pulls me down to the sidewalk.

The PROPRIETRESS *laughs more deeply.*

One time at one of those very tiny café tables we both exploded laughing at the same instant, and our heads shot forward just as the waiter was lowering my omelette between us . . .

She bursts out laughing and slaps her thigh. Music: sharply. He sees this and his smile remains. The tea kettle whistles behind the counter.

PROPRIETRESS. Milk or lemon?

He watches her a moment, smiling.

Lemon?

MAN. Lemon, yes.

(*She goes and pours tea. The* MAN, *with a new anticipatory excitement.*) You're not busy?

Music dies away.

PROPRIETRESS. After Christmas it all dies for a few days. (*She hands him a cup.*)

MAN. It's more like somebody's home in here.

PROPRIETRESS. I try to sell only what I'd conceivably want for myself, yes.

MAN. You're successful.

PROPRIETRESS. In a way. (*Confusing.*) . . . I am, I guess. – Very, in fact.

MAN. But a baby would be better.

PROPRIETRESS (*a flash of resentment, but then truth*). Sometimes. (*She hesitates.*) Often, actually. (*She looks around at the shop.*) It's all simply numbers, figures. Something appalling about business, something totally pointless – like emptying a pail and filling it again every day. – Why? – Do I look unhappy?

MAN. You look like you'd found yourself . . . for the fiftieth time and would love to throw yourself away again.

PROPRIETRESS. You try to avoid hurting people.

MAN. Yes, but it can't be helped sometimes. I've done it.

PROPRIETRESS. No wonder she loves you.

MAN. I'm not so sure. I really don't know anymore.

PROPRIETRESS. Oh, it must be true.

MAN. Why?

PROPRIETRESS. It would be so easy.

MAN. But I'm so old.

PROPRIETRESS. No.

MAN. I'm not sure I want her to. I warned her not to, soon after we started. I said there was no future in it. I said that these things are usually a case of loving yourself and wanting someone else to confirm it, that's all. I said all the blunt and ugly things I could think of.

PROPRIETRESS. And it didn't matter at all. (*Slight pause.*)

MAN. It didn't?

PROPRIETRESS (*with a hard truthfulness*). Of course it mattered – what you said made her stamp on her feelings, and hold part of herself in reserve. It even humiliated her a little.

MAN (*in defence*). But her independence means more to her than any relationship, I think.

PROPRIETRESS. How do you know? – You were the one who ordered her not to love you . . .

MAN. Yes. (*Evading her eyes.*) But there's no tragic error, necessarily – I don't think she wanted to love anyone. In fact, I don't think either of us said or did anything we badly regret – it's Nature that made the mistake; that I should be so much older, and so perfectly healthy and she so young and sick.

PROPRIETRESS (*unnerved, an outburst*). Why do you go on assuming it has to be the end!

He looks at her with surprise.

Thousands of people survive these things. And why couldn't you ask her what exactly it was?

MAN. I couldn't bear to make her say it.

PROPRIETRESS. Then all she's actually said was that an operation . . ?

MAN. No. Just that the 28th of the month was a big day.

PROPRIETRESS (*almost victoriously*). Well that could mean almost anything.

MAN (*in anguish*). Then why doesn't she let me come and see her!

PROPRIETRESS (*frantically*). Because she doesn't want to load her troubles onto you!

MAN. I've thought of that.

PROPRIETRESS. Of course. It's a matter of pride. Even before this happened, she never encouraged you to just drop in, for instance – did she?

MAN. Oh no. On the contrary.

PROPRIETRESS. Of course not! She wanted her hair to be done and be dressed in something you'd like her in . . .

MAN. Oh, insisted on that, yes.

PROPRIETRESS. Then you can hardly expect her to invite you to see her in hospital! (*Slight pause.*)

MAN. Then it *is* pretty superficial, isn't it?

PROPRIETRESS. Why! – it could be the most important thing in her entire life.

MAN (*pause. Shakes his head*). No. Important – but not the most important. Because neither of us have burned our bridges. As how could we? – If only because of my age?

PROPRIETRESS. Why do you go on about your age? That's only an excuse to escape with.

MAN (*smiles*). But it's the only one I've got, dear. – But whatever age I was, she wouldn't be good to be married to.

PROPRIETRESS (*hurt, almost alarmed*). How can you say that!

MAN. What's wrong in saying it? She's still ambitious for herself, she still needs risks, accomplishments, new expectations; she needs the dangerous mountains not marriage in the valley – marriage would leave her restless, it would never last. (*Pause.*)

PROPRIETRESS (*dryly*). Well, then . . . you were both satisfied . . .

(*As he turns to her, surprised.*) . . . with what you had.

MAN. That's a surprise – I never thought of that. Yes; very nearly. (*He thinks further.*) Almost. Yes. (*Slight pause.*) That's a shock, now.

PROPRIETRESS. To realise that you were almost perfectly happy.

MAN. Almost – You see, there was always – of necessity – something so tentative about it and uncertain, that I never thought of it as perfect, but it was – a perfect chaos. Amazing.

PROPRIETRESS. And your wife?

MAN (*slight pause*). My wife is who I should be married to. We've always helped one another. I'll always be grateful for having her. Especially her kindness.

PROPRIETRESS. She's not ambitious.

MAN. Yes; within bounds. We're partners in a business – advisory service for town planners. She's tremendously competent; I oversee; do less and less, though.

PROPRIETRESS. Why? Isn't it important?

MAN. Certainly is – we've changed whole countrysides for the next hundred years.

PROPRIETRESS. Then why do less and less?

MAN. I won't be here in a hundred years. – That struck me

powerfully one morning. (*Pause.*)

PROPRIETRESS. So – all in all – you will survive this.

MAN (*catching the implied rebuke*). That's right. And in a while, whole days will go by when her anguish barely crosses my mind; and then weeks, and then months, I imagine. (*Slight pause.*) And as I say this, I know that at this very moment she may well be keeping herself hidden from me so as not to wound me with her dying.

PROPRIETRESS. Or wound herself.

He looks at her questioningly.

If she doesn't have to look at what she's lost she loses less. – But I don't believe it's as bad as you make it. She's only keeping you away so that you won't see her so frightened of the knife. She has sense.

MAN. But why! – I would try to comfort her!

PROPRIETRESS (*strongly, angrily protesting*). But she doesn't want comfort, she wants her power back! You came to her for happiness, not some torn flesh bleeding on the sheets! She knows how long pity lasts! (*Slight pause.*)

MAN. Then what are you saying? – That there is really no gift I can give her at all? – Is that what you say?

PROPRIETRESS, *silent, lowers her eyes.*

There is really nothing between us, is there – nothing but an . . . uncommitment? (*He grins.*) Maybe that's why it's so hard to think of something to give her . . . She asked me once – as we were getting up at the end of an evening – she said, 'Can you remember all the women you've had?' Because she couldn't remember all the men, she said.

PROPRIETRESS. And did you believe her?

MAN. No. I thought she was merely reassuring me of her indifference – that she'd never become demanding. It chilled me up the spine.

PROPRIETRESS. Really! Why?

MAN. Why say such a thing unless she had a terrific urge to

hold onto me?

PROPRIETRESS. But now you've changed your mind . . .

He turns to her surprised.

MAN. No, I kind of think now she was telling the truth. I think there is some flow of indifference in her, cold and remote, like water flowing in a cave. As there is in me. (*Slight pause.*) I feel you're condemning me now.

PROPRIETRESS. I never condemn anyone; you know that. I can't.

MAN. I know. But still, deep, deep down . . .

PROPRIETRESS. No. I'm helpless not to forgive everything, finally.

MAN. That's your glory, but in some deepest part of you there has to be some touch of contempt . . .

PROPRIETRESS. What are you saying? – You carefully offered only your friendship, didn't you?

MAN. But what more could I offer!

PROPRIETRESS. Then you can't expect what you would have had if you'd committed yourself, can you.

MAN. What I would have had . . ?

Music resumes.

PROPRIETRESS. Yes! – To be clung to now, to be worn out with weeping, to be staggered with your new loneliness, to be clarified with grief, washed with it, cleansed by a whole sorrow. A lover has to earn that satisfaction. If you couldn't bring yourself to share her life, you can't expect to share her dying. Is that what you'd like?

MAN. I would like to understand what I was to her.

PROPRIETRESS (*protesting*). You were her friend!

MAN (*shakes his head*). There is no such thing. No! No! No! What is a friend who only wants the good news and the bright side? I love her. But I am forbidden to by my commitments, by my age, by my aching joints – great God almighty, I'm sleepy by half-past nine! The whole thing is ludicrous, what could she have seen in me? I can't bear the sight of my face in the mirror – I'm shaving my father every morning!

PROPRIETRESS. Then why not believe her – you were . . . simply one of her friends.

Music dies away.

MAN (*pause*). One of her . . . friends. Yes. – I'll have to try to accept that. (*Slight pause.*) But why doesn't it empty me? Why am I still filled like this? What should I do that I haven't done – or say that I haven't said to make some breakthrough? (*Weeping.*) My God, what am I saying! (*Imploring.*) You know. Tell me!

PROPRIETRESS. Perhaps . . . that it's perfect, just as it is?

He slowly turns from her, absorbing her voice.

That it is all that it could ever have become? (*Pause.*)

MAN. You feel that? – You believe that?

PROPRIETRESS. Yes.

MAN. . . . That we are as close now as we ever can come?

PROPRIETRESS. Yes. – But she believes she's going to make it, she knows she'll live.

MAN. So she's simply . . . momentarily afraid.

PROPRIETRESS. Oh, terribly, yes.

MAN (*with gathering hope*). That's possible; and it's true that she'd never wish to be seen that scared, especially by me. She has contempt for cowardice, she rises to any show of bravery – any! I think you're possibly right; she'll want to see me when she's made it! When she's a winner again!

PROPRIETRESS. I'm sure of it.

MAN. On the other hand . . . (*He breaks off suddenly; as though a hollowness opens beneath him his face goes expressionless.*) . . . it's also possible, isn't it . . . that . . .

PROPRIETRESS (*cutting him off, with dread*). Why go further? You'll know everything soon.

MAN. Not if I can't see her. She won't say the name of the

hospital.

PROPRIETRESS (*she touches his hand*). But why go further?

MAN. But if she . . . dies?

PROPRIETRESS. She doesn't expect to.

MAN (*with confidence, an awareness*). Or she does expect to.

And he turns to her; she is filled with love and anguish; he speaks directly to her, gripping her hand in his.

Either way, my being with her now . . . would only deepen it between us when it should not be deepened, because very soon now I will be far too old. If she makes it . . . it would not be good for us – to have shared such agony. It won't cure age, nothing will – *That's* it.

She offers her lips, he kisses her.

It's that she doesn't want it spoiled you see, by deepening.

PROPRIETRESS (*she embraces him, her body pressed to his, an immense longing in it and a sense of a last embrace*). She wants to make it stay exactly as it is . . . forever. (*She presses his face to hers, they kiss.*) How gently! (*He kisses her again. With a near cry of farewell . . .*) Oh how gently! (*He slips from her embrace; a new thought as he looks around the shop. Filled, directed by his grief.*)

MAN. Then what I ought to send her is something she could definitely keep for a long time. (*He is quickened as he looks about, as though he almost knows beforehand what to seek. He moves more quickly from object to object, and at a tray of costume jewellery he halts, draws out a watch on a gold chain.*) Does this work? (*He winds it.*)

PROPRIETRESS. Oh yes, it's exact. It's an antique.

MAN (*puts the watch to his ear, then couches it in his hand, hefts it, then hangs it from the neck of the* PROPRIETRESS *and stands back to look at it on her.*) Yes, it's beautiful.

PROPRIETRESS. I know.

He starts to take out his wallet . . .

Take it.

Music resumes but more rapidly now.

She takes it off her neck and holds it out, hanging it before him; he puts back his wallet. The implication freezes him.

Go ahead – it's just the right thing; it will tell her to be brave each time she looks at it.

He takes the watch and chain and looks at them in his hand.

You never said her name. (*She starts to smile.*)

MAN (*starting to smile*). You never said yours. (*Slight pause.*) Thank you. Thank you . . . very much.

On each of their faces a grin spreads – of deep familiarity. The light begins to lower; with the smile still on his face he moves away from the setting until he is facing front, staring. The woman and the boutique go dark, vanishing. He strolls away, alone..

Music dies away.

SOME KIND OF LOVE STORY

CAST

ANGELA
TOM O'TOOLE

The action takes place in ANGELA's bedroom, in an American city. Time: the present.

A bed in a darkened room. A window. The headboard of the bed is white plastic tufting with gold trim, Grand Rapids Baroque. A door Upstage to the bathroom. Another at Right to the living-room. Skirts, bras, shoes, articles of clothing dropped everywhere. ANGELA *is barely visible sitting up on the bed. The Right door opens.*

TOM O'TOOLE *sticks his head in.*

TOM. Are we decent?

ANGELA. Christ's sake, close the door.

TOM. Lemme get in first! (*He shuts the door behind him, pushes back his narrow brimmed hat, unbuttons his raincoat, and is forced to peer through the murky air to see her face.*) Well! – You're sounding nice and spunky, how's it goin' tonight?

ANGELA. Philly out there?

TOM. In the kitchenette, lip-readin' his racin' form.

ANGELA. Say anything to you?

TOM. Nooo. Just laid one of his outraged-husband looks on me again. What do you say I buy you a spaghetti? – Come on.

ANGELA. You can turn on the light. And lock the door, will you?

TOM. What's with the rollers? You going out?

She undoes a roller now that her attention has been drawn to it. He locks the door and switches a lamp on. She is sitting up in bed, permed hair, black slip, pink wrapper. She lights a cigarette.

Jeeze, you really are swollen. You want ice?

ANGELA (*works her jaw, touching it*). It's going down.

TOM (*sitting on a stool beside the bed*). Hope you don't mind, darlin', but a man who takes his fists to his wife ought to be strung up by his testicles one at a time.

ANGELA (*a preoccupied air*). Nobody's perfect. He can't help himself, he's immature.

TOM. Well, maybe I'll understand it sometime – It's amazing, I always leave here with more questions than I came in with.

ANGELA. He's still the father of my daughter. (*She gets off the bed, tidies up the room a bit.*) By the way, she called me from L.A. She's going to apply to the University of California, being she's so fantastic in basketball.

TOM (*dropping into a chair, hat and coat still on*). Well, that'd be nice, wouldn't it? You're lucky to have a kid these days who loves you.

ANGELA. Don't yours?

TOM. Yeah, but they're exceptional. Anyway, I'm unusually loveable. (*He guffaws.*)

ANGELA. What're you laughing at? – It's true. (*Sadly.*) You're probably the most loveable man I've ever met.

TOM (*to get down to business*). You caught me climbin' into bed when you called.

ANGELA. I appreciate you coming, Tom – this had to be my worst day yet. (*She moves to a window to look into the backyard.*)

TOM. No kiddin'. On the phone you sounded like you seen a ghost.

ANGELA (*a wan smile*). You ever going to love me again?

TOM. Always will, honey – in spirit.

The answer turns her sadder; she restlessly walks in sighing frustration.

I explained it, Ange–

ANGELA. What'd you explain?

TOM. You are part of the case in a certain way; and I can't be concentrating on this case and banging you at the same time. It's all wrong. I'm being as straight as I can with you. – What happened today?

ANGELA. I don't know – it just hit me again like a ton of bricks that Felix is still sitting in that cell.

TOM. That's right; it'll be five years October.

ANGELA. You tend to get used to it after so long but today I simply . . . I couldn't stand it all over again.

TOM. I can't stand it *every* day.

ANGELA (*as though reawakened to his value*). You're a wonderful man, Tom. You're really one of a kind.

TOM. Personally, I wouldn't mind sharin' the distinction, but I don't see too many volunteers on *this* case.

ANGELA (*she looks off, shaking her head with wonder at his character*). Be proud of yourself – I mean with all the great people in this state, the colleges, the churches, the newspapers, and nobody lifts a finger except you . . . I simply can't believe he's still in there!

TOM (*sensing attenuation*). What'd you want to see me about, Ange?

ANGELA (*glances at him, then gets up again, moves*). I'm really teetering. My skin is so tight I could scream.

TOM. What happened today?

ANGELA. God how I love to see you sitting here and the sound of your voice . . . (*At the window.*) . . . Is that drizzle comin' down again?

TOM. But it's kind of warm out; you want to try to walk it off? Come on, I'll take you to the boardwalk, buy you a chowder.

ANGELA (*moves restlessly*). God, how I hate this climate.

TOM. I thought it reminded you of Sweden.

ANGELA. I'm a Finn, not a Swede; I said it was *like* Finland

– Not that I was ever *in* Finland.

TOM (*a grin*). So how's my standing tonight?

ANGELA. You're always in my top three; you know that.

TOM (*wryly*). Not always, Ange – last time I was practically wiped off the scoreboard.

ANGELA (*genuinely surprised*). What are you talking about?

TOM. You ordered me never to show my face again, don't you remember?

ANGELA (*vaguely recalling a probability*). Well, you were probably pressuring me, that's all; I will not submit to pressure . . .

TOM. Well, *you* called *me* tonight, kid. So what's it about?

ANGELA. What the hell is this goddam rush, suddenly?

TOM (*laughs*). Rush! You have any idea how long we've been bullshitting around together about this case? It's damn near five years!

ANGELA. And every single thing you know about it came from me and don't you forget it either.

TOM. Well . . . not everything . . .

ANGELA (*a shot of angry indignation*). *Everything!*

TOM (*a sigh*). Well, all right. – But I'm still nowhere.

ANGELA. This is a whole new side of you, isn't it?

TOM (*sensing her fear – gently*). Baby Doll, the last time on Thursday I spent seven-and-one-half hours in this room with you . . .

ANGELA. It was nowhere *near* seven and . . .

TOM (*suppressing explosion*). Until two-thirty a.m. when you give me such a kick in the balls that if it'd landed I'd have gone into orbit. So we can call tonight a strictly professional visit to hear whatever you got to say about the case of Felix Epstein . . . and *nothing else*. – Now what'd you want to tell me?

ANGELA (*dismissing him*). Well, I can't talk to you in a mechanical atmosphere.

TOM (*gets up*). Then goodnight and happy dreams.

ANGELA. What are you doing?

TOM (*a strained laugh*). Gettin' back into my pyjamas! – I have driven here through half an hour of fog and rain!

ANGELA (*open helplessness*). I'm desperate to talk to you! Why don't you give me a chance to open my mouth? (*Turning her back on him, moving* . . .) I mean, shit, if you want a mechanical conversation go see your friendly Ford dealer.

TOM. I'll tell you something, Angela – you're just lucky I'm still in love with you.

ANGELA (*she smiles now, tragically*). You wouldn't be kidding about that if I wasn't a sick woman – I'd have walked you off into the sunset five years ago and don't think I couldn't have done it.

TOM. My wife thinks you could still do it.

ANGELA. Go on, she knows why you see me nowadays.

TOM. Maybe that's why she's talkin' separation.

ANGELA. One of the nicest things about you, Tom, is that you're so obvious when you're full of shit.

TOM. She thinks we're still making it, Angela.

ANGELA (*breaks into a smile, warm and pleasured, gets up and comes to him, takes off his hat and kisses the top of his head*). Honestly?

TOM. I mean it. From the way I talk about you she says she can tell.

ANGELA (*sliding her hand towards his crotch*). Well as long as she believes it, why don't we again?

TOM (*grasping her wrists*). Y'know . . . I had to give up the booze twenty years ago, and then the cigarettes because the doctor told me I have the make-up of an addict. If I went into you again I'd never come out the rest of my life.

ANGELA (*seizing the respite*). Were you ever really in love, Tom?

TOM (*hesitates, then nods*). Once.

ANGELA. I don't mean as a kid . . .

TOM. No, I was about twenty-five.

ANGELA. What happened to her?

TOM (*hesitates, then grins in embarrassment*). My mother didn't approve.

ANGELA. Why not, she wasn't Catholic?

TOM. She was Catholic.

ANGELA (*a wide grin*). A tramp?

TOM. No! But she knew I'd stayed over with her a couple of times. And we were a strict family, see.

ANGELA. You've still got a lot of priest in you, Tom – I love that about you.

TOM. You do? I don't. Leaving Maria was the biggest mistake I ever made. In fact, five or six years later, I was already married but I went back looking for her – I was ready to leave my wife – But she was gone, nobody knew where.

ANGELA (*romantically*). And you really still think of her?

TOM. More now than ever. In that respect I lived the wrong life.

ANGELA (*she is staring at him, an open expression on her face. On her knees beside his chair she rests her head on his shoulder*). Life is so wrong – a man like you ought to be happy all day and all night long.

ANGELA *sings 'When Irish Eyes Are Smiling'. He corrects a couple of mistakes.*

TOM (*intimately, breaking into the song*). Tell me the truth, Angela – are you ever going to unload what you know about the Epstein case?

ANGELA (*slight pause. She is deeply fearful, but taking pleasure, too, in his concern*). I'm so worried about myself, Tom. I think I did some kind of a number today, right in the middle of Crowley Square.

TOM (*grinning*). I know when you're changing the subject, kid.

ANGELA (*angered*). It scared me to death, for Christ's sake! – I'm still shaking!

TOM. What happened?

ANGELA (*a moment to let her indignation sink in*). I'm walking along past the piano store – Ramsey's?

TOM. And?

ANGELA. All I remember next is I'm sitting on the fender of a parked car with a whole crowd of people around me. A couple of young guys were sniggering – like I'd done something indecent or something – they had that look, y'know? (*A deepening of overtly fearful breathing.*) I've really got to get to a doctor, Tom.

TOM. Okay.

ANGELA. I go blotto for longer and longer stretches, I think. Sometimes I get the feeling that I don't know where the hell I been all day, or what I said, or to who I said it.

TOM. You want me to arrange a psychiatrist?

ANGELA. With what, though?

TOM. Maybe I can get one on the tab. You want one?

ANGELA (*a sigh*). I don't know, everyone I ever went to ends up trying to get into my pants. Anyway, I know what they'll tell me – I'm a split personality. So what else is new? Why are you so resentful tonight?

TOM. Honey, it's the same split personality conversation we had fifteen different times, and it's eleven p.m.

ANGELA. What I am trying to tell you is that my heart is hanging by a thread, I haven't got very long. Or is that important?

TOM. Then why don't you tell me what you know before it's too late? The man is still innocent and he's still dying by inches in prison; his wife is a walking wreck, her parents are ready for the morgue, and you have the key to this case, Angela – I know it as sure as I know my name – and you jerk me around month after month, a crumb here and a crumb there. . . . I'm so exhausted I can't sleep! – And now you take to dragging me out of bed every other night to chat me up? (*She covers her eyes suddenly.*) Maybe it'd be good if you saw Felix again – you haven't been up there in a year, I could drive you . . .

ANGELA (*this touched a nerve*). I don't want to see him.

TOM (*surprised*). You mean *never?*

ANGELA. I've done more for Felix Epstein than you or anybody. I led the fight all by myself, for Christ's sake!

TOM. Honey, I don't know too much about the head, but as one ex-Catholic to another . . .

ANGELA. I'm not 'ex'.

TOM. Well, semi-ex. What's eatin' you alive is not split personality, kid, it's your conscience.

ANGELA (*with shaky sarcasm*). You been talking to your friendly Jewish psychiatrist again, I see.

TOM. He's not my psychiatrist, he's interested in the case.

ANGELA. Well if that's what he thinks I'm up to, you can tell him from me he's full of shit.

TOM. I'll send him an immediate wire. (*He makes to leave.*) I'm really beat . . .

ANGELA (*instantly stopping him*). Wait, I just want you to tell me one thing. Sit down a second. Don't be this way – (*They sit.*) Why are you on this case?

TOM (*shocked – a near screech*). *What*!!

ANGELA (*sharply*). Well, don't be mad, I'm trying to tune myself! They're yelling tonight.

TOM (*quieting*). You're hearing them now? (*She nods. He is awkward making this absurdly obvious explanation.*) Well, the Epsteins hired me to clear Felix, they paid me five thousand dollars. – How do you pop a question like that after all these years?

ANGELA. Simply that if I told you what I know . . . (*A near stutter.*) . . . what, what . . . when would I ever see you again – on television? The great detective who broke the Epstein case . . . ?

TOM. In other words you backed me out of my pyjamas to be the Ladies Home Companion again.

He starts angrily for the door, but she flies to him in what he sees is a genuine terror.

ANGELA. No! Tom, you can't go! Oh, God you can't leave me tonight . . . Tom, Tom, please, you mustn't . . . ! Not tonight! (*She has a grip on him and pulls him back to the chair, forcing him into it.*) . . . you got to stay . . . just a little while . . .

TOM. God Almighty, what has got you so scared?

Trembling, she returns to sit on the bed.

ANGELA. Let's just be peaceful for a while, okay? (*Making conversation.*) What . . . what's it like out?

TOM (*reaching into his side pocket, ignoring her question*). You know what I done?

ANGELA (*grateful for the diversion, smiles, mimicking*). What'd you done?

TOM. Finally bought myself a notebook . . . (*He takes out a black looseleaf notebook.*) This is amazing – you askin' me why I'm in the case – because I sat down after lunch and started making a resume of the case right from day one, and it suddenly jumped off the page at me. (*A grin.*) That I had no explanation why *you* were involved in this case in the first place. At all and whatsoever. That funny?

ANGELA. Why shouldn't I be?

TOM. But why should you be, honey? (*A grinding laugh.*) You never knew Felix before his arrest; *or* the parents. And there you were in the courtroom every single day of the trial, and startin' up a defence committee yet! – I'd just always taken it for granted that you belonged there!

ANGELA. Why not! – I had nothing to do in the daytime and I kept reading about the case in the papers so I came to see.

He glances up at her with a look of open scepticism.

Why don't you come out with it?

She is almost visibly swept by a furiously pleasurable release, a sense of her real self; she stands, throwing out one hip, arms akimbo, mouth distorted into a tough sneer and her voice goes rough as gravel.

What you mean is how does a fuckin' whore come off attending a . . .

TOM. Now wait, I did not call you a . . .

ANGELA. Go on, you're full of shit – you know I've been a hooker!

TOM. I never said . . .

ANGELA. Oh, fuck off, will ya! You've snooped around, say it! – I've hooked the Holiday Inn, Travelodge . . .

TOM. Cut it out, Angela.

ANGELA. . . . Howard Johnson's, Ramada Inn . . . I've spread my ass on every barstool in this misbegotten, reamedout village . . . why don't you say it?

TOM (*helplessly*). I did not mean that you . . .

ANGELA. Say it! – How does a common slut *presume* . . .

TOM (*erupting*). I did not cast any such aspersion, Angela . . . !

ANGELA (*bending over to shout*). . . . *Presume* to involve herself in high class causes!

TOM (*mystified and alarmed*). What *is* this?

ANGELA (*she seems actually blind, enraged*). Well, you can get your filthy parish mind off my ass, you Irish mutt!

TOM (*suddenly aware, stepping back from her*). . . . Oh, God, is this a number?

ANGELA (*cupping her breasts to thrust them forward, mimics him*). 'Oh, God!' Grab onto this you jerked-off choir boy

. . . come on, get your finger out of your yum-yum and try some of this!

TOM (*holding his head*). Holy God.

ANGELA. Go on, you don't kid me . . . (*Turning and trying to force his hand onto her buttocks.*) Grab hold, you fucking milk-face, you think you're better than anybody else?

TOM. Angela, Jesus . . . !

(*A struggle; he forces her onto the bed. She screams and tries to fight him off, loses her wind, and gasping, as he stands up, watching him . . . pushing his hands off.*)

ANGELA. Well, if you can't get it up get goin'. I've got a line into the street tonight. Tip the hatcheck girl – if you can part with a dollar. And the name is Leontine in case you want to ask for me next time. (*She has gradually lost an inner pressure and seems to fall asleep.* O'TOOLE *goes and bends over her, moved and mystified. He drawsa blanket over her. Then he straightens up and peers into the air, goes to the phone and dials.*)

TOM (*sotto voce, with glances toward the bed*). Hello? That you Mrs Levy? Tom O'Toole here. (*Charmingly.*) You sounded like your daughter! – Oh, pretty fair, thanks; the doctor said I could call anytime and I . . . – Oh, thanks very much, I'm really sorry for the hour. – Really! – I never thought you people watched TV! Thanks. (*He waits, glances over to* ANGELA, *then stares front with a certain eagerness.*) Hey, Josh, how are ya! – (*Nods.*) I'm there now but I might have to hang up, she just blew herself out. – Yeah, just like I described to you. Listen, something just struck me; could a person have delusions, but like inside the delusion is the facts? What I'm trying to say Josh . . . is that I got a gut feeling tonight that *somebody might really be threatening her life*. – I mean it's very hard to watch her tonight and believe that she's stoking the whole thing up from the inside, and if they really want to get rid of her it explains a lot of what she's been hinting, you see? – Right! 'Cause I can't help it, Josh, I still believe that the key to this case is under that pantyhose. (*Listens avidly.*) Oh, but she's definitely had Mob connections, that's objective! (*He listens.*) In what sense, my relation? (*Blushingly.*) Well, you must've guessed, didn't you? We rolled around together last spring but I finally decided to go back to the *status quo ante.* – Well, I got some bad feelings; started to wonder if they had her back working for them again. – Ya, basically prostitution. In fact, I think hubby may be the pimp, he's been punching her around again lately and that's typical pimp relationship. – Ya, but I thought she'd gotten out of that a long time ago. Even on the Vice Squad as a young guy I never touched them; I don't even like public swimming pools! (*Sees* ANGELA *moving.*) She's moving around . . . – I read you . . . – But I think I'm *being* objective; maybe sometimes you've got to go to crazy people for the facts, though . . . Maybe the facts are what's making them crazy unless I'm bananas too, by this time. (*She is sitting up, looking around.*) Gotta go. (*He hangs up.*) How you doin', dear? (*She turns to him, sharp surprise.*) . . . I been here a few minutes.

ANGELA. How long you been here?

TOM. Few minutes.

ANGELA. Was that Philly knocking?

TOM. I didn't hear any knocking, you must've been dreaming.

ANGELA (*slight pause – she stares at the door*). Would you go and see if they're still out there?

TOM. Who's that, dear?

ANGELA. The cops.

TOM. What cops you mean?

ANGELA. The cruiser. They've been parking a cruiser on the

street almost all the time. Didn't you see it when you came?

TOM. . . . Well, no, I didn't notice.

ANGELA. Well, go and take a look out front. Go ahead.

TOM (*suspending disbelief, hoping it is true.*) Okay. (*He unlocks the door, exits, as . . .*)

ANGELA. Look out the bay window – usually towards Rodman Street.

She turns front, fear in her face, an attempt at concentration . . . he re-enters, shuts the door and walks into the room. She rather quickly goes and locks the door, always glancing at him for his report.

TOM. Don't see any cruiser, Angela.

ANGELA. Well, believe me, they're always there.

TOM (*nods . . . only half pretending to disbelieve her*). Cops are leaning on you? (*She barely nods, turns away.*) When did *this* start?

ANGELA. About . . . three, four weeks.

TOM. You mean since I began coming around so much again?

ANGELA. I think so.

TOM. Well, that would be nice, if I'm makin' them nervous. But I have to say it, honey – there's no cruiser down there now.

ANGELA. You're . . . not leaving, are you?

TOM. I'll stay a few minutes, if you want. (*He removes his coat. She goes to the bed and sits. He sits in an armchair.*) Who's Leontine?

ANGELA. Leontine?

TOM. Yeah, you just went into her; she come after me like the wrath of God.

ANGELA. I never heard that name.

TOM. She's quite a broad.

ANGELA. Why – what'd she say?

TOM. Nothin' much. She sounds like a whore in a house.

(*This seems to wilt her a little with yet another grief.*) You really don't remember *none* of it?

ANGELA (*pressing her temples apprehensively*). No. But listen . . . there is always a cruiser, Tom. (*He looks at her, silent.*) I'm telling you, they're down there all the time.

TOM. Sit down. (*He puts her in a chair, sits opposite her and claps his hands together to inspire hope.*) I have a feeling tonight is going to break the ice.

ANGELA (*she is glad for their unity, and also digging in against it*). . . . Just let me get my wind a little.

TOM. Good, get your wind. (*Feeling some semblance of control, he spreads out on the chair, chuckles . . .*) I never knew anybody where everytime I see her there's some big surprise – you're a soap opera. I keep waitin' for the next instalment.

ANGELA (*with tragic pride*). Yeah, well – I've had a life, kid.

TOM. So what you're telling me is – it's the cops that've got you scared. Right?

She glances at him, loaded with other considerations.

You wouldn't want to give me a definite yes or no on that.

She turns to him, her gaze unreadable.

Okay, then it's yes.

ANGELA. Tom?

TOM. Uh huh?

ANGELA (*another message runs parallel with her words*). You're not realising the problem . . . (*Slight pause.*) I'm talking about *you*.

He was momentarily turned away from her; now he faces her. Slight pause.

TOM. What about me?

ANGELA (*cautiously*). You've got to start being more careful and watch every step you take . . .

TOM (*affects a grin, blushing with anger*). I hope I'm not hearing this right, Angela.

ANGELA (*with apology*). . . . I'm only telling you what I know. You should start being more . . .

TOM (*cutting her off*). – Honey, listen to me. I was a New York cop for twenty-four years; I been threatened by *experts*, so you can imagine that some Mack Sennett Police Department is not my idea of the Holy Terror, y'know? And I wish you would say this in case somebody should happen to ask you . . .

ANGELA (*trying to be testy*). . . . Nobody's asking me anything.

TOM (*seething*). But just in case they did, though – you tell them that I am on the Epstein case to the end of the bitter end . . .

ANGELA. . . . I'm not trying to . . .

TOM. . . . And there is nothing anybody can do about that, Angela – right?

ANGELA. That couldn't be better with me, Tom.

TOM. It wouldn't matter what it was with you, honey, or with anybody else. Get the picture?

ANGELA. You're one of a kind; honestly, Tom, you really stand tall. (*She comes to him, kisses him.*) Take me some place, let me make you happy again. Come on.

TOM (*holding both her hands*). Listen, never be the only one who knows something . . .

ANGELA (*looking contritely at the floor*). I know . . .

TOM. If somebody else knows it too, that's your best protection.

She nods agreement. He mimes playing pool.

The table's all set up, you want to start hittin' a few?

The moment of decision is on her, and she gives him a lost smile and turns away again.

I know you want to, Angie.

ANGELA (*a desperate little laugh*). You know? – Sometimes you talk just like Jimmy Cagney.

TOM (*sighs*). Oh, honey, are we gonna talk about Cagney now?

ANGELA. Well you do, you get that same sweet-and-sour thing. And the same brass balls.

TOM (*flattered despite himself*). Well, let's face it, Cagney was my god. (*Snaps his fingers, still seated he goes into a light little shuffling tap dance with a chuck of his head.*) 'Take me out to the ball game . . .'

ANGELA (*genuinely delighted, relieved*). Hey, wonderful!

TOM. Sure, and Pat O'Brien, Spencer Tracey . . . Christ, all those great Irishmen, tough and honest to a man. The moves in them days was Mick-Heaven. The only crooks were Italians.

ANGELA. You'd been great in a movie.

TOM. What as – the dumbest bookie on the block?

ANGELA. No, something dignified – like the first Irish Pope.

TOM. Jesus, you really like me, don't you.

ANGELA. I adore you, Tom. You've saved my life more than you'll ever know.

She draws him to her on the bed and snuggles onto his lap. He doesn't mind at all, and grins at her.

Do me once more.

TOM. No more, Ange, I'm sorry – it does something to my judgment.

ANGELA. I could make you fly around the room. You're my ideal, Tom.

TOM. Come on, kid.

ANGELA. You know, Father Paulini once said that if I'd known a man like you earlier in my life, I'd have turned out a completely different person. But once my father'd raped me, I always expected a man to go right for my ass.

TOM. Mmmm.

ANGELA (*slaps his cheek lightly*). Can't you get your mind off the case for *one minute* and just talk to me like a person?

TOM. It's after eleven p.m., Ange, I'm tired.

ANGELA. Know what I love? When you talk about being a cop in the old days in New York. Would you? – It soothes me. Talk about the Communion Breakfasts. (*She rests her head on his chest.*) And how important the Church was, right?

TOM (*sighs in boredom – although he likes it, too. He glances down at her, sensing his power . . .*). Oh yeah, the Church was really important in the Department in those days. Like any cop who took money from whores . . . or like dope money . . . the priest lay his head open.

ANGELA. Really? Even dope?

TOM. Sure . . . even the Mafia wouldn't touch dope in those days . . .

ANGELA (*incredulously*). Jesus.

TOM. It was a whole different world. (*Grins.*) Like one time they had me guarding the money in the Yankee Stadium office; great big piles of cash on the table. And I ask one of the officials – bein' that they were getting me for nothin', with the city payin' my salary, and all – if I could maybe get a hot dog sent up. So he says sure, gimme fifty cents, I'll send down. Imagine? – I'm watchin' half a million bucks for them and I couldn't even steal a free dog.

ANGELA. I can just see you there . . . with all that money . . . and nobody even giving you a dog. (*Her fear returns in a sweep and she is suddenly welling up.*) Oh, God, Tom . . .

TOM (*turning her face to him*). What is it, honey . . . come on, tell me! (*He hesitates before her vulnerability, then suddenly kisses her on the mouth.*)

ANGELA. Come on, Tom – please! Screw me, split me. I'll never forget that last time. You're a bull. Please! I want you!

He gets to his feet, disturbed by his unforseen kiss. She is sent into a real outpouring of sobbing – in mourning, as it were, for her wasted life which denied her a man like this . . . he tends to her, smoothing her hair.

TOM. Listen now – I could arrange protection. I could have you taken where it's safe. Just tell me what's got you so scared? (*She reaches for him again . . .*) I'd love to, honey, but I'm goddamned if I ever change this subject with you again. It's my professional reputation, my livelihood!

ANGELA (*even here there is a faint air of her improvising*). I'm going to die.

TOM. I hate hearing you say that.

ANGELA. I can't get air. (*Slight pause.*)

TOM. You been to confession?

ANGELA. Yes. But I . . . (*Breaks off.*)

TOM. You couldn't tell him about this, huh? (*She shakes her head.*) Why are these cops leaning on you, can you just tell me that?

ANGELA (*she is silent for a moment; some resolve seems to harden*). Tom.

TOM. I'm listening.

ANGELA. I want you to tell me one thing from the heart. – What's the single main thing you want from this case?

TOM (*uncomprehending*). The single . . . ?

ANGELA. Well is it to get Felix out on the street, or . . . ?

TOM. Well, no, I want the people who put him in there too.

ANGELA. Why? You want revenge or something?

TOM. There's such a thing as the administration of justice, honey – which in this county, is laying on the floor like a busted dozen eggs, it is a fucking farce. Callaghan's got to be blasted out of the prosecutor's office for falsifying evidence, okay? And Bellanca and his whole crew of detectives for conspiring with him . . . (*Grinning.* Now tell me why you asked a question like that?

ANGELA. Well, I agree with Bellanca . . .

TOM. Why? – Callaghan's worse; publicly calling me a 'ridiculous pseudo-detective' and trying to lift my license . . . but we're back in this tic-tac-toe again. Are you going to tell me why the cops are so heavy on you, or not? (*She moves as though framing an answer.*) And I beg you on bended knees, don't start wrappin' me in another ball of wool.

ANGELA (*looks down at her hands, almost patently evading*). The thing, y'see, is that I was so humiliated after what my father . . .

TOM. (*impatiently*). Darlin', I *know* your father raped you, but . . .

ANGELA. Oh, am I boring you?

TOM. I didn't say you . . .

ANGELA (*fish on the line, she swims away, half sobbing, half furious*). Well, I beg your fucking pardon!

TOM (*furiously*). Angela, I am just about convinced starting this minute that you are full of shit! I don't think you know a goddamned thing about this case!

ANGELA (*in great alarm*). Can't we talk for two minutes without the case . . . ?

TOM. I want an answer to what I asked you – what got you into this in the first place? Where are you comin' from, Angela, what is your connection!

ANGELA (*gripping her head*). I'm going crazy!

TOM. I'm turning into a laughing stock! I walk into the Burrington Court House the other day and I had a hard time not to put a fist through some of the stupid smiles on those cops standing around – they all know I'm still on this case after nearly four years . . .

ANGELA. Well, fuck' em!

TOM (*takes a beat – quietly*). Well, you're really chock full of solutions. I understand a very colourful description of me is goin' around the courthouses – I am the detective who couldn't track a diuretic elephant on a glacier.

ANGELA. A diuretic elephant . . . ? (*She breaks out laughing.*)

TOM (*grinning*). Gives you a vivid picture, doesn't it?

Their eyes meet and she sees the steel in his eyes and turns away.

All right, baby – take care of yourself. I guess tonight ends it between us, kid. And I may as well tell you straight – I am humiliated. (*He waits for her to start it going again; then . . .*) And I'm sorry for your sake; that you couldn't level with me; cause in my opinion, the reason you're sick is that you lie. (*He starts to leave, he sees her near paralysis of fear.*) It's okay. I've got a whole other way to move ahead. It would've been easier with you but I can make it alone. Take care, kid – I'm out of your life.

He crosses the room to the door, starts getting his arms into his raincoat – stalling, but not too obviously. She watches him in desperation. Her voice trembling, her anxiety pitched high . . .

ANGELA. Can you believe . . . ? (*She breaks off.*)

TOM (*alerted*). Believe what, dear?

ANGELA (*wringing her hands, struggling in fear of going on . . .*). That a man can be a fine and good man and still do something that's . . . just terrible?

TOM (*avid now*). Sure.

ANGELA. I mean a thing . . . that is not really in his nature to do, but that he has to because . . . it's all so . . . (*Almost crying out.*) . . . rotten in this place?

TOM (*more warmly now*). Absolutely. I believe that. If I thought life was straight lines I'd be workin' for the Highway Department. (*Slight pause.*) . . . Like who are you referring to?

She sends him a terrified glance; there is some longing in her look, too. Her breathing now becomes raspy and he helps her to the bed where she sits, gasping and glancing up at him half in terror and half in hope.

I always said you had class, darling, you know why? – 'Cause of your conscience; most people would just sign out and butter their own potatoes, but not you. You suffer.

His expectations high, he watches her regain her breathing, but she doesn't venture any further.

Who were you talking about?

She glances at him, but nothing more.

Kid, now listen to me and hold on tight – I am six inches from thinking that *you* were part of the frameup they laid on Felix . . .

ANGELA (*furiously*). How can you be such a stupid son of a bitch!

TOM. . . . And that you're still part of it right now, and trying to keep me from finding out what went down! Which would make you about the lowest cunt since Hitler! (*Pushing up his coat collar as though to leave.*)

ANGELA (*with breathless veracity, and really trying* not *to break down in weeping*). After five years you don't know the first thing about this case.

TOM (*pause. He turns to her at the door*). . . . Jesus, the way you say that goes right down to my haemorrhoids.

ANGELA. Believe me, darling . . . zee-ro. (*She holds up forefinger and thumb, touching.*)

TOM. You telling me that Felix Epstein is guilty? (*Long pause.*)

ANGELA. Felix is innocent. (*She heaves for breath; a real attack, she lies down.*)

TOM (*goes to her quickly*). What should I do! You want a doctor?

She rises on one arm, gasping.

Tell me what to do!

She rocks back and forth; he bores in filled with aggressive need.

All right, can you confirm one fact – did Callaghan fake the picture that nailed Felix? Or don't you know?

She screams, frightened of him.

– What are you doing? . . . Oh, no, Angela!

She presses her fists against her chest and her elbows against her sides with her shoulders pushed upward as though she were trying to become small, like a young child. He recognises this.

Don't do that – ! Please stop that, Angela!

He makes a move toward her.

ANGELA. Don't you touch me! (*She skitters into a corner, blindly staring at him.*)

TOM (*reaching toward her protectively*). Ange . . .

With a frightened scream, she cowers all scrunched up, terror in her face. A sound from her mouth, high and childlike.

Is it 'Emily'?

ANGELA. Don't, please . . . !

TOM. Okay, Emily . . . (*Opening his coat and holding out his palms.*) . . . see? Nothin' on me at all. Okay, darling? Why don't you come out and we get a little ice cream from the corner? Your father's gone, honey – honest, he won't be comin' back tonight.

He takes one step toward her but she reacts in fright so he backs up.

Okay, dear, you stay there and I'll just make a call, Okay? Take your time, have a little nap if you want. (*He goes and sits beside the phone, dials. As he waits, he playfully twiddles his fingers at her.*) Hya, darlin'. (*Into the phone.*) Sorry to bother you again, Mrs Levy . . . thanks a lot. (*To* ANGELA.) How about a chocolate fudge later? – I'm sorry, Josh, – No, no, I hate to bother you so late . . . – Oh, zonked out again, being Emily now, all scrunched up like an eight year old, it's pathetic. Listen, bad news . . .

she's been seeing two police cruisers parked on the block every single night . . . but I looked and there's absolutely no sign of them down there. I'm getting the sinking feeling that I've blown four and a half years . . . on a dream! (*Resistance hardens his face.*) Except, goddammit, Josh, she was the first one who told me about Carl Linstrom; – yes, the man who was seen covered with blood, running away from the Kaplan house. And now I have four separate witnesses to corroborate and I can't get the police to make an arrest! You see what I mean? – She knows too many facts for just a crazy, fantasising whore . . . ! (ANGELA *sits up, he sees her.*) . . . We're back on the air, I'll be in touch. (*He hangs up. She approaches him, staring.*) Well! What do you say, Bubbles – welcome back! (*She stares at him, puzzled, suspicious. He is defensive* . . .) I made a little call. (*Her stare is unrelenting.*) To my friend, the psychiatrist. Sends his regards. (*Her stare remains.*) I told you – he's my quarterback sometimes. He's still very interested in the case . . . You know, Felix being Jewish . . .

ANGELA. Some Jew! He didn't have the balls to join my committee.

TOM. Well, let's face it kid, neither did anybody else, that was a one-woman committee. (*He stands.*) Well, take care. I really got to hit the pike.

ANGELA. Wait, wait . . . we didn't even talk. What've you been working on lately?

TOM. Oh, nothing great.

ANGELA. Like what?

TOM. Corporation stuff mostly. Big ball bearing company; in fact – I've got to go out to Phoenix, investigate a guy they're about to make the vice president.

ANGELA. They still doing that shit?

TOM (*shrugs*). Well, you know – you can't have a homosexual vice president of a ball bearing company.

ANGELA. But how do you do that?

TOM. Ah, it's boring. I get his old airplane ticket stubs for the past few months; they usually travel on the company account; and see if he's been to some off-the-track town . . . you know, Ashtabula, Ohio; Grim City, lowa; and I go to the gay bar and show the bartender his picture with a hundred dollar bill clipped to it, and he tells me if he's ever seen him there. I didn't used to mind it, but I don't like it anymore. But . . . (*He shrugs, with a sigh, rubbing two fingers together.*)

ANGELA. And for that he can't be vice president?

TOM. Well, they're scared of blackmail. And you know, he's supposed to be a good example.

ANGELA. To who?

TOM. Who the hell knows anymore? (*At the door.*)

ANGELA (*the same lostness and tension grip her but she no longer pleads for him to stay*). Would you take another look down the street before you go?

TOM. For you, I'll do it. (*He goes, opens the door, exits. She remains absolutely still, facing front. He returns.*) I don't see them.

ANGELA (*awakened*). Heh?

TOM. There's no cruiser down there.

ANGELA. Who?

TOM (*impatiently*). The cruiser! The cops you were so worried about.

ANGELA (*preoccupied*). Oh.

TOM. Why don't you try to relax now, Okay? – Maybe I'll see you sometime. (*She is lost in thought. He turns her face to him.*) . . . Ange? – goodnight.

ANGELA. I used to be with Charley.

TOM (*electrified*). . . . Callaghan?

She is silent.

Talking about the prosecutor?

ANGELA (*hard as a nail*). I will deny everything if you ever try to hurt him with it – I'm myself now, Tom, you understand what I'm saying to you? I will never hurt Charley. (*She takes a sudden inhale.*)

TOM (*stunned*). Okay. – Was this like one or two shots or . . . ?

ANGELA. Three, four times a week over two years. We went to Canada and Puerto Rico, couple of times.

TOM. And when did it end? (*Slight pause.*)

ANGELA. He's come back to me.

TOM. You seeing him *now*?

ANGELA (*a sudden expressiveness, closeness*). He's the love of my life, Tom.

TOM. Right. – This is quite a blow to my mind, darlin'. (*Slight pause.*) You mean like . . . you were exercising with him while he was prosecuting Felix?

ANGELA. Yes. (*Slight pause.*) – You don't believe me.

TOM (*slight pause*). – Well . . . it sure ties certain things together. That's the reason you came to the trial every day, is that it? – to buck him up?

ANGELA (*hesitation*). I wasn't there to buck him up. (*Slight pause.*) I was there taking notes – which you saw me do, and which you read.

TOM (*apologetically*). That's right, honey . . .

ANGELA. Some whores can take notes, y'know – I went to Mary Immaculate, which just happens to have the highest academic record in the state. I can also add, subtract and multiply . . .

TOM. Now, don't go off into a . . .

ANGELA (*deeply agitated*). Sometimes I don't understand why the fuck I talk to you at all, O'Toole. I mean, Jesus . . . (*He lets her find her calm as she walks about shaking her *head.*) I may come off the street but that don't mean I've still got rocks in my head. I'm going to get out of this situation, you know.

TOM. I hope so, Angela. – Out of what situation?

ANGELA (*retreating*). Never mind. Just don't forget what I said about hurting Charley. I can murder you if you do that.

TOM. How you going to murder me, Ange?

ANGELA. Don't worry, I can do it.

TOM. We're gonna forget you said that, Okay?

ANGELA. I'm not threatening you!

TOM. The second time tonight . . .

ANGELA. I didn't mean that I . . .

TOM. Stop-right-here-Angela! Charley Callaghan has tried to get my Investigator's Licence lifted because I have gotten reversals on two of his biggest cases, just like I am going to do on this one . . .

ANGELA. I did not mean . . . !

TOM. . . . So you can ask me not to hurt Charley but please do not try to scare me with him because that is to laugh! Now what'd you want to say? – I mean I hope you are not conveying some kind of a threat from somebody.

ANGELA. You know? – Sometimes I think you ought to see a psychiatrist.

TOM. Oy gevalt! – Kid, you are going to end me up pluckin' chickens in the funny farm!

ANGELA. But you suspect everything I say! You tell me to trust you, but do you trust me?

TOM. Darlin', look – let's get back to taking those notes during the trial;.can I ask what they were for?

ANGELA. 'Cause I knew Felix had nothing to do with Kaplan's murder, and I wanted to prove it.

TOM. I'm still not getting the picture, dear, forgive me. You were in the hammock with Charley at nights and in the days taking notes to *dis*prove his case?

ANGELA. We broke up over the case.

TOM (*impressed*). Oh!

ANGELA. I couldn't stand what it was doing to him. He'd come back from the court and we'd go out to the beach and build a fire and he'd stare into it with tears pouring down his cheeks. Sometimes he would look up into the stars and try to pray. Charley studied for priesthood, you know . . .

TOM. I heard that.

ANGELA. He still does retreats.

TOM. Yeah, well . . . I guess I must've missed his spiritual side.

ANGELA. You have a closed mind: I'm telling you he's a whole other person than you believe.

TOM. Listen, I'm always ready to learn. – What were the tears for though?

ANGELA. . . . We even went to churches in San Juan.

TOM. Together?

ANGELA. Well, we sat in different parts . . .

TOM. In other words, the tears were that he was rigging the Epstein case, or what?

ANGELA *doesn't answer at once.*

Ange? Please. – What were the tears?

ANGELA. It wasn't his fault. The chief of detectives handed him the case, all tied with a ribbon and ready for trial . . .

TOM. Bellanca. (ANGELA *nods.*) So *Bellanca* faked the photograph that nailed Felix? (*She nods again.*)

ANGELA. Charley didn't want to touch the case. They made him push it. I know how you hate him, Tom, but you have to believe me . . .

TOM. Tell me something – why did they pick on Felix in the first place? Why him?

ANGELA. Total accident – he just happened to have come to town to visit his uncle, Abe Kaplan; it's exactly like he claimed – he was trying to get Kaplan to take him into the accountancy firm.

TOM. But why did they have to go through that whole charade when they could have just gone out and picked up Linstrom? – They had to know Linstrom was covered with blood that night – they *had* the killer any time they wanted him.

ANGELA (*slight pause*). Because Linstrom was a runner.

TOM. A runner?

ANGELA. For Kaplan. (*Slight pause.*)

TOM. Abe Kaplan was in drugs?

ANGELA. In! – Abe *ran* the drugs in this town. – God, you are stupid. You're pathetic.

TOM (*embarrassed*). I knew Abe was the big loan shark . . .

ANGELA. That was the front.

TOM. . . . So they latched onto Felix . . . tell me again, will ya?

ANGELA (*impatiently*). To make it look like a family argument – the uncle and the nephew . . .

TOM. But Charley's the chief . . . (*She silently assents.*) . . . if he felt so bad about it, why did he have to go ahead and make the case against Felix?

ANGELA is staring.

Don't go out on me, will you? (*She stares. He bursts out.*) This is horrendous. – You cannot go out on me now! Why couldn't they arrest Linstrom?

ANGELA. Because it could open the whole can of worms.

TOM. What can is that, honey?

ANGELA (*this is deeper than she wanted to go. Barely audible*). The police connection.

TOM. To the drugs.

ANGELA. That's why they're parking down there.

He gives her an evasive nod.

They are, you know.

He gives her a deeper nod of assuagement. But his thought has moved to something else at which he stares now . . .

They are parking down there, Tom . . . (*She starts angrily for the door, but he forces her into an embrace.*)

TOM. If I was to ask you, Angela – how do you know Abe Kaplan was in drugs . . . can I ask you that?

ANGELA. *doesn't answer at once, moving away from him.*

. . . Because I'm trying to be as objective as I can, you see, dear? I mean let's face it, Abe was one of the pillars, right? With the synagogue and the Boys Town and you name it, and a lot of people are going to find that hard to believe, you know?

ANGELA (*decides, faces him*). I used to be with Abe.

TOM (*rocked*). . . . No kiddin', *Abe*?

ANGELA. A lot. We went down to Bimini together.

TOM. Bimini.

ANGELA. Twenty, twenty-five times.

TOM. Isn't Bimini one of the . . . ?

ANGELA. I carried for him coming back. I would deliver the stuff to Bellanca.

A long pause. He moves now, facing front.

That's why I'm so upset with them parking down there, you see?

TOM (*he sets his jaw*). But they are not parking down there, honey.

ANGELA (*springing up, gripping her head*). They are parking down there!!

He shuts his eyes.

And you . . . you've got to start taking precautions.

TOM. We must be on some kind of wave length together . . . (*He takes a snubnose revolver out of his pocket.*) I never carry this, but I'm leaving the house tonight and, for some reason . . . I stuck it in my pocket before going out the door. (*He puts the gun away.*) Incidentally, if Bellanca's holding any kind of . . . like a drug rap over you, the best thing you could do is level with me, you know; the Feds would protect a witness against drug dealers, they have a witness-protection programme and it's serious . . . You're not going out on me, are you?

ANGELA. – No, I'm here. (*Her voice breaks in the tension and she moves, holding down a sobbing fit.*)

TOM. How long can you go on with this tension? You're going to explode.

She simply shakes her head.

Has anybody said exactly what they want from you? – Is it to get me to stop coming around? – or what?

ANGELA (*staring ahead, almost stupidly*). For me to give him his letters back.

TOM (*this is new . . . he uses a fine degree of charm*). . . . Which letters we talkin' about?

She stares.

Charley wrote you letters?

She turns to him blankly.

About your relationship, or what?

ANGELA. About his struggle.

TOM. Like with his conscience.

She is staring ahead.

– He wrote you a letter about it?

ANGELA (*nodding*). Nine.

TOM. No kiddin' – (*With the faintest tinge of doubt now.*) – nine letters?

ANGELA (*reaches for his hand*). Don't leave me, Tom.

TOM. I'm with you, Ange. And where are they – these letters?

ANGELA. . . . I have them some place.

TOM. Oh.

ANGELA. I always had to have candles for him in the apartment.

TOM. Candles.

ANGELA. It helped him – to look into flames. I was the closest to him, closer than his wife. He couldn't keep it to himself anymore. I begged him. I prayed for him but he had to push the case, or he'd lose everything. I told him, I said, 'You could be anything, you could be President of the United States! – Don't do this to an innocent man, God will take it out of your flesh!' – I thought if he saw me in court taking notes he'd realise that I meant business and I would not let Felix rot in jail . . . and it would make him stop the case. (*She breathes in suddenly, deeply, and the eyes seem to be going blind.*)

TOM. Don't leave me, Angela.

ANGELA (*gripping his hand*). I'm staying. I'm trying . . . Oh, God, Tom, you don't know, you don't know . . .

TOM. Tell me, what, what?

ANGELA. . . . They picked me up off the street today. (*She is in open terror.*)

TOM. Cops?

ANGELA. I lied to you before . . . When I was walking past Ramsey's piano store, they suddenly came up beside me and jammed me into the cruiser, and drove me around, two cops and a detective. Caught my hair in the goddamned door!

TOM. Bastards! – What'd they want?

ANGELA. That if I didn't straighten up I'd be floating in the bay. (*She weeps. He holds her in his arms.*)

TOM (*he turns to the door*). So they're leaning on you for the letters, is that bottom line?

ANGELA *nods.*

Why don't you give them to them?

ANGELA. But I'd never see him again.

TOM. You honest to God see him now?

ANGELA. He comes, once or twice a week. But now it's only to get them back.

TOM. You're not making it with him anymore.

ANGELA. Only once in a while. (*Now she curls up on the bed.*)

TOM. Can I see the letters? (*She doesn't react.*) You want to go somewhere? My valise is in the car. (*She stretches a hand to him, tempted, conflicted.*) Get your coat on, come on, we'll ride somewhere and talk more. (*He holds her hand.*)

ANGELA. I'll die before I hurt him, Tom.

TOM. All right – Suppose you don't show me anything, just read me the relevant parts – you keep them in your hands. – Go on, get them.

She is in a fever of indecision. She gets off the bed, one moment covering her eyes with her hands, the next glancing at him as though trying to judge him. She opens a drawer off the dressing-table; hesitates, then takes out a brush and brushes her hair.

Darlin', listen to me – with that kind of evidence, I can put Felix back on the street by noon tomorrow.

ANGELA (*pressed*). I said I can't hurt Charley!

TOM (*furiously.*) Then why've you told me this?

ANGELA. I can't give you them now.

TOM. When then?

ANGELA. When I can!

He watches her for a long moment.

TOM. Angela – explain to me – why'd you tell me all this?

ANGELA. So you'd help me!

TOM. Help you how?

She looks directly into his eyes in an open appeal.

Are you telling me to drop Felix? You're not telling me that, are you?

She is silent.

Honey – you mean I just drive home now and go to sleep?

She is silent – furiously.

Talk to me.

ANGELA (*scared of him now*). I don't owe Felix Epstein – I fought for him!

TOM. How! You had a cannon and you threw some beanbags! And for five whole years you cold-bloodedly watched me chasing up one deadend after another and never said boo about this?

ANGELA. You never trusted a word I said, did you? Do you trust me even now? You know you don't!

TOM. What other man in your life ever believed in you like I did! How dare you say that to me! I'm damn near a laughing stock for believing in you. – Now give it to me straight – did you call me here tonight to get me to quit this case?

The load on her is crushing . . .

ANGELA. Ssssh! – Don't talk so loud . . .

TOM (*to the door*). Fuck Philly and fuck them!

The violence in the air sends her into quicker movements seeking escape and air . . .

Where are you comin' from, Angela, whose side are you on? What is happening here? (*With a cry in his voice, he grips her.*) Are they running you? Do they make you keep calling me?

ANGELA (*violently breaking from him, shaking a finger at him*). You know . . . you know . . . (*Groping breathlessly, she becomes rigidly straight; a new personality, a terribly austere, dignified lady with upper-class speech.*) . . . it might just be a terribly good idea for you to think a little more highly of me and stop irritating me!

TOM. Who's this now?

ANGELA. You are irritating me!

TOM. I refuse to talk to Renata!

ANGELA. Stop irritating me!

TOM (*even though knowing she is hardly able to hear him – in fact, she is softly hooting to herself as he speaks in order to block off his sounds and mock him*). Irritating *you*! You knew all these years where the bodies were buried and I'm irritating you? You're lucky I quit the booze, your face'd be running down that wall by now! (*Swelling, pulling up his pants.*) The enormity!

ANGELA. Enormity? (*She bursts out laughing rather merrily.*)

TOM. And what if I don't quit? Would that . . . put you in some kind of an emergency?

ANGELA (*as though quite beyond all harm*). Me!

TOM. . . . In other words, sweetie . . . are you trying to tell me that we're not really all that great friends? – Is that it?

ANGELA (*confused, but adopting an indignant stance*). Now you listen . . . !

TOM. You listen to me – this is still the United States of America, you don't have to lay down in front of those punks.

ANGELA. Well, I must say . . . what astounds *me* is how you get to think *you're* such a high grade cultured individual and such a great Catholic . . . !

TOM. All right, Renata, come! I'll find a doctor for you in Boston.

ANGELA. . . . But all you really are is gutteral!

TOM. Will you just blow that out your ass and talk straight?

ANGELA. . . . You can't help it, your whole manner is gutteral because your whole background is gutteral.

TOM. You're not even using the word right.

ANGELA. I mean who do you imagine you fuckin' are – just because you read some magazines without any pictures?

TOM (*eyes rolling upward*). Jesus Christ . . .

ANGELA. *You* have the audacious contempt to call the Lord's name in vain?

TOM (*defeated*). Okay, Renata, let's just forget the whole

ANGELA. *You* can call me Miss Marshall. Stupid bastard.

TOM (*laughs, despite everything*). By this time Miss Renata Marshall ought to know that a respectable lady like her doesn't call people stupid bastards.

ANGELA. Which I would be delighted to do if these stupid bastards had the mental competence to understand any other kind of language, you dumb shit.

TOM. Touché. (*He spreads his arms out.*) Okay, pull out the nails. I want to come down. I'm through, hon . . . for tonight. But I'll be back and we can start *all over again*!

She is surprised, frightened too as the air goes out of her.

(*In a mixture of laughter and fury . . .*)

That's right, Baby. (*Partly toward the door.*) I will never give up until Felix Epstein is walking the street! Plus lover-boy Callaghan gets a long number across the back of his shirt – if, in fact, you ever really laid him at all outside of your mental waterbed!

ANGELA (*exhausted, she starts to droop*). Well, you don't say . . .

TOM. Then where's his letters? Show me one single proof that this is not another one of your spitball delusions?

ANGELA. *My* delusions! *My* delusions! And what about your delusions? All of a sudden *I'm in the United States of America*? (*Tears are pouring into her eyes.*) And *I've* got *delusions*? This town is in the United States? This police force . . . ?

TOM (*his pain surges and he protectively embraces her, chastened*). I gotcha, honey.

ANGELA (*weeping*). Help me – for Christ's sake, Tom!

TOM. Sssh! (*He cuts off her weeping by kissing her mouth and holds her against himself with great force. And turning her face up . . .*) Did you really think you could get me off the case?

ANGELA (*covers her face and sobs in defeat*). My God!

The phone rings: they are both caught off guard. She goes and picks up the phone with high tension, her voice fearful, very faint – clearly, she has some specific caller in mind. Yes? (*Surprised and pleased – charm suddenly warms her voice.*) Oh! – Oh, I'm so sorry, I forgot all about it! (*A near stutter.*) Well . . . well . . . well, yes, sure . . . (*She looks confused at her watch but can't quite focus on it . . . and with a glance at Tom,* sotto voce.) What's the time?

TOM (*sotto voce*). Ten to twelve.

ANGELA (*with a warmly thankful glance at him*). Sure, I can make it, I have have to get dre . . . (*But glancing down at herself, she breaks off.*) . . . in fact, I am dressed already . . . (*Feels her hair, surprised that it is in place.*) . . . in fact, my hair's practically done . . . Ah . . . (*Ineffectually shielding the phone – oddly – with a half-turn away from Tom.*) . . . where is it again? Oh, right! (*Nearly whispering.*) And what's the room? Okay. (*Smiles.*) . . . You too, pussycat! (*She hangs up. She has expanded with a new pleasure-shame, an identity that is palpable. She turns to face him.*) I had an appointment I forgot all about.

TOM. You did? How come?

ANGELA. I don't know, I just blew it.

TOM. They say that means a person really doesn't want to go.

ANGELA. You got time to drop me?

TOM (*this is more difficult*) . . . Where's that?

ANGELA (*evasively*). Well . . . like the corner of Main and Benson would be okay.

TOM (*an instant – he looks at her almost incredulous, then turns away, and with dry rage, humiliation*). Come on.

ANGELA (*with fresh energy*). Just got to fix my face, be right with you. Put your feet up. (*She turns to go up to the bathroom.*)

TOM (*with an open resentment*). Why don't I drop you right at the hotel instead of on the street – it's only a few more yards? (*She turns back to him, ashamed – as it were – for his sake.)*

ANGELA. . . . The corner would be okay.

He doesn't reply, his head turned angrily away from her, although he is attempting to grin. She breaks the moment, hurries into the bathroom . . . another moment . . . and in a dispirited way he picks up the phone and dials. He waits, greatly tired, an inward look in his deadened face.

TOM. This could be tapped, you want to hang up? – Good, turn it on. You rolling? (*As for a record.*) Abe Kaplan was hit by one of his own crazy runners. – That's correct, he was into drugs, Josh . . . with the detective squad. – Why is it incredible? – Because she was Abe's broad. And Callaghan's too, incidentally. (*He listens.*) Look, talk to you later, I just wanted to tell you this much before I go outside. – No don't worry. I'll be all right – What do you want me to do, call the police? – Well, that's nice of you to offer, but she's only going to twist you around too, isn't she? I mean I've got to stop looking for some red tag that says 'Real' on it; I don't have the education, but I have the feeling and I'm just going to have to follow my nose, wherever it takes me, y'know? – If something's real for me then that's the last question I can ask, right? and to me what this lunatic says is real. (*A laugh.*) – It *is* all a mystery, yes, but I still have my ignoramus opinion, Josh; I think that somewhere way upstream the corruption is poisoning the water and making us all a little crazy. – Her? No, she's feeling great now! In the toilet getting saddled up for some honcho in the Hilton, and ten minutes ago rasping out her last and final breath! (*He laughs.*) – No, kid, it's not unreal, it's just horrendous!

ANGELA *enters.*

And here she comes now, riding on her elephant, our Lady of the Hilton, looking like seven million bucks!

She laughs delightedly.

You hear her? She's laughing, fulla beans.

ANGELA (*calls into phone*). Hya, Doc!

TOM. Now if only Felix could get the joke – Right, talk to you soon. (*He hangs up.*)

ANGELA. Before we go down – if those cops give me any trouble, we're going to midnight mass at St Jude's, Okay?

He laughs brazenly.

What are you laughing at?

TOM. What cops?

ANGELA (*gesturing toward door*). In the cruiser downstairs.

TOM (*totally loose and lost, he laughs*). What cruiser downstairs?

She looks shaken, distraught.

You stole five years of my life, you goddamn lunatic! I ought to wrap you around a lamp post.

ANGELA (*gathering herself in protest*). But there's always one there!

TOM (*mimicking*). There's always one there! (*Clenching his fists to keep them off her.*) How did you get into my life!!

With a look of apprehensive uncertainty mixed with indignation, she turns and dashes out the door. He strides about, full of self-hatred.

How did I get into this goddamn dream! My brain died! She murdered my brain . . . !

She enters, rather slowly, glancing at him with a new air of mock indignation. He reads this look, and takes an uncertain few steps toward the door, then halts and turns back to see her looking at herself in her hand mirror with bland assurance. He rushes out the door. She stares front. He re-enters.

ANGELA. Who's crazy now?

TOM. Angela . . . Christ, I'm sorry. Forgive me, will you?

She gives him a peeved look. Approaching her, arms extended . . .

Oh, Darlin' . . . Oh, Ange . . . I can't help it, I love you!

(*He starts to embrace her but she frees herself.*)

ANGELA. Hey, watch the hair, for Christ sake! I'm serious, you've got to get yourself some help!

TOM (*apologetically*). But, honey, they weren't down there a little while ago . . .

ANGELA. Well, don't cops take leaks?

TOM (*anxious to forestall*). Look . . . what do you say we go and get a ravioli and a nice bottle of wine . . . ?

ANGELA (*imperatively*). *I have to go*!

TOM (*surprising himself, a cry*). *Why*! They don't have to run *every thing* in this world! . . . Listen . . . get in my car. Let me take you to Judge McGuire's house – you remember, he and I are close; he'll arrange federal protection; we can bust this case and you can start a whole new life, darling. (*She stares into his face.*) And who knows, maybe we could still walk off into that sunset together? (*Taking her hand.*)

ANGELA. I can't.

TOM. Yes you could, if you believed in me.

ANGELA. No, not only you, Tommy, – I think you got me too late; all that went by. Come on, I'm late. (*She takes her coat off a chair, she starts upstage. He rushes to intercept her.*

TOM. Wait! I want to tell you something Dr Levy told me.

ANGELA. Levy! Levy's gutless.

TOM. He said I haven't been in love since I was twenty-five, so you like woke me from the dead, sexually, so . . .

ANGELA. Did he really say that?

TOM. So I handed you almost magical powers, like you could see in the dark through a slab of concrete.

ANGELA. Oh, Tommy . . .

TOM. . . . But I see now that whatever you know you're never going to tell me, because you don't want me off and away. That's it, isn't it – never, never, never.

ANGELA. Listen! – maybe if we could meet for a good long

lunch tomorrow . . .

TOM. No more lunches!

ANGELA. Give me one more chance to try to tell you, Tommy; that makes me happier than anything I've ever heard in my life – that I woke you from the dead. How about Pinnochio's, one o'clock?

TOM. No! Come, I'll drop you. I've got a man in jail. I've wasted too much time. (*He gets his coat and hat.*)

ANGELA. So this is it, then?

TOM. This has to be the last long night, yes. But you get evidence, something I can take into court, call me anytime – I just have to get to work, Okay?

ANGELA. Okay. Then I should tell you something to keep in mind. *There's a whole side of this case you never even heard of.* (*He goes stock still.*) Don't believe it, I don't care – but I have to tell you. You're not just leaving a crazy woman, you're leaving the case. 'Cause I'm the only one alive who knows. There are names that'd knock your head off, all the way to Boston, Washington, Providence and New York. The whole criminal justice system could be picked up by the tail like a dead rat. All you got now is the tip of the tip of the iceberg. – Good Luck. (*She opens the door and glances back.*) You still dropping me or is that out too? (*She sees him wipe a tear from his eye.*) What're you doing? (*She comes to him, incredulously.*) Why are you crying?

TOM (*shrugs, shakes his head*). . . . I guess because I still believe you.

ANGELA (*she draws his face to her and holds him*). Lunch tomorrow. I'll be at the corner table at the end of the bar.

TOM. NO!

ANGELA. Please come! (*She lowers her hands.*) It's all in me, Tom. And you're the only one who can ever get it out.

I want to talk . . . quietly and . . . honestly (*She is staring ahead.*) And then maybe it'll all fall out . . . all the rottenness; and then it'll drop away. And then, maybe I *could* start to change my life. I'm going to expect you. You might just be amazed! (*She goes out. From the next room . . .*) Philly? Where are you? I'll be back in a couple of hours! (*Calling.*) Tom? Are you coming?

TOM (*eyes lifted*). Sorry, Felix . . . but hold on, don't let go, baby!

ANGELA (*from further off, calling*). What are you doing, you're making me late!

TOM (*shutting his eyes*). Dear God . . . make it only one more time!

ANGELA. Tom!

TOM. Yes! Coming, coming, coming . . . (*Hurrying out as the scene quickly blacks out.*)

Afterword

Two Way Mirror consists of two complementary plays which question the nature of the real. One, powerful and even melodramatic, examines the problem of recovering truth in a world marked by personal and social psychosis; the other, elegiac in tone, exists in the border territory marked out by memory and desire. Taken together with his extraordinary study of the theatrical content of private and public experience – *The Archbishop's Ceiling* – these plays mark a new phase in the career of America's leading dramatist.

Some Kind of Love Story is, on the face of it, a detective story but, like John Fowles' *The Enigma,* it is simultaneously a parody of the genre. The model of a concealed truth slowly exposed by rational process defers to an account of the problematic nature of reality and the complex motives of those who imagine themselves to be concerned to recover it.

Tom O'Toole is a detective, apparently anxious to solve a five year old murder. The key to the crime is Angela, a call girl whose clients, it seems, include both the criminal world and the public officials with whom she alleges they have colluded. But Angela is unstable to the extent that her personality is in constant danger of fragmenting. Profoundly frightened, she retreats into a series of alternative personalities. Manoeuvred into an emotional corner she opts for catatonia or offers only fragments of information, hints of further revelations. She promises evidence but offers none. The effect on the detective is wholly destabilising. If her accusations are true and those who investigated, charged and prosecuted the crime are the real guilty parties then moral distinctions begin to blur. He has to assess the credibility of a woman whose personality is disintegrating in front of him, in a world whose values seem no more than a convenient fiction. And there is a further complication in so far as the detective and would-be informant seem once to have been lovers. Since their justification for meeting is his investigation of the crime, what is it that maintains his interest? Is it, in short, a love story or a detective story? So long as she refuses to reveal the whole truth, assuming her to possess it, he continues to visit her. In that sense both perhaps have a vested interest in the game which they play, a game in which truth is pursued on the understanding that it must never be discovered. And with corruption apparently at the heart of things how can the real be recovered and a system of meaning maintained? As Tom O'Toole remarks, 'I've got to stop looking for some red tag that says 'Real' on it . . . I think that somewhere way upstream the corruption is poisoning the water and making us a little crazy. All that remains, it seems, is a plausible fiction. As he says, 'If it's real for me then that's the last question I can ask'. That, of course, leaves us with no agreed fictions let alone realities; not even, perhaps, the supposedly irreducible authenticity of a shared relationship. But this is only some kind of love story, a partial truth at best. The real thing seems beyond recovery. And yet, the murder itself was real enough and, if the detective is right, an innocent man is incarcerated. Perhaps, after all, his dogged determination is just what it appears to be even if his desire for justice leads him to wrestle with phantoms which make him doubt his own motives no less than the possibility of tracing truth to its lair.

Some years ago Arthur Miller found himself involved in a local criminal case. He intervened to secure the release of a man falsely accused of murder, in doing so exposing the public officials who had secured ther indictment. The experience plainly lies behind this play. The fascination, however, lies in the extent to which what, earlier in his career, might have been recast as social drama is now forged into a metaphysical work of great subtlety. And what appears as melodrama is in effect a highly self-conscious study of a dislocating sensibility, a hunt for meaning and security conducted on the very borders of madness by those who can scarcely understand their own motives let alone press the question of truth and reality to the point at which it may destroy them both.

Its companion piece – *Elegy for a Lady* – is in a different mood but is no less disturbing. It, too, seems to dissolve the very characters which it presents. Starting with the simplest of dramatic gestures – a figure alone in a darkened stage – it creates character, plot and language only to make them problematic, only to negate such meaning as has begun to coalesce.

A man enters a boutique, tentatively, apparently seeking a present for a dying woman. The proprietress responds, slowly exposing, or so it seems, something of the man's relationship with the absent woman. In the course of the play, however, an act of transference seems to occur as the proprietress is invested with some of the characteristics of that woman. But in this play there are few if any certainties. It begins, indeed, with the man alone, in a single beam of light, staring, we are told, deep into himself. Slowly the light rises and the details of the set become apparent, fragmentary, barely sketched in, suspended in space. It is almost as though it were being summoned into being by his mind, or, indeed, as if he were a product of the proprietress's mind as she also appears, motionless, in passive thought. She may or may not be the dying woman and this her final fantasy; she may or may not exist. At the end of the play the light fades, the man remains for a moment and then he, too, disappears from the stage.

It is tempting to see this as a play about the process of artistic invention since the characters and their setting are themselves, of course, summoned into being by the writer who sits at his or her desk in passive thought. But then perhaps it is concerned with memory or that world which is the product of need or hope. Or maybe it is an elegy for more than a single woman, lamenting and celebrating a life which begins with darkness and returns to it. But, like Beckett's or Pinter's work (and plays like *Krapp's Last Tape* and *Monologue* come to mind), it is best not decoded in terms of single meanings. It is a chimerical work, deceptively simple in its language and effects; a threnody for the self which creates but which is itself inevitably decreated by the pressure of time or the sheer fragility of its own inventions.

Two-Way Mirror, as its composite title suggests, contemplates the deceptive nature of the world in which its characters exist. At times they suspect a hidden world of meaning and coherence but when they look they see nothing but their own anxieties and desires reflected back at them. Like the figures in Plato's cave they see only shadows which they must take for reality until the chains which bind them are loosed. Miller no longer believes that reality to be as easily claimed or readily defined as once he did. But the need to do so remains – a phantom, a lure, an illusion, but, in some critical and inescapable sense, a necessity.

CHRISTOPHER BIGSBY

Lightning Source UK Ltd.
Milton Keynes UK
UKHW020204260319
339895UK00007B/50/P

9 781408 111321